The Anatomy of Philosophical Style

For Helen

The Anatomy of Philosophical Style

Literary Philosophy and the Philosophy of Literature

Berel Lang

Basil Blackwell

First published 1990

Basil Blackwell Ltd
108 Cowley Road, Oxford, OX4 1JF, UK

Basil Blackwell, Inc.
3 Cambridge Center
Cambridge, Massachusetts 02142, USA

British Library Cataloguing in Publication Data

A CIP catalogue record for this book is available from the British Library.

Library of Congress Cataloging in Publication Data

Lang, Berel.
    The anatomy of philosophical style: literary philosophy and the philoso-
phy of literature/Berel Lang.
       p. cm.
    ISBN D-631-16494-4 − ISBN 0-631-17546-6 (pbk.):
       1. Literature − Philosophy. 2. Style, Literature. 3. Style (philosophy) I.
Title.
PN49.L34 1990
801 − oc20

Typeset in 11 on 13pt Sabon
by Best-set Typesetter Ltd
Printed in Great Britain by T. J. Press Ltd, Padstow

Contents

Acknowledgements

I am indebted to a number of friends and colleagues who in response to my impositions on them have been generous with their time and learning (and sometimes, it seemed to me, with their criticism). So, thanks of many different kinds to Ralph Cohen, Josiah Gould, Robert Howell, Joel L. Kraemer, Richard Lee, Howard Needler, William Sacksteder, and Forrest Williams. A reader for Basil Blackwell also offered several valuable suggestions of which I have tried to take advantage.

My wife, Helen S. Lang, who has herself developed a sustained account of "literary philosophy" in the contexts of classical and medieval philosophy, has, as always, read the manuscript of this book acutely, inventively, generously. The book is dedicated to her with thanks, and with love and esteem.

B. L.

Introduction

Discussions of the relation between philosophy and literature have typically focussed on the role of philosophical ideas in literature – the large questions about morality and mortality often designated as philosophical, one suspects, more because of their apparent intractability than because of the willingness of their readers (or authors) to follow them to their theoretical ends. This conception of philosophy *in* literature is, however, only one rendering of the relation between philosophy and literature; the arbitrariness of many discussions which restrict themselves to it has been due, it seems to me, to the exclusion of other formulations of that relation on which this one depends. To call attention to a literary "idea," for example, presupposes an explanation of how ideas "occur" in literary texts (as well as of how – or if – they can be conceived apart from them) and of the process by which they are inferred from such sources which often do not mention them explicitly at all. And these questions, also on the verge between philosophy and literature, are rarely acknowledged in the discussion of individual themes in literary works, however significant philosophically those themes are otherwise held to be.

It becomes evident, then, that there is a need to consider what other formulations or modalities are implicated in the conjunction of philosophy "and" literature, and I shall be referring in this book to two of them in particular. In Part I, "Philosophical Discourse and Literary Form," the topic is addressed of philosophy *as* literature; Part II, under the heading of "Literary Form and Non-literary Fact," affords a view of the philosophy *of* literature. These two modalities of the general conjunction of philosophy and literature are related not only to each other but also to the role of philosophy in literature – a now triadic connection which can be made clear, it seems to me, even though the third of these is not itself elaborated here.

The premise motivating the discussion of "Philosophical Discourse and Literary Form" is that philosophy, however it is otherwise conceived, is also, perhaps even first, a form of writing. To the extent that this is true, moreover, the critical means that have been found relevant to more conventionally "literary" texts can be – *ought* to be – also applied to philosophical writing, up to the point at least that the writing itself demonstrates its irrelevance. The past neglect of this aspect of the relation between philosophy and literature has been due to those sources themselves. From the standpoint of literary criticism and theory, there are many, more typically literary texts than those of philosophical discourse by which the practical or theoretical understanding of literature can be enlarged. The need to decipher often technical presuppositions in the connection between idea and form in philosophical writing has sometimes been a barrier for literary interpreters (at other times, the failure to recognize the existence of this barrier has itself been a problem).

From the other side, philosophers themselves have posed discouraging objections. Not only individual writers, but certain schools and traditions have argued for a radical distinction between philosophy and rhetoric – a distinction which among its other consequences entails that philosophy's literary or aesthetic character is related only accidentally, if at all, to its philosophical content. In this view, the commitment of philosophical discourse is to truth – whether in description or conceptualization but in any event as distinct from the manner of representation in either. In these terms, a proposal to read philosophy literarily is at best an irrelevance, at worst a distortion.

The latter claim, spoken "professionally," might understandably be intimidating to readers who are not philosophers; it is more difficult to excuse the philosophers themselves who have pressed it or agreed to it. Even if the traditionally central issues of metaphysics or epistemology were finally judged to be more fundamental than (and separate from) questions about the means of their representation, this judgment itself could only be made as the evidence had been gathered and argued. In fact, however, the conclusion has appeared as an *obiter dictum* which only *asserts* that the association between philosophy and writing has no significant connection to philosophical understanding. That conclusion may in the end be warranted; but to show this *or* its contradictory requires that the status of philosophical discourse as both discourse and philosophy must at least be considered. The relation between philosophy and the means of its representation thus emerges as a philosophical as well as a literary issue – with implications for philosophy and literature *whatever* conclusions the analysis leads to.

The discussion of philosophy as literature in Part I attempts initially (in chapter 1, "The Anatomy of Philosophical Style") to outline the theoretical issues entailed by a general conception of "literary philosophy." In the chapters following this, the relevance to philosophical writing of such literary categories as authorial point-of-view, genre, tropes, and figurative discourse is considered. The thesis that emerges at that point – perhaps also now – may not be surprising: that the "literariness" of philosophical writing is not accidental or ornamental but unavoidable – imbedded in that discourse and so also in its substantive questions and proposed solutions. It has become a methodological commonplace even in the natural and social sciences where the means of representation are most often slighted, that those means persist as substantive elements: if the medium is not the whole of the message, the message is at least in part the medium. The argument advanced here similarly criticizes the myth of "immaculate perception" in philosophical writing – the traditional and still common ideal of the philosopher as disembodied mind or reason in direct contact with the contents of the "real" world. Also the Owl of Minerva, the claim is made, sees through the eyes of the text.

Admittedly, this general prescription does not specify the terms in which it is to be applied. And the examples then elaborated: the role of philosophical genres (chapter 2), the pivotal instance of Descartes' writing, and then certain more limited examples in philosophy's history (chapters 3 and 4), the conceptions of philosophical irony (chapter 5) and of the status of beginnings and ends in philosophical discourse (chapter 6) – are obviously not, and not proposed as, exhaustive. In this sense it is an ideal of literary philosophy that is presented, not the systematic results of a research program. Given philosophy's characteristic lack of self-consciousness, however, this "provocation" is not as small or preliminary a matter as it might appear. To the extent that the examples developed demonstrate an immediate relation between philosophy and its written "body," they also establish the difference that recognition of this relation can make in the writing and reading of philosophical texts and in understanding the corporate or institutional discipline of philosophy; they also argue, beyond this, for a substantive connection between philosophy and other types of discourse.

In Part II, "Literary Form and Non-literary Fact," the focus of discussion shifts to the philosophy *of* literature and its starting point in the "literariness" of literary texts. Philosophy, preoccupied else-where, has nonetheless persisted in returning to a set of concentric questions about the distinguishing features of literary texts – begin-ning with the status of literary representation to which Plato first called attention, and extending to subsidiary although still large questions about the distinctive features of literary style, interpreta-tion, and evaluation. The discussion here relates the philosophy of literature to the earlier topic of literary philosophy by addressing the role of non-literary fact in literary discourse. That role – so the argument goes – underlies the persistent question, wherever philoso-phy and literature are joined, of the status of the claims (or denials) of truth in the many and varied representations of that conjunction. For philosophy and literature separately, to be sure, the relation between text and world has been a central issue (including, of course, the disputed question of whether such a relation exists at all). The analysis here of the connection between non-literary fact and literary form, although setting out from the side of the literary text, extends also to the issue of truth in literary philosophy, appearing there most markedly in proposals on the relation between the apparently con-flicting intentions of philosophical method and philosophical style.

That the concept of truth has in its own systematic appearances been fundamental for philosophy hardly needs saying; the most basic substantive and institutional distinctions have been governed by it. So, for example, the distinction between realism and skepticism – and then the many stages of dialectical relation between the two for which that basic opposition is a source. One might reasonably surmise that the nature of philosophy itself is at stake here – with this question, as Simmel suggested, the most central of all those asked by philosophy. An analogous issue of truth, moreover, has been hardly less persistent on the side of literature, impelled there by attempts to understand the complex but unmistakeable influence of literary texts on their audi-ence. In those attempts, the role of fact and truth has been denied as well as affirmed – but never ignored: the conception of literature as a "mirror of nature" has itself been a mirror of the history of literary experience. The intensity of these references to truth from the sides of philosophy and literature independently might be regarded as a reason for believing that to relate them would only compound the difficulties found in each. I shall be suggesting, however, that joining the two sources in fact promises a likelier resolution of the issues each raises than does continuing to address them separately in what is mistakenly held to be their "own" terms.

Part II focuses, then, on one aspect of the role of truth as it straddles philosophy and literature, namely, the "factual" substructure of literary texts. This substructure is constant, first as a source and later as figured in literary representation; it is the more consequential in both those roles, I suggest, because of efforts in the texts themselves to conceal or to divert attention from it. Even the most deliberately "self-consuming" literary texts incorporate non-literary facts that refer those works (and their readers) beyond themselves; as their authors cannot escape history in the act of writing, so what is written – the literary representation – also bears that mark. The evidence of this incorporation is most apparent in borderline genres (borderline between fiction and nonfiction) like autobiography and the fable (the subjects respectively of chapters 8 and 9); it is also present, however, and methodologically even more telling, in central literary genres such as drama and the novel (chapter 7). The sources in non-literary fact of literary figure impinge, moreover, on the discourse of criticism and interpretation, as these, too, claim places within an enlarged – historicized – conception of literature (chapters 10 and 11). If the presence of history is recognized at the origins of texts, we should not be surprised that the act of reading and the later reflections evoked by that act must also make room for it.

The recent emphasis among poststructuralist authors on the non-referential character of language and literature has disclosed important features of reflexivity in literature – literature as its own subject – that had otherwise been ignored or repressed. But the dangers in this revision have also become clear: that by it literature may be seen as removed from history and the non-literary basis the latter provides in fact and experience. Without this ground, I should claim, the texts of literature, both in their own immediacy and in the broader framework of which they themselves are part, become quite simply unintelligible – victims, in Whitehead's phrase, of the "fallacy of misplaced concreteness' in which abstraction is mistaken for the thing itself. At issue here is not merely a strategy of reading or a question of style, but a basic, finally an ontological commitment. To deny a role for non-literary fact within the domain of literature is to undo the writing of the literary text and the act of reading not only as each has been practised (that practice *might,* after all, amount to one large and persistent mistake), but to their very possibility. The latter claim is not stipulative, as it might seem, but empirical: to the extent that literary history – and history *in* literature – are denied or excluded from the literary understanding, what remains is radically different from literature as it has been practised and even as its possibilities have been imagined. At the very least, theorists who would exclude history from the writing and reading of literary texts have an obligation to provide an alternative account of the evidence of its presence there; they have so far, it seems to me, failed to do this, probably because of the very rejection of history that is at issue.

Obviously, to admit a role for fact in the origins of literary form does not itself establish a conception of truth adequate for judging the literary text as literary; nor does it provide a framework for determining the relation of that conception to the (also) textual claims of philosophical – or scientific or commonplace – truth. But the admission and the understanding it assumes are necessary conditions for these larger projects. The *assumption* of the literary irrelevance of non-literary fact is an analogue to the assumption in literary philosophy of the irrelevance of philosophical method to philosophy's literary form. But a connection is demonstrable in both those cases, and the studies in Part II, although addressed mainly to literary texts, will, I believe, further support the argument presented in Part I with its emphasis on philosophical texts.

The reliance of authors on non- or extra-literary facts in projecting the imagined world of literature and their assumption of this knowledge also on the part of the reader disclose broad resonances. Even the supposedly "hard" facts of biology or physics which writers of fiction cannot escape (literary characters, too, for example, conform to physical laws) have interiors and historical pasts – although *this* relation to fact is not one that the scientists themselves have been quick to welcome. From a different direction, the cultural and social conventions that shape the expectations of author and reader (as in the deployments of genre or style) are also complex and subtle examples of the incorporation of an historical ground in literary representation. In these respects, then, the most original literary text presupposes an unoriginal basis; the writer's reference to the world as-it-has-been is, if anything, more fundamental to the world he imagines literarily than are his more distinctively artful projections of what might or ought to be. Viewed from this standpoint, the work of the literary imagination is constantly ironic, not as a trope but intrinsically, persistently maintaining a contrast between what is actual and what is possible – the former presupposed by the writer even when it is not explicitly "written" by him. The requirement that the literary text should reflect such a basis of non-literary fact is no less compelling than the requirement that it should also go beyond it.

This literary role of the actual or factual may seem, even if admitted, trivial. Why would an author (or reader) *care* whether Hamlet had a non-literary grandmother (cf. chapter 7) when there is the literary Hamlet himself to reckon with? But it is a principal point of what is argued here that "Hamlet-himself" cannot be known or even imagined without recourse to a history aside from the prince and indeed aside from *Hamlet* as well – a history which although often vague in outline, is quite precise in its effects. That authors and readers do not dwell on these effects or their causes, perhaps do not, strictly speaking, even think of them, is more aptly understood as evidence that they take the existence of those details for granted than that they ignore or reject them. The not unreasonable response that any such framework of causal or historical connectives "goes without saying" itself attests to the presuppositions of that "saying" – the historical ground from which the imagined literary world emerges and which is efficacious at least in part *because* it goes without saying.

Philosophy as literature and the philosophy of literature are thus viewed here as instantiations of the general relation between philosophy and literature. Certain issues – including the "forms of fact" – are important to each side of that general relation, and questions taken up from the perspective of one of those sides will accordingly also have consequences for the other. That this connection is more than accidental is underscored by the convergence of these two modalities of the relation between philosophy and literature on the third one which has been mentioned but is not part of the discussion here. This is the conception of philosophy in literature, with its focus on the ideas or themes that the literary work is (in a rudimentary formulation) "about." For that rudimentary conception, too, draws on the two modalities of philosophy and literature cited earlier. The sense in which a literary text can be "about" an idea (or anything else) does not itself represent a literary idea; it assumes a variety of conclusions from the philosophy of literature, including a response to the question of *how* readers find or grasp such ideas in the text. To deal with even this one question, furthermore, involves additional claims about the literary form of ideas in themselves – for example, about what in them empowers their translation into poetry from history or science or philosophy – and whether that medium itself has a form. The modalities of philosophy as literature and the philosophy of literature suggest that even the most abstract ideas or concepts more than assume, *require* a literary body – a conclusion, it will be suggested here, that has consequences in turn for the more general concept of truth as the latter, too, must then allow for the bodily presence, the factuality, of form.

One way of summarizing the project represented in this book is, then, as intended to uncover the substructure of the superficially transparent and easy conjunction of "philosophy and literature." Taken by itself, the conjunction implies that philosophy is not literature and (conversely) that literature is not, certainly not intrinsically, philosophical; that somehow the reader must bridge an initial gap between the two in order then to determine what connections if any, link them. The account here, however, argues to the contrary point: that it is the alleged division between philosophy and literature, not their conjunction, that requires explanation and justification – the conjunction being prior to and more immediately given than the other. This does not mean that there are no distinctions there to be made – only that the burden of justification is on them rather than on the broader starting point I propose which holds that the thinking of philosophy is also literary and that literary texts also live a philosophical life. The latter claims themselves require elaboration and evidence, of course – but it makes a difference for this process if we recognize that the prima facie warrant is on its side.

Versions of a number of chapters in this volume have been published before this; and although these have been revised, certain differences in emphasis and tone remain that reflect the differences in occasion for which they were written over a period of eight years. Notwithstanding these variations, the themes within and joining the chapters are, I believe, both explicit and consistent; the "aspectival" structure of the argument, addressing a common center from a number of directions, is nonetheless cumulative. Certain claims made in the volume are left in the form of promissory notes, including a large one indeed in respect to the ontology of the literary text. I trust, however, that the relevance to the relation between philosophy and literature of what is in these cases only promised will be clear; readers can then judge for themselves whether the proposals are worth following further. In any event, the discussion of these and other issues bearing on the relation between philosophy and literature have been the focus of so much attention recently that readers are unlikely to be dependent only on the formulations presented here. There is arguably more interest now in the conjunction of philosophy and literature than at any time since the classical origins of rhetoric which in its counterpart to the category of "literature" excluded virtually nothing that was written or said. That inclusive ideal did not hinder the making of distinctions among the varieties of writing and speaking. Indeed, it provided specific terms by which such distinctions could be sustained: author, audience, and world would not be dissociated from the process of discourse. Some version of this framework remains also now a requirement for understanding the relation between philosophy and literature.

Part I

Philosophical Discourse and Literary Form

1

The Anatomy of Philosophical Style

Style is the physiognomy of the mind.
                            Schopenhauer

Although the history of western philosophy is almost entirely a history of written texts, philosophers have lived in that history – and written and thought in it – as if the role of the unusual artifacts we recognize as manuscripts and books were entirely incidental. The assumption here is that the act of writing has nothing – at least nothing *essential* – to do with the act of philosophy; that philosophy as spoken, "oral" philosophy, would have the same character that written or "literary" philosophy does, and that the two of them would be identical to philosophy as it might be thought but not yet expressed, or even to philosophy in its hidden truth before it had been thought at all. The conventional means of writing, in other words – of syntax and of language – have no more to do with *what* is written than do the further literary possibilities exemplified by individual style with *its* marks of the author's voice. All that counts philosophically in this view of the history of philosophy – past or future – is the "what" which is asserted there, not the "how" by means of which the "what" puts in an appearance.

It would be arbitrary simply to reject out-of-hand this conception of the relation between philosophy and the act of writing, and indeed the claim that this conception is *possible* is a premise of what will be said here. For to consider it as a possibility means at least that it is not self-evident or necessarily true; that it can be tested by evidence and argument and also – most importantly – that it bears comparison with *alternate* possibilities. I shall in fact be defending one of those alternatives, but whether that defense succeeds or not is itself separate from the claim that there *is* an issue here, that the body of philosophy – its faces and limbs – cannot simply be assumed to be an accidental encumbrance on its mind and thought, indeed that the likelier connection between those two is far from accidential. The ideas of philosophy, in other words – its mind – do not only constitute a history; they appear always *within* history, subject to the same constraints that any form of action or making is subject to and mirroring those constraints in the ideas themselves.

I shall be attempting to call attention here to one aspect – the literary and stylistic appearance – of this location of philosophy within history. If my suggestions about the relation between the literary features of philosophical texts and the substantive work of philosophy turn out in the end to seem obvious, the fact remains that they have much more often been held to be obviously false than they have been admitted as even possibly true. Certainly the claim has not been part of any sustained view of philosophy by philosophy itself, and this is, it seems, but another example of the larger indifference of philosophers to their own history: acutely tuned to the metaphysical categories of space and time, philosophers have been notably reticent about their own locations in space and time. Thus, the argument that philosophical writing is shaped by its formal character as written discourse as well as by its other, more explicitly philosophical purposes – and beyond this, that those two determinations are themselves related – has still to be made (and probably, if the history of philosophy serves as a guide, more than once).

In considering the relation between the thinking and the writing of philosophy, we are obliged, it seems to me, to choose between two alternate and opposed models. On the first of these – what I call the "Neutralist" model – the form or structure of philosophical discourse is denied any intrinsic connection to its substance as philosophy; the relation is viewed as at most ornamental, at its least as accidental and irrelevant, even as a hindrance or occasion of philosophical obfuscation. This view might be willing to agree that certain philosophical writers (Bacon or Hume, for example, or Kierkegaard) had keener ears for literary mood and style and a more deliberate involvement with those literary means than other thinkers did; but such accomplishments make no more *philosophical* difference, either for the writer or for the reader, than does the fact that certain philosophers (Nietzsche and Moore, for example) had good ears for music and others were tone-deaf or at least tune-deaf, as Kant apparently was.

The premise on which this conception of philosophical discourse depends is much like the principle that underwrites the possibility of translation among lanuguages. For even if we concede that nuances in one language may be missing from another or if we maintain, more formally, some version of the slippage that Quine finds between all (ostensibly) synonymous terms – still we take for granted in much of what we say and do a common thread of meaning that enables us to distinguish better or worse translations of the same text, or at a more immediate level, that enables us to make (or break) appointments across several languages with no more than a nod at the incommensurable features that may separate them. Just so, this first "Neutralist" model holds, there is also a single and common ground of philosophical discourse: propositions which tie predicates to subjects and which, in doing this, ascribe or deny existence to the variety of objects, theoretical or palpable, that comprise the reference of philosophical discourse. Thus, for Plato's dialogues, Aquinas' commentaries, Montaigne's essays, Hume's inquiries: it is only a matter of extracting from each of them the common linguistic core that has been imbedded as a proto- or meta-language among the several historically distinct languages in which those authors respectively wrote; and then, after that (*soon* after that) of extracting the structure of philosophical assertion which enables the reader to place the thoughts of such various figures in a single, homogeneous field of philosophical discourse. We read the quite different texts of these and other philosophical authors, then, as addressing each other (and us) about a common set of problems in a philosophically neutral medium of discourse, and we place them on a continuous and fairly even line in the history of philosophy.

There are, of course, powerful attractions to this view. Practically, it enables critical comparison and contrast, the elaboration and (more important) rebuttal of philosophical texts, without the burden of historicism, without requiring more than passing attention to the specific contexts from which philosophers have written or to the sociological and psychological – as well as literary – conditions that would otherwise be assumed to distinguish those contexts. Philosophically, it also provides support for what has been a constant and perhaps necessary (even if illusory) starting point for philosophical reflection: the sense that the individual philosopher stands always at the point of a new beginning on which the lines coming out of the past, united because of the insufficiency of that past, converge. It underwrites, then, the hope of philosophical progress. Psychologically, too, it offers the comfort of thinking of the otherwise solitary profession of philosophy as a large (albeit diverse) corporation in which philosophers have carried on a single and lengthy conversation.

Even if we accept this prospect of a context-free or neutral medium of philosophical discourse as an ideal, however (as many historians of philosophy and philosophers do), it is quickly apparent that the difficulties of finding that ideal realized in philosophical writing are substantial – sufficiently so, it seems, to indicate the need for a quite different model on which to base the anatomy of philosophical style. The difficulties themselves suggest the form that this alternative will have. It seems obvious, for example, that a reader of the *Republic* who identifies the speeches of Thrasymachus as representing Plato's point-of-view – even if we grant that Plato himself in one sense *did* say or write those speeches – would be making a serious mistake. But the only way we come to know this, whether we explicitly identify the process or not, is by recognizing that in the genre of the dialogue, authorial point-of-view (for the *Republic*, Plato's) looks out of the text by means that are quite different from the means by which authorial point-of-view asserts itself (for example) in a treatise or commentary. *There*, unless notice appears to the contrary, we feel justified in attributing the statements of the text directly to the author: whatever other problems of interpretation we encounter in understanding those statements, it is the author's own commitments that speak. There are different ways, then, in which an author can look out of a text – out of philosophical texts, as well as out of novels or poems; and this makes a difference – it *should* make a difference – to the way in which a reader looks into the text, the philosophical text as well as those others.

Once we admit the relevance of this principle of interpretation to the reading of the *Republic* at the elementary point at which we distinguish Thrasymachus' presence from Plato's, moreover, we encounter the inevitable next question about the *true* location of authorical point-of-view in that work. Do the speeches or words of Socrates himself represent Plato's point-of-view (as, for example we later would identify Philonous with Berkeley in *his* dialogues), or – as seems likelier here – do we have to make further distinctions even among the occasions of Socrates' words? For if Socrates speaks differently (not only in manner but in what he says) as he addresses different interlocutors, and if, in addressing different interlocutors or even sometimes the same one he contradicts himself egregiously or makes mistakes in elementary logic (the more obvious the blunder, the rule of interpretation goes, the more likely that it is intentional), then we must follow the search for authorial point-of-view one step

further, beyond even Socrates' statements. We find here in fact a
conception of method – the Platonic method – in which the reader
together with the speaker articulates the philosophical process and
the conclusions to be drawn from it. The authorial point-of-view
appears here as a ground against which the reader himself then
appears as figure; the collaboration is unavoidable. We thus learn
that the form of the Platonic dialogue is itself associated with a
conception of learning (and behind that of knowledge) and so, finally,
with a conception of philosophy itself – all of them animated by what
would otherwise appear to be "only" a device of literary artifice. At
the very least, as we recognize again and again the implausibility of
identifying Plato's position with any single proposition or argument
simply because it *appears* in the dialogue, we have then also to
consider that this suspicion or bracketing of discourse is itself an
intention of the dialogue form.[1]

   To be sure, much has been written along these lines about Plato's
dialogues, and it might be objected that any general conclusions
based on that source are likely to represent no less an anomaly in the
history of philosophy than Plato does himself. The implication I draw
is stronger than this, however; namely, that if the conventional
literary category of authorial point-of-view makes a difference (ultimately a philosophical difference) in reading Plato's dialogues, then
the same literary features also may be of consequence to understanding other philosophical genres. At least it would be arbitrary as well
as imprudent simply to assume that this is not the case, and that
means, of course, that we have to look and see *whether* it is the case
or not.

   Even the reasonable claim that the role of authorial point-of-view
in other philosophical genres is usually less striking or crucial than in
Plato's dialogues is in no way inconsistent with this first conclusion of
philosophical interpretation. For we are familiar with the saying that
"art conceals art;" and as point-of-view sometimes serves philosophy
as a literary (and so artful) mechanism, the fact that it is less obviously
a causal presence in certain instances of philosophical discourse than
in others may mean only that there are artful reasons why that should
be so. Indeed one can readily think of both literary and philosophical
reasons why the concealment or repression of the author might well
be attempted as a tactic of philosophical discourse. If, for example,
philosophical writing is conceived along the lines of scientific discourse – that is, as a reflection or mirror of the "facts" of a philosophically accessible reality – then, in the interests of consistency,
the authorial point-of-view would approximate that of nature itself:

impersonal, disinterested, universalist, hardly a point-of-view at all. It is not surprising then that for philosophical writers who take scientific or mathematical discourse as a model for their discourse (I think here of writers otherwise as dissimilar as Spinoza and Husserl, Leibniz and Carnap), the persona of the philosopher should appear in the text – more accurately, be repressed in the text – through the various stylistic corollaries of impersonality, detachment, replicability of evidence and argument. Thus, stylistically, the third person tends to be used rather than the first as the subject of assertions, the passive voice rather than the active. The stance of authorial point-of-view here is that of an observer who, in contrast to the point-of-view that animates Plato's dialogues, is simply reporting disinterestedly and objectively on a body of philosophical principles and arguments to a reader who is assumed to be in much the same position as the author (minus, of course, the author's knowledge). Philosophy intends here only to describe the world, not to change it, much less to be changed by it – and this conception of philosophy is displayed or represented in the text itself no less clearly (sometimes much more so) than it is asserted there.

The persistent appeal of science as a model for philosophy owes a good deal to the Cartesian method, and this makes it the more ironic that as we identify different forms assumed by authorial point-of-view in the topography of philosophy, Descartes himself, in at least one of his works, takes up quite a different stance from either of the two just cited. The "I," of course, is a constant presence in Descartes' *Meditations*, and indeed the meditation as a genre is itself a distinctively egocentric form of discourse which could not exist without such constancy. But there is more to the connection between the authorial "I" and the genre of the meditation than only the repetition of the former – and we see this especially vividly in Descartes' insistence that the reader of the *Meditations* must replace the Cartesian "I" in the text always with his or her own "I." The reader, Descartes tells us, is not to read "*about*" the process of meditation but, in reading the *Meditations*, actually to meditate. So the *Cogito* argument works for the reader – insofar as it works at all – only when it is the reader's "I", not Descartes' "I" and not even the reader quoting Descartes, who utters or asserts it. That "I," moreover, must carry on the process of meditation without interruption, as a single and continuous activity. Descartes' insistence that the reader should not interrupt him (or himself) with objections or questions may seem no more than the plea of an author for a sympathetic reader – but Descartes formulates a specific justification here which he also acts on in gathering the Objections at the end of the *Meditations*, namely, that meditation (the act *and* the genre) is (in Austin's term) "performative." In it, the authorial "I" appears not as an observer or even as an agent actively engaged by some other object – but as constituting itself in the discourse, in effect creating itself in the act of expression. Only so is the systematic doubt from which Descartes sets out and which threatens the reader's self as well as Descartes' to be overcome. This process, although carried on successively, step by step, requires in Descartes' view a distinctive combination of continuity and memory, an incorporation of each preceding step which interruption or counter-argument would not only interfere with but destroy: once interrupted, it would have to begin over again. There is, then, a progressive construction of the reader's "I," for which the philosophical meditation is intended to provide a means – in contrast, for example (as Descartes himself points out) to the genre of the treatise which he could have written but chose not to and in which the reader's "I," like the author's would figure as a presupposition, something that *already* existed.

What we find then in these several references is the outline of a typology in philosophical writing for the role of authorial point-of-view, with three points mapped onto it (I call them elsewhere the "reflexive," the "expository," and the "performative" conceptions of point-of-view) – with much empty space remaining to be filled in, and with room as well for certain problematic variations: So Nietzsche, for example, argues in *The Genealogy of Morals* for a perspectival conception of knowledge from what seems itself to be the disinterested and universalist stance of the expository point-of-view that he is attacking. Or again, Hume, raising doubts in the *Treatise* about the status of personal identity and the external world, manifests no such doubts about his own identity as philosopher, or about the (apparently) external objects of his philosophical investigation. There is a question then in such cases of whether we may not learn more about the author from his written text of literary presuppositions than from the explicit one of philosophical assertions – but once again, on either count, text it is. In any event, the objection seems to gain force in these examples as well, *against* the first, Neutralist model of philosophical style as it argues for the irrelevance and certainly for the inconstancy of philosophical style as a factor in philosophical writing and reading. The correlation between variations in the role of implied author, on the one hand, and substantive differences in philosophical method, on the other, argue for the need or at least the plausibility of an alternate anatomy of philosophical style.

I propose that we consider as such an alternative, then, an "Interaction" model which introduces a version of the "Heisenberg Effect" for philosophical discourse. That is, in contrast to the Neutralist model in which the philosophical writer draws on an independent and supposedly "style-less" body of propositional assertions that the philosopher first discovers and then arranges or reformulates, the writer in this second model, in choosing a form or structure for philosophical discourse, is, *in that act*, also shaping the substance or content which the form then – very loosely speaking now – will be "of." The form in other words is an ingredient of philosophical content – as the impingement of light, in the "Heisenberg Effect," influences the activity or location of the particles identified, and as the question of what identity the particles would have *without* the process of identification is then placed in the limbo of indeterminacy. The "Interaction" model thus alleges an intrinsic connection for philosophy between those sometimes dichotomous terms "form" and "content"; put more broadly as a gloss on Buffon's familiar line, that "style makes the man," it asserts that style makes the philosopher (and then the philosophy).

This proposal may seem to move to the side of excess as the Neutralist model had suffered from scarcity, and certainly, the systematic objections that can be anticipated here are formidable. A possible implication of this alternative – one which is realized in Croce's nominalist aesthetic, for example – is the contention that with it, the several genres of philosophical writing and beyond that even the individual works *within* a genre cannot be compared or criticized. If the form of each text is unique and determinant, then the hope of subsuming any one of them under a general category, of evaluating it or even of interpreting it by trans-individual criteria (such as truth or adequacy) is doomed beforehand. Since we are required to address each text in its own terms, the only alternative simply to reiterating the individual text would be to write a new and different one. More strongly than the Romantic ideal according to which the most adequate response to one poem is the writing of another, this alternative would hold that that is the only response *possible*. Even if one qualifies the "Interaction" model so as to admit the existence of philosophical genres, moreover, the question persists of whether what is expressed philosophically in one generic form could not be expressed in another – for example, whether Plato's metaphysics or the conception of philosophical method represented in the *Republic* could be expressed in a critique or treatise, or Hume's *Treatise* as a meditation, or (perhaps most pointedly) Descartes'

Meditations as a discourse, without significant philosophical loss (or more neutrally, difference).

What is at stake in such questions is the issue of exactly how strong the claim for interaction in the "Interaction" model is. If any conclusions emerge from the discussion so far, they are, first, that the latter issue would indeed be a test of the "Interaction" model (and perhaps of much else as well); and secondly, that resolution of the issue is possible only by looking and seeing – by examining case by case and literary feature by literary feature the extent to which the means applied in the literary analysis of texts generally (as, for example, the category of point-of-view) are fruitful when applied to philosophical writing.

It may be useful in this light to consider the directions in which such analysis may go, and especially then the important structural element already referred to, of philosophical genre. From Aristotle on – indeed before him as well, at the basis of Plato's attack on the poets – the tradition of literary theory finds a central and pivotal feature of "literariness" in the varieties of genre and literary type and in the structural differences which those varieties entail. On the Neutralist model of philosophical discourse, the authorial voice, together with all other central features of the text, is homogenized both across individual works and across genres: all authors, notwithstanding their superficial differences, speak with a single philosophical voice, overriding the many *apparent* differences of genre and style. But even the concession that these latter exist as *apparent* is a sufficient starting point for the proposal made here – since once we admit among groups of texts of even apparent differences (which may be all that genres ever are, after all), we have then to distinguish the genres, to see *what* they are, and then most important, to determine what if anything underlies the appearances.

I have already noted for a number of philosophical genres (the dialogue, the treatise, and the meditation), that like the standard literary forms of the novel or the lyric, they serve certain functions more aptly than others: it would, for example, be as unlikely to find a philosopher writing a refutation of another philosopher's work in the form of a meditation, as it would be to find a poet writing a sonnet whose intent was comic. This does not mean that either of these would be impossible – but that they are unlikely to occur, and if they occur, unlikely to succeed. We find, moreover, built into the generic structures of philosophy, philosophical presuppositions (like the relation between the philosopher as he writes and the reality about which he writes) which make the study of genres potentially even more significant for philosophy than for other disciplines where such presuppositions may or may not bear directly on questions of content. We recognize otherwise as well, that the history of philosophical genres (for example, in the medieval attentiveness to the commentary, or in the development, beginning with Montaigne and Bacon, of the genre of the essay) is linked to the social history of philosophy – to the selection of canonical or authoritative texts and to the changing role of canonization, for example, but also, to external developments: to the history of printing with its impact on the expanded audience of philosophy, and to the development of vernacular languages – all factors that also influence the articulation by philosophical writers of the genres within which they work. What is required here (and what will be further developed in chapters 2 and 3) is an enumeration and typology of philosophical genres, a map keyed in such a way as at once to acknowledge the apparent variety of those genres as they range from aphorism and pensee to critique and treatise – and yet to find in common, for those instances, the correlations between the literary means and philosophical purpose.

Beyond the category of genre appear many other literary themes and issues, some of them more speculative than others in their likely effect on philosophical discourse, but hardly, any one of them, prima facie irrelevant. The use of figurative language, for example, is itself a recurrent methodological issue for philosophers and has often in fact made strange bedfellows of empiricists and rationalists; it turns out to be an issue in terms of their philosophical *practice* as well as of their theories. Both Hobbes and Locke, for example, object explicitly to the use in philosophical discourse of figurative language as it moves away (in their view) from the plain sense and direct reference of literal usage (a "perfect cheat," Locke castigated it); but we know that this did not prevent either of these writers from making use of such figures and Hobbes, most egregiously, of a large one – a "Leviathan" of one – at that. Viewed more systematically, there are considerable differences in the use of certain literary figures by philosophical writers. Kant, for example, uses metaphors more often than similes, where with Plato the proportions are the other way round, and in both cases there is a relation between the literary figure used and the philosophical intent – as there is also in Hegel, for whom any philosophically historical fragment will eventually disclose the whole: so his use of metonymy as a literary figure.

Differences are also evident *within* the individual literary figures with respect to the philosophical significance ascribed to them. Stephen Pepper, for example, identifies four "root-metaphors" which,

in his view, exemplify or even determine the metaphysical commitments of the principal systems in the history of philosophy.[2] It is at
least arguable, moreover, that philosophical examples – which themselves often take the form of figures of speech – play various roles in
philosophical writing: from simple illustration to a role as paradigm
or as evidence and even to a position like that of a crucial experiment
on which a thesis may stand or (more usually) fall. It would surely be
important to know what correlations exist between the varieties of
philosophical example and patterns of philosophical method and
metaphysical commitment. The evidence suggests that there *are* such
correlations – and if there are, this is unlikely to be accidental.

Again, at a more distant remove, if we consider the possibility of
reading philosophy in terms of the standard literary tropes, we recall
Hayden White's tour de force in applying that schematism to the
writing of history by the great nineteenth-century historians – and his
conclusion that beneath (or above) their ideological differences there
was also a consistent literary impulse: that Marx had written history
as tragedy, Burkhardt as satire, and Ranke as comedy.[3] The historian
is thus viewed as "emplotting" the data, and in doing this quite
naturally, even inevitably, as making use of literary modes of narrative. The question will persist of course, of how far one can press or
extend such characterizations; but it seems to me more than merely
whimsy to associate the causality of Hegel's *Phenomenology* – what
motivates the discourse – with a version of what we otherwise
recognize as the *Bildungsroman* in the narration of which the novice
figure of *Geist* (spirit) after overcoming a number of serious adver-
sities (for which, naturally, *Geist* itself is responsible) then realizes its
true nature and destiny. This is, after all, a standard pattern of what
in literary history we recognize familiarly as the Romance. Similarly,
Leibniz's *Monadology*, often taken to be only humorously inventive,
may in fact be more seriously comic. We see there a piecemeal or
monadic world in which objects which superficially look quite different from each other, with specific shapes and physical bodies and
taking themselves seriously in those individual appearances, are
found by Leibniz to resolve themselves into a perfect harmony; they
thus restore a lost equilibrium or balance to the world. This is, after
all, the standard combination of reduction and restoration, replete
with happy ending, that comedy *characteristically* has, whether inside
philosophy or (more usually) out.

Again, the question of what or how much we might gain by
classifying philosophical writings in this way is open – but that same
question is far from closed even with respect to the categorization of

much more conventional literary works. And if it turns out that the standard literary tropes of romance, comedy, tragedy and satire *do* apply (even painted with broad strokes) to the discourse of history or philosophy, then the question of what those "tropic" categories signify becomes increasingly important as a philosophical question. Surely if there are standard narrative patterns that cross the disciplines – or that cross some disciplines but not others – the significance of those patterns becomes a substantive question for (and across) the disciplines themselves. Notwithstanding the difficulties faced by such explanations as the account of archetypes that Frye proposes or the account of class consciousness and social displacement which a Marxist writer like Lukacs gives for the same phenomenon, it would be in the direction of such formulations that the discovery of common patterns in literary and philosophical texts would move us.

Even without this larger implication, it is necessary now, on the "Interaction" model, to begin to think of philosophical texts, like other literary structures, as composed around "actions" and characters, with the philosophical author "emplotting" the actions for a variety of purposes (inside or outside the text) – rather than simply discovering or thinking the philosophical system as a static or unified whole. The image of philosophical thought as atemporal and undramatic, as itself non-representational, has been very much taken for granted in the historiography of philosophy since the nineteenth century; it has in certain respects been part of the profession of philosophy since its origins. Any attempt to assert authority – a feature, after all, of all rhetoric – will also be inclined, even with the best of intentions, to disguise its own means which, so far as they are disclosed, would undermine that authority. Philosophers have persistently seen themselves and persuaded readers to see them as engaged in knowing, in contrast to doing or making and thus as beyond the reach both of time and of rhetoric. To speak of philosophical texts as literary artifacts, then, whatever difficulties it encounters in the way of literary analysis, forces philosophy to an awareness of its historical character – a necessary step if philosophy is to follow its own advice of knowing itself.

These then, albeit sketchily drawn, are some of the features that an anatomy of philosophical style will, on the "Interaction" model, hope to identify and which promise a view of the body of philosophy – that is, of its corpus, of its texts. Admittedly, the discussion thus far is preliminary and programmatic; the "Anatomy" itself which flourished as a genre in the sixteenth century (as in Burton's *Anatomy of Melancholy*),[4] also raises self-referentially the same questions of philosophical style referred to above more generally. Nor do I mean to suggest that the analysis of philosophical style will be decisive for every or any particular instance of reading or interpretation. What I have been arguing is that the evidence on which the reading and interpretation of philosophical texts depends will also, unavoidably, take a position with respect to the literary or stylistic character of those works – and that this is the case because of their own status as writing, a condition that, not alone but also, makes philosophy possible.

For philosophers and readers who find nothing startling or exceptionable in this conclusion, the task now is to go on to develop the critical instruments – a finer anatomy – for which the literary study of philosophical discourse still waits. Only the philosopher who takes as his goal the ideal of a disembodied text, the literary equivalent of jumping out of one's skin, will be reluctant to acknowledge that whatever else we recognize about the origins of philosophy or its habitat, its methods or its purposes, philosophy characteristically lives inside the text. This is moreover, not an accident: there is no philosophy as we recognize it in non-literate societies, and it is unlikely that philosophy will survive the transition to a post-literate society if that should occur. We need then a theory and practice of literary philosophy for the same reason that we need philosophy itself.

Notes to Chapter One

1 For a fuller statement of this view of Plato's conception of his own writing, see Berel Lang, "Presentation and Representation in Plato's Dialogues," *Philosophical Forum*, (1974), pp. 224–40. Cf. also Ronna Burger, *Plato's Phaedrus: A Defense of a Philosophic Art of Writing* (University: University of Alabama Press, 1980); Paul Friedländer, *Plato*, translated by Hans Meyerhoff (Princeton: Princeton University Press, 1958–70) 3 vols; Charles Griswold, *Self-knowledge in Plato's Phaedrus* (New Haven: Yale University Press, 1986); Jacob Klein, *A Commentary on Plato's Meno* (Chapel Hill: University of North Carolina Press, 1965).

2 Stephen Pepper, *World Hypotheses* (Berkeley: University of California Press, 1942).

3 Hayden White, *Metahistory: The Historical Imagination in Nineteenth Century Europe* (Baltimore: Johns Hopkins University Press, 1974).

4 Robert Burton, *The Anatomy of Melancholy* (1 edn, 1652), (London: J. M. Dent, 1932).

2

The Plots and Acts of
Philosophical Genre

When Hegel wrote that philosophy's Owl of Minerva takes wing only
at the falling of dusk, he did not mean that philosophy is always
tardy, only that it comes late in the day. It may, however, seem both
late *and* tardy to call attention now to the role of genres in philosophical writing, and still more beside the point to assert the importance of philosophical genres to our *philosophical* and not only to our
literary understanding. Even if we find a way past the objections of
aesthetic nominalism for which *any* allocation to genres is a snare and
a trap – recall here Croce's declaration of "eternal war" against the
obscurantism of genres[1] – we confront the growing skepticism of
literary theory as it now disputes not only the formalism presupposed
in all distinctions of genre, but also the mimetic or representational
function of discourse more generally.[2] If texts as such can no longer
rely on a mimetic ground, it would be impossible for the traditional
features of genre, rooted in the now obsolete distinction between
form and content, to represent a literary (or indeed any kind of)
idea; that is, it would be impossible for them to be philosophically
significant.

This difficulty only intensifies, of course, for philosophical writing:
philosophy, we learn, ought no longer to delude itself with hopes for
success as a "mirror of nature" (in Rorty's phrase of opprobrium),[3]
and it would then be delusion added to delusion to believe that the
genres of philosophical discourse might, at another remove, mirror an
object which philosophy had mistakenly been supposed to represent
in the first place. That original "representation" turns out now to
represent nothing at all – and Plato's attack on the deceptions of art
thus discovers a new and finer object in philosophy itself (his own

indictment at least supposed that there was something for art to be deceptive *about*). In this postmodernist account, then, there could be no philosophical point in plotting the course of philosophical genres; and indeed there could hardly be any other point except perhaps on the part of antiquarians who would find a place for genres among the other historical curiosities which philosophers, quite inexplicably, once took seriously, like Descartes' piece of wax of Plato's aviary or Berkeley's tar water.

Such intimations of the death of genres, however, may be not only premature but misdirected. For even in a less suspicious age, when the prima facie claims for the existence of genres might also have been accepted at face value, their role was shadowy, consigned to a rhetorical limbo. Evidently (or so I shall argue), there have existed generic conventions of which philosophical writers have been aware and to which their writings conformed. But even among authors in whom this pattern is most explicit, it is not as though the writer, after first reviewing a list of possible genres, would then simply *choose* one among them that most recommended itself. No doubt, a writer's style – including his use of genre – is deliberate, in *some* sense a matter of choice. But the status of "choice" in this context is unusual. Plotting genre cannot be like trying on suits until one finds a likely fit – because this would imply that when the philosopher is trying out various possibilities, an original philosophical text that is itself genre-free exists in the philosopher's own mind, somewhat transcending the constraints of all genres. (We might suspect, here a claim for the genre of all genres that is not itself, however, the member of a genre.) And although it is *possible* that such a philosophical bedrock exists – it would be, in a way, a true philosopher's stone – all that philosophers have turned up in their history as a matter of fact is a considerable number and variety of – well, it has to be said – philosophical genres.

Genres, in other words, have rarely been read or written as "natural kinds", and yet they have surely been read and written. The distinctions among them and even the broad title of genre itself, like other stylistic categories, have typically been awarded retroactively, only after the literary – or philosophical – fact. This suggests that the distinctions of genre reflect a specific purpose, like a wedge driven into the text by which readers no less than writers attempt to gain leverage on it – and I hope to show how this functional explanation applies to the individual members of genres as well as to the taxonomies in terms of which genres collectively are categorized. That genres have this retroactive cast is, in fact, a further reason for treating with caution announcement of their obsolescence. Since we *always* have to wait for the designation of genres, an announcement of their death may mean only that signs of life have not been sought long enough. We run the risk of discovering that these announcements, too, as they purport to speak of the history of genres or the history of philosophy, represent a standard literary form: both those histories, after all, include the genre of the obituary.

This caution may seem tendentious, and I do not in any event mean to suggest that in order to test the viability of genres we have to wait for that long run in which they and everything else are bound to be dead. But to wait circumspectly seems a reasonable counsel at a time when pronouncements have circulated not only of the obsolescence of genres but of philosophy itself: its recent death for Heidegger, its prospective death for Wittgenstein, its recent *and* prospective death for Rorty. Obviously, if philosophy has "come to term" – in that ambiguous phrase of Heidegger's[4] – then the genres of philosophy would also be over, passé. But this inference also leaves open the converse possibility: if philosophical genres continue to assert themselves, so then would philosophy itself. Perhaps, a radical defense of genres might argue, philosophy itself is nothing more or other *than* this – that is, a family of genres.

I shall be following here something close to this rather oddly-ordered and backward-looking course of argument. But viewed from this direction or some other, any analysis of philosophical genre does well to begin with its historical role – only then moving to the more decisive question of whether that role remains one of "mere" history, or whether we find in it, as I suggest, something that verges on philosophy itself.

Genres As They Have Been

Philosophers no more than other writers deserve to be taken at their word; but since the only evidence we have for judging them originates with that word, even a systematic review of philosophical genres might look first at what readers ordinarily read first of philosophical texts, namely, their titles. These are at times, to be sure, an unreliable indicator, since titles – inside or outside philosophy – have a history closely tied to the social institution of publication: to the shifting composition of audiences, to the invention of printing, to the emergence, in post-Renaissance writing, of the use of vernacular languages, and so on. And to these general considerations, we have also to add the idiosyncratic genealogies of individual titles – the checkered careers, for example, of the titles we now know familiarly as the

Metaphysics or the *Nichomachean Ethics* of Aristotle, or still more to the generic point, the "dialogues" of Plato.

Yet, even allowing for such instances, we also recognize a large number of philosophical titles which were devised and assigned by their own authors – and with this, the fact that these titles often include a reference to the genre of the work designated. The genre, in other words, is named as part of the title. Admittedly, the frequency of this occurrence underscores the difficulty of deciding what any specific title is a title *of* (for example, in distinguishing philosophical method from philosophical style: is the "Critique", in Kant's usage, a methodological or a generic designation? Or both? Or does it begin as one and turn into the other?). But even conceding this problem, the number and the variety of such references is notable.[5]

It might be argued, of course, that when a single author like Descartes gives a central place in the titles of his writings to such genre-terms as "Discourse," "Meditations," "Rules," and "Principles," this is evidence of no more than the hand of an unusually self-conscious author – or perhaps even a systematic attempt at disguise (he had, after all, admired Horace's line that "Who has hidden himself well has lived well.") But an alternate explanation might propose that only the number of genres named is distinctive here, since the practice of announcing the genre in a title is itself a common occurrence, both before and after Descartes.

So, for example, one might move backward to the appearance of the *Sentences* (of Peter Lombard), to the *Commentary* (as of Albert on Aristotle's physics and biology), to the *Epitome* (Averroes, on Aristotle's metaphysics), to the *Questions* (of Buridan or Ockham on Aristotle's logic), to the *Guide* (as Maimonides' address to the perplexed) to the *Confessions* (of Augustine), to the *Essays* (of Bacon and Montaigne). Or one can push past Descartes to his successors, early or late, to find such "genred" titles as the *Pensees* (of Pascal), again the *Essay* (*Concerning Human Understanding* by Locke, and the "New" Essays by Leibniz), the "Treatise" (*Theologico-Political* by Spinoza), the "Dialogue" (as in Berkely's Three and Hume's one), further "Discourses" (Leibniz, *On Metaphysics*); the *Prolegomenon*, (as in Kant); the "Genealogy" (as well as the "Polemic") in Nietzsche's *Genealogy of Morals*); the "Autobiography" (as for Mill or Croce); the "Letter" (as in Schiller's, *On the Aesthetic Education of Man*) or in the more literal "Correspondence" of many writers (the latter, with the strange feature usually of being a posthumous genre).

These, again, are only a sampling of philosophical titles which include generic self-reference. Even a fuller list would be exhausting before it could claim to be exhaustive, and that is to say nothing yet of genres which for reasons also having to do with the requirements of genre have been less readily incorporated into titles – the aphorism, for example, or the fictional nonfictions of Kierkegaard or of Barthes (although it is not difficult to imagine "mythologies" as indeed a genre). Titles are, moreover, only a single and preliminary indication of the historical role of genres in philosophical writing. Other evidence ranges from explicit statements by philosophers concerning the act of their writing to the obviously deliberate (but unspoken) internal literary structures of their philosophical texts themselves. Especially because the latter phenomenon reflects what philosophers do rather than what they *say* they do, it must be central to any argument concerning the importance of philosophical genre, and I return to this point shortly. Even what has been said so far, however, suggests a two-fold thesis about the historical role of genres in philosophical writing – a thesis which admittedly appears here as no more than a promissory note, one that can be made good only by a full taxonomy of philosophical genres. The thesis is quite straightforward: first, that on even the most non-committal definition of genre, the history of philosophy has been a history of genres; and, second, that this history of philosophical genres has been deliberate – one in which philosophical authors and readers have collaboratively defined the relation between function and form as a basis for the varieties both of genre and of philosophy.

Admittedly, neither part of this thesis would survive if it had to depend only on prima facie evidence such as the appearance of genre-terms in philosophical titles – but then, they do not need to. No other philosopher, it seems, has devoted a full work to the general topic as Kerkegaard does in *The Point of View for My Work as An Author*; but when authors otherwise as unlike as Plato and Kant, Descartes and Wittgenstein, Hobbes and Collingwood, speak explicitly and recurrently in their writing not only of what that writing is about as philosophy, but also about the writing as writing – there is no reason to believe that they mean the latter less than they mean the former; one would do well in fact to suspect a connection between the two.[6] Writing itself is a frequent – arguably an inevitable – subject for philosophical writing, and much, if not all, of that reflexive discourse is focussed on the elements of genre.

The Proof is in the Act

Is there a way of demonstrating rather than only of asserting that philosophical genres have mattered to their authors because they also matter *philosophically?* This last term, of course, makes all the difference, since it costs nobody anything – hence almost everybody has been willing to pay the price – to concede that some philosophers have been more attentive than others to the act of writing and to the literary artifice that goes under the title of style. It does not matter *which* names are filled in here – the point is that there is agreement about the invidious comparison itself. So, for example, there are readers who admire Hume's style and readers who are moved by Heidegger's. These are unlikely to be the same readers – and in fact, for these particular readers to reach agreement about *anything*, it would probably have to be about other judgments implied by this first one (for example, that they each prefer the writing of their own first choice to that of Dewey). But these comparative judgments may in the end reflect less on the philosophical significance of the authors mentioned than on certain habits of taste nourished in a cultural context for which philosophical discourse (and truth) is one element of a number of related ones. Such judgments, in other words, may have more to do with style than with philosophy.

On the other hand, it might also be granted, also without much cost of disagreement, that there often seems to be a kind of stylistic "fit" – a kind of prosaic justice – between the use by an author of a particular philosophical genre and the themes or commitments that the author proposes in it. Since Socrates' method was Socratic, the argument here would go, it is obviously suitable to have Plato embody Socrates in the form of the dialogue; given the medieval Church's conception of authority and thus of authoritative texts, the importance attached to the commentary in medieval philosophy is understandable and expressive; since William James means to attack both the tradition of systematic philosophy and the concept of a systematic or monistic reality, it is fitting that he should write mainly in the essay form – that is, pluralistically, starting each time anew. And so on.

But taken at this level, genres would be of only literary interest in the pejorative sense of that term – "literary" as meaning incidental or ornamental, a mere means intended to serve another, weightier end. Admittedly, even in this accidental dispersion of genres, one might find something in the way of a history and perhaps something in the way of local meanings: the slightest stylistic feature, after all, looked at hard enough, may disclose what that style is "of". But philosophers, whether reading philosophy or plotting it themselves, would find little compelling in these examples – since for every instance that might be cited of generic fit, there may seem also to be others, hardly less obvious, of misfit. So Hume, in the *Treatise*, questions the claims of personal identity but does not doubt the identity of the authorial "I" who speaks steadily and firmly in that text; Nietzsche, in the *Genealogy of Morals*, argues for a perspectival epistemology from an authorial point-of-view that seems anything but perspectival; Derrida writes grimly and with authoritarian severity in defense of the values of play and freedom. Such apparent inconsistencies may themselves have a deeper – and consistent – meaning. But viewed on the surface, they seem likely to leave us discounting any *philosophical* tribute paid to philosophical genres as only another one of the "likely stories" that Plato identifies in the *Timaeus* with mere empirical analysis – the stock-in-trade of literary criticism, it seems, precisely because that genre does not have as its object truth or knowledge in any theoretical sense. One can, it seems, either take or leave such stories without making any great differences to *philosophical* claims that philosophers assert and which, in this sense, seem not to be stories at all.

I wish, however, to argue a stronger case than this for the role of philosophical genres – and the evidence that would support, or as I see it, *require* such a conclusion comes from two directions. One of these is negative, to be found in the consequences which follow if philosophical readers *deny* the role of genre; the other is positive, disclosing itself in the power which the conception of genre provides if it is taken seriously. First then, the *via negativa*, according to which either the differences among philosophical genres are ignored, or – what in practical terms amounts to the same thing – the various genres are treated as if they were all one (whatever that one is).

In that sourcebook for all subsequent accounts of genre, the *Poetics*, Aristotle records a few ostensively commonplace remarks about the categories of length, size, and order which he places at the periphery of his account of the genre of tragedy. (Tragedies, like other candidates for beauty, must be neither too large nor too small, their beginnings must come before their middles, their middles, before their ends, etc.). But as with so many of Aristotle's commonplaces, these too, may serve elsewhere as Prime Movers.

So, for example: Nietzsche wrote what he – and we – recognize as aphorisms. Thus (from *The Gay Science*): "The object of punishment is to improve him who punishes." This aphorism could, one supposes, be a bit longer than it is in Nietzsche's words; it might, stretching a point, extend to two sentences or even to three, and the theme itself, we recognize, is taken up elsewhere by Nietzsche himself, in non-aphoristic form and at greater length. But try then to imagine this aphorism or indeed *any* aphorism which goes on for 260 pages, is divided into chapters and sections, with a preface and (later) an afterword – and see then how the aphorism survives. It is not, here, that we also have Nietzsche's own defense of the aphorism as a genre ("Systematic form," he writes, "attempts to evade the necessity of death in the life of the mind as of the body . . . and so it remains dead . . . . The rigor is rigor mortis . . . . Aphorism is the form of death and resurrection: 'the form of eternity' "); but that we know, by imagining it and by having seen much other writing, that whatever the 260 pages which replace the aphorism do or say, they will not constitute an aphorism, or ensue in whatever the aphorism was meant to. Or again: Hegel's *Encyclopedia of the Philosophical Sciences* includes 577 entries, divided into three main sections, together with an introduction explaining the principle (the genre-principle) of his *Encyclopedia*. Imagine now a volume with "Encyclopedia" written on its title page, but with only a single, one-line entry in it, the length of Nietzsche's aphorism. We would no doubt suspect a joke here, possibly a profound one and one which might (like any aphorism) require time and space to elaborate. But whatever we in the end discover about or add to this text, it is unlikely to be or to do what a philosophical encyclopedia (Hegelian or not) is understood to be or do.

Admittedly, this version of the negative argument risks begging the question. *Of course*, a 260 page book is not going to be an aphorism – or one sentence, an encyclopedia. And even if we overlook the fact that neither of those genres has been central in the history of philosophy; even if we also put aside the fact that differences in length are often misleading indicators of genre (we all know treatise-size volumes that are essays or notes writ too large), a question still remains: are not the differences that such odd thought-experiments are assumed to make exactly what is at issue here? If an aphorism that turned into a treatise lost its status as aphorism; or an encyclopedia that was somehow compressed into an aphorism lost its standing as an encyclopedia, they might nonetheless, all four of those categories of genre together have the *same* philosophical standing, be tested by the same philosophical criteria, be read for the same purposes and by the same methods and attentiveness. At least this, it seems, is the crucial question on which the alleged significance of philosophical genres turns: are those genres not all, in the end, *philosophically equal* – or, less tactfully, philosophically trivial? Well, perhaps, but at this point, even with no more than acknowledgement of the contingency or mortality of genres, the burden of proof begins to cut two ways; it rests as much on those who claim that there is no philosophical difference in supplanting one genre by another as on anyone – me – who claims that the difference here is both visible and philosophical. Once taken, the first step – acknowledgement of the deliberate existence of genres – may lead in either of these directions; there is now no a priori reason for privileging one of them rather than the other.

The negative argument itself, furthermore, can be moved to a more substantial basis, one in respect to which the charge of question-begging will not arise (at least no more than it does elsewhere within the circle of interpretation). The words that we read in the *Republic* are, we generally assume, as much Plato's words as the words in the *Nichomachean Ethics* are Aristotle's (perhaps more, if the *Ethics* has indeed reached us in the form of a set of notes). This proprietary claim on Plato's behalf includes, of course, the words attributed to Thrasymachus as well as those attributed to Socrates, as those two sets of words are reported in the *Republic* – and here the problem begins. Thrasymachus finds himself compelled to retreat in Book I by the force of Socrates' argument – but this is not true of Socrates and surely not of Plato himself. What, we ask, is Plato's own view of justice here? – and we draw a quick line, for starters, between Plato and the views expressed by Thrasymachus, even though Thrasymachus' words *are*, in another sense, also Plato's. Well, does it not seem likelier that Plato speaks through Socrates – the words of the latter being the commitments of the former? No doubt, but at times even this does not seem very likely – for example, when we detect, in Socrates' arguments against Thrasymachus, reasoning so obviously faulty that elementary logic texts might later use them to illustrate the informal fallacies (for example, of equivocation, or division). It was not, of course, that Plato did not have the advantage of reading such texts. Indeed we can hardly avoid identifying here the exemplification of an elementary rule for all reading: the more obvious the blunder, the more obviously deliberate the "blunderer". But deliberate for what end?

The point hardly needs to be labored: the words, no doubt, are all Plato's – but he wrote them in the form of a dialogue which means that probably not all the words are equally his, that some of them are unlikely to be meant as his at all. When Philonous refutes Hylas in Berkeley's *Dialogues*, we recognize not only a victor but Berkeley himself. In the *Republic*, we discover from the text that if we are to find Plato in it, we are going to have to look beneath or around the words, even those of Socrates – indeed that certain constraints, of distance and reflexivity – are being asserted in respect to the character of philosophical discourse itself. Those conditions are structural features of the Platonic dialogue as a genre; the reader who fails to recognize them risks making a series of errors ranging from the gross to the subtle – from confusing Thrasymachus with Plato (a gross error) to questioning whether the method of dialogue yields a conclusion at all (a sutble error, but error nonetheless as it misses the possibility that the method might be the conclusion). To fail to recognize these potential errors *as issues*, moreover, is to make another mistake which is more serious than the first ones, in effect, of a different order; it verges on the denial of a role to genre altogether and, with this denial of textual conventions, brings into question the act of reading itself. But contrary to this: that the distinctions which have been cited in reference to the *Republic* may seem so obvious as hardly to need saying means no more than that the difference that genres make in general is also – or should be – obvious.

To be sure, it may be objected that the Platonic dialogue is an historical anomaly – and hard cases, it might further be objected, make bad philosophy or at least bad generalizations. But although the chaos that would result from reading the *Republic* as if it were a treatise is an egregious example of what happens with the denial of genre, there are too many other likely examples for this one to be seen as idiosyncratic. So – for one other large example – Descartes instructs the reader of his *Meditations* that the reader is to read that text not as though it were *about* meditation, but *as* meditation. There might well be – there *were* – treatises about meditation and handbooks of how to do it: but for meditation itself and philosophical proofs that depend on it, only meditation itself will do. Thus, the "I" of the *Cogito* has to be an actual "I" – the reader's "I" – if the proof of which it is part and whatever then depends on it is to work. The meditation, in other words – that is, in the words of genre – is not a treatise or dialogue, not even, to bring matter closer to Descartes, a discourse. *Can* the arguments of the *Meditations* be read otherwise, *im*personally – for example, in the case of the *Cogito*, as a hypothetical ("If I think, then I exist"), or "All thinking beings are existent beings; I am a thinking being; therefore, etc."? The *Cogito* can be and has been so read; the result only happens to yield a different form of proof (and genre) from the one conceived by Descartes.

Inside Genre, Looking Out

Slow as the process has been, we come back now to genre itself. What I have outlined so far is, first, evidence of the role of genre provided by philosophers themselves; and then other evidence of mistakes that would follow insofar as the readers of philosophical texts might confuse one genre with another or, at an extreme, choose to ignore the role of genre altogether. None of this speaks substantively about the why or how of philosophical genre, or about the distinctions among philosophical genres that are worth making or preserving. This last issue especially is important for the present discussion, since if, as I have claimed, definitions of genre are characteristically contextual and functional, then – given the indefinitely large number of *possible* functions – there will also be an indefinite number of possible taxonomies of genre. The question then arises of where to begin that will not seem arbitrary.

Here again, however, it is useful to return to Aristotle's *Poetics*, and to recall the distinction he draws among a basic triad of literary genres which then reappears with great regularity in the history of aesthetics, through the Renaissance and into the twentieth century (in such authors as T. S. Eliot). (Strictly speaking, the distinction is due first to Plato, but in a rudimentary form.)[7] Admittedly, it may seem unlikely that a distinction among the lyric, the epic and the dramatic genres could be applicable to *philosophical* genres (although I shall in fact suggest a connection); but the *basis* of the Aristotelian distinction is worth noting, since it persists in contemporary theory with its ascription of a role to the phenomenon of authorial "point-of-view" or "implied author". Some poetry, Aristotle notes, is uttered in a single voice that does not itself appear as a character in the text; some poetry – drama – is uttered only in the voices of individual characters who appear in the drama, with differences that distinguish them from each other and from any independent narrative voice. Some poetry – as, for example, in the epic – combines these two versions of representation: at times we hear the narrative voice, at other times we hear the characters speaking for themselves.

Aristotle does not himself attempt to establish a causal relation between these differences in authorial point-of-view and the genres with which they are associated (although he does do this for other stylistic features, distinguishing, for example, between the formal as well as the moral characteristics of comedy and tragedy). But as the Aristotelian distinction persists in later literary history, the causal connections also become more explicit (so, for example, it seems essential to the function of the lyric poem that it should be uttered in the single voice of the speaker). Exactly why the role of authorial point-of-view should be so central a distinguishing mark among genres is an important and still largely unresolved question for literary theory – but the fact itself is evident, and this is also the case for the understanding of philosophical genres.

Consider, for example, the very different roles of authorial point-of-view in two groups – "meta-genres" – of philosophical texts. In one of these, the implied author positions himself outside or at least independently of what he is writing about, conceiving the role of philosopher as directed to analysing the features of a reality already formed and given. This positioning in itself reflects a metaphysical disposition – and the same disposition, now both rhetorical and metaphysical, assumes a standard form in such genres of philosophical writing as the treatise, the critique, and the discourse. In these all, the author's voice is distinguished from the objects referred to, to the extent that it often is entirely unmentioned (the authorial pronoun "I" or the more attenuated "we" do not appear); or, if it is mentioned, it may take an impersonal form, standing for a typical or "ideal" observer rather than an actual one. The author, moreover, proposes to disclose to the reader the view of an object which is assumed to be identical for both author and reader. So, for example, in *Concerning Body*, Hobbes defines philosophy as "such knowledge of effects or appearances, as we acquire by true ratiocination from the knowledge we have first of their causes or generation; and again, of such causes or generations as may be had from knowing first their effects."[8] And we see here, both from within the statement and by viewing it as itself a representation, a conception of philosophy in which the philosopher (whether Hobbes or his reader) makes no difference, and *is made* no difference in, by the causes and effects which comprise its subject matter. The world, including the philosopher himself, remains essentially what it was before or without philosophy. This "meta-genre" of philosophical writing does not have a standard name, and I suggest for it a term I have used elsewhere – the meta-genre of "exposition".[9] This meta-genre is analogous to the "drama" in the original Aristotelian distinction among genres: in the philosophical text, it is the facts of the world which appear in the role of characters; these are understood to be speaking for themselves, without the obtrusion of a narrative or interpretive voice.

Consider, by contrast, a second generic form where the "I" of the authorial point-of-view is part of the subject of the philosophical discourse – and where both that "I" and the world in which it is situated are contingent on the discourse itself. This is, it seems to me, a standard condition of the personal essay: it also appears, more radically, in such other genres as the dialogue, the aphorism and the meditation. In all of these, both the point-of-view and the objects viewed (as they are disclosed or presented by the "I") are at least to some extent constituted in the act of discourse itself: the authorial "I" is not fully shaped – nor is there a complete or fully structured world in which the "I" (the writer's *or* the reader's) is situated. The discourse itself is in motion, constituting its elements at the same time that it refers to them. So this meta-genre might be referred to as "performative") – and the conception of philosophy involved here, in contrast to the theoretical emphasis of the expository genre, is practical. On the Aristotelian distinction among the forms of literary mimesis, the contingent and unstable point-of-view in this genre would correspond to the contingent self that speaks in the "lyric" mode.

These two examples of difference at the level of meta-genre are sketchy, but it is possible from them to begin to identify the features of a more general theory of philosophical genres. The most fundamental requirement for the latter will be a map of conceptual boundaries – the categories in terms of which genre distinctions are relevantly made. Authorial point-of-view has been mentioned here as one such category on the grounds of its centrality to the function of philosophical texts (and also the conception of philosophy represented in them). Again, such "grounds" are not fixed: the appearances from which they are inferred can and often are given alternate descriptions: in this sense, genres are always embedded in a theory (for philosophical genres, in a theory of what philosophy itself is). Once again, it is relevant to note here the analogy to more traditional literary analysis for which questions about genre are the most persistent of all questions, and where the grounds proposed for making distinctions among genres are set at very different levels of generality. These range from the narrowly structural alternatives provided by Aristotle – to the more speculative alternatives of a writer like Frye who finds a hierarchy of grounds for the taxonomy of genres: a "trope-ic" level which distinguishes the genres of tragedy, comedy, romance, and irony; and then, still more fundamentally, an assortment of psychological or moral archetypes on which the tropes themselves depend.[10] There is no way of circumscribing, let alone of predicting these possibilities, and there may be advantages as well as liabilities to such a lack of definition. I suggest in chapter 5, for example, that even the tropes of tragedy, comedy, romance, and irony may be usefully applied to philosophical texts.

Is there a way of bringing order into what, with these suggestions, promises to be an indefinite number both of the grounds or categories of genres and still more, of individual genres? So far in this chapter alone, about 25 genres or meta-genres have been referred too – and this is without mentioning other lesser but popular ones (from the medieval "Quodlibeta" to the contemporary "Book Review") which come readily to mind. The number of genres distinguished historically is itself suggestive (why, for example, is that number so sharply reduced in contemporary philosophy?) – and that number only underscores the potential usefulness of distinctions among the genres as they reflect (and disclose) the relation of philosophical form to philosophical function. This is what I have attempted in the distinction between the expository and the performative meta-genres based on authorial point-of-view; the category of "implied reader," would be a second pertinent ground of generic distinction, related to, although distinct from, the first. In the texts of certain genres, for example – especially those of "exposition," the conceptions of implied author and implied reader are almost identical: the latter lacks only certain items of information which the former possesses, and even this difference will have been made up by the end of the text. In "performative" texts, by contrast, it is the contingent nature of the reader that is addressed: the act of philosophizing also represents the constitution of the reader's self, often with a lack of predictability about the outcome of that process. The reader of a Platonic dialogue who is engaged by the dialogue is evidently meant to continue that activity beyond the dialogue itself; the Elenchic dialogues, which conclude with questions, only bring into the open this underlying – and genred – characteristic. In this sense the writing itself is a *preface* to philosophy.

A third such factor that might be cited is textual intention – the purpose(s) realized in the space *between* writer and reader. This third category is based on a recognition of the philosophical text as not passive but in motion, as entailing a transaction between writer and reader in which each recognize that the other imposes certain constraints and opens certain possibilities. The change effected in this transaction may be as slight as the replacement of one item of information by another, or as large as the redirection or reconstitution of the reader's self. In either event, the action initiated will reflect the protocols of a genre that is itself a template for literary "doing".

To be sure, even within the bounds of a single genre, intention and act may vary: so, for example, Moore and Ayer come to contradictory conclusions about the status of ethical properties by way of (roughly) the same genre. Furthermore, there may be similarities *across* genres: the ostensively impersonal descriptions of expository genres *might* reconstitute a reader's life. (It is conceivable that such descriptions could *gain* power because of their impersonality.) There are, moreover, textual features (such as syntactic or grammatic structure) which evidently have little to do with the role of genre. Yet, beyond these qualifications – qualifying *them* – is the textual (and generic) intention – the sense of what the philosphical text is meant to *do*, as that shapes, and is shaped by, the genre. "We are given genres," Bakhtin writes, "in almost the same way we are given our native language."[11]

I recognize that the characteristics of genre that have been cited would require elaboration before they could serve as the basis for a taxonomy of philosophical genres. Even in the terms cited, however, something can be said about the single most decisive question that faces any claim for the importance of philosophical genres, namely, the question of translatability or synonymy among them. Can what is "said" in one genre also be said in others? In *all* others? In *some* others? Exactly? Approximately?[12] Since these questions are questions about meaning, they bear directly on the philosophical significance of genres: philosophy would be independent of genres to the same extent – no more, no less – than meaning is.

It has to be stipulated early on in respect to all these qusetions that to affirm translatability among genres does not in itself presuppose the existence of a common genre–neutral philosophical "core." This relation might rather be understood operationally or functionally, and it seems evident that viewed in those terms, apparent differences among genres will often be relatively unimportant philosophically – as, for example, among the various "expositional" forms in which the main parameters of genre (point-of-view, implied reader, textual intention) are roughly identical. Thus, although the commentary is recognizably different from the treatise, they share in common a conception of the status of the implied reader; even the textual intention of the commentary which is to interpret a prior text in such a way as to demonstrate its truth does not move far from the intention of the treatise to reflect or mirror the philosophical facts of the matter. In this sense, a commentary on Aristotle's *Physics* and the text of Aristotle's *Physics* itself may, in stylistic terms, come to much the same philosophical thing.

On the other hand, for the extremes of the expository and performative meta-genres described above, no such reconcilation is possible. In the latter of these generic forms, the author and/or reader are constituted by or in the text, in the former, they are already extant, given prior to the text – and this difference between the two meta-genres is prima facie unbridgeable. To be sure, either of the two sides can produce a *version* of the other: an "exposition" can be given, for example, of a "meditation" (Spinoza does this in his treatise on *Descartes' 'Principles of Philosophy', Demonstrated in the Geometric Method*; indeed, Descartes himself does it, to show in effect that it can be done, in responding to the Objections to the *Meditations*). But such efforts amount only to the claim that a paraphrase of *some* sort be given for any text – a possibility that seems undeniable whether applied to *King Lear* or the American Declaration of Independence, to the Book of Job or to Aesop's *Fables*. The crucial philosophical question in respect to the individual works that constitute philosophical genres is whether the *full* design of a work in a particular genre can be realized in its translation into an alternate genre – and here, it seems clear, that as between *some* genres, the answer to this question is a straightforward "No."

To be sure, a pertinent description or expository statement can be formulated that refers to a Platonic dialogue. But insofar as the genre of that dialogue proposes to engage the reader in a philosophical method which is dialectical and non-expository – to involve the reader as an agent and not only as a viewer of the process – the proposed substitution of genres, although it does not take the reader entirely away from the dialogues, runs up against a *philosophical* barrier between the two genres and the meanings of which they are capable. A treatise on justice, no matter how faithfully Platonic in its intent, *cannot*, because of their differences in genre, stand in for the *Republic*. Or again: Descartes involves apparently common themes in the *Meditations* and the *Discourse on Method* – although in terms of the distinctions I have cited between performative and expository genres, those two works might seem to be quite disparate. Does the apparent generic difference override the apparent commonality? And, if not, what does this say about the alleged distinction between those genres?

My own response to the latter questions will be elaborated in chapter 3, but can be summarized here: notwithstanding its earlier date of publications, the *Discourse on Method* is in fact dependent on the *Meditations*: the two works do not in fact represent two distinct genres but are internally connected, with the *Discourse on Method* thus not a "true" or generically independent discourse. I recognize the dangers of tendentiousness in this strategy; it is not intended in any event as a general means for reconciling all works which belong to apparently opposed genres. But since the lines that separate genres are *always* defeasible, always subject to the shifting designs of the individual author, this possibility of transvestism among genres – one assuming the guise of another – is constant. Genres themselves have a history in the life of the individual writer if only because their forms follow their function – the latter originating, after all, with the author's decision on what philosophy is or should be.

Outside – and After – Genre

The view of philosophical genre outlined so far has been largely involve institutional and conceptual factors and indeed the relation *external* history of genre is also, it seems, relevant philosophically. The fact that genres have a history within the history of philosophy – with some genres flourishing at one time but not at others – suggests the likelihood of a connection between genres and the movements or shifts in philosophical speculation. Such correlations undoubtedly involve institutional and conceptual factors and indeed the relation between them. So, for example, we may well ask why the genre of the dialogue which has such a rich philosophical history should have no place in contemporary philosophy especially when, in terms just of quantity, more philosophy is being written at one time than ever before. And one likely reason here is that with the professionalization since the eighteenth century of philosophy and philosophers, the role of professional expertise has been so emphasized in philosophy as a discipline that the texts and genres of philosophy are bound to reflect it. In such terms, the textual instability of the dialogue could only clash with the authoritarian self-image of philosophy and its writers. So, too, for at least some of the same reasons, we see virtually the elimination of the commentary in its medieval form: what contemporary philosopher would subordinate himself to such a degree as to will truth through a text he had not written himself?

At the same time, one might also suspect that the history of individual philosophical concepts has links or associations with the varieties of genre. Only the most rudimentary analysis has yet been attempted of the causal – social, psychological, aesthetic – origins of philosophical ideas, but it seems obvious that such connections do exist. So it has often been pointed out, for example, that the form of the essay flourished in conjunction with the rise of skepticism (as in its origins with Montaigne and Bacon); and similar correlations can be identified in respect to systematic philosophical issues. Is not the problem of 'other minds' or the proofs required of an external world related to the appearance of genres (like the *Meditations* of Descartes) in which the constitution of the self – from the inside out – is the first requirement of the philosopher? Any such beginning would inevitably leave the constitution of everything other than the I in a precarious position – that is, as a "problem". (One might contrast here the form of the dialogue in which the genre *itself* presupposes the existence of "other minds.")

I recognize that the emphasis of these last comments but also of the earlier structural analysis here is on genre as viewed by the *reader*, for whom the philosophical text exists as an object to be grasped and for whom, then, the categories and elements of genre would provide a means. But what, it might be asked, of the philosopher who as *writer* brings that object into existence in the first place? For if, as has been suggested, the categories of genre are retrospective and readerly, of what use could talk about genre be to the writer – except, perhaps, as a means of acquainting him with readers' expectations which the writer might then choose either to respect or to violate.

This issue is in one aspect part of a more general question about the *definition* of the philosopher as reader and as writer. No one expects a "professor" of literature who speaks about the work of Flaubert or Keats also to write as they did; what the professor of literature does is in these terms entirely readerly (although he may also write *about* his reading). The distinction is much less easily made, however, between the teacher or professor of philosophy, on the one hand, and the philosopher, on the other – and the reasons for this difficulty are related to what has been said here about the writerly status of philosophical genres. Certain consequences which follow from acknowledging a role for genre in the reading of philosophy are writerly as well. The very recognition of "a" genre has the effect not only of disclosing the writing of philosophy as resulting from certain philosophical decisions about that writing – but of relating those de-cisions to the more general philosophical transaction which as a whole then – the hand of the philosopher now included in the body of the philosophical act – becomes representationally significant. We see here again, in a more compelling form that we would otherwise, that writing is itself a subject of philosophical writing, indeed that at times there is no way for philosophy to distinguish between *that* subject and its other, more overt ones.

Again, the philosophical author does not necessarily deliberate about the act of writing or reflect on it. The conventions of writing, including the conventions of genre, may be so strongly embedded, carrying such ideological conviction, that they are invisible. But the philosopher cannot outstrip history or jump out of his philosphical

skin – and the very consciousness that this is so will make a difference. The alternative to it – a road often taken – is to view the writing
of philosophy as filling in the blanks of a set piece, where the project
of philosophy and its methods are assumed as given and fixed.
Philosophy, on this account, purports to be independent of history –
of the history of philosophy and the history of writing, as well, of
course, as the history of individual philosopher. But quite to the
contrary: the texts of philosophy are indebted to each of these. We
can hardly imagine what philosophy would be if this were not the
case, and one large reason for this is the role that genre plays in
defining first the possibility and then the actuality of the philosophical
text. Genre, I have been proposing, is philosophically both functional
and inevitable – functional because it serves a philosophical purpose,
inevitable because there is no way of realizing any other philosophical
purpose without realizing that one as well. In this sense, the status of
genre is much like that of history itself: contingent in each appearance, but unavoidable as a kind.

Even the inevitability of philosophical genre, it should be pointed
out, does not mean that the question of its specific functions does not
remain an issue – for philosophical texts individually or for philosophy as a whole. Rorty, when he speaks gratefully about the passing of
"that literary genre we call 'philosophy' – a genre founded by Plato,"
implies that by calling the whole of philosophy a genre, we not only
assert the contingency of philosophy (i.e., that it *has* a history) but
also diminish its traditional importance, assuring or at least hastening
the end of that history. On a more robust view of genre, the fact that
philosophy as a whole might be viewed as a genre (this would,
incidentally, have to be accompanied by its distinction from other
genres of the same order; what would *they* be? History? Religion?
Astrology? Crossword puzzles?) would imply only that we – writers
and readers alike – ought to take more seriously than we have the
question of what it is that philosophy *does*, with a richer knowledge
now, on the basis of the study of genre, of what the medium of that
doing is. This does not, as it could not, provide the philosophical
writer with a ready-made genre within which he places himself. Quite
to the contrary, it focuses the philosopher's attention on a contingent
present where, after all, philosophy begins and where (the irony is
essential to the fact) it has begun again and again in the past. Plotting
philosophy by way of its genres, then, only leads us back to this
obvious point – the same point, we recognize, to which all philosophical discussion eventually returns. If what I have been saying is
correct in principle, however, it is only when we plot philosophy by its

genres, that we become fully aware of the act to which that plotting leads and for which it is then a necessary condition – the act, that is, of *committing* philosophy.

Notes to Chapter Two

1 Benedetto Croce, *Problemi di Estetici* (Bari: G. Laterza, 1910).
2 See here, e.g., Jacques Derrida, "La Loi du Genre/The Law of Genre," *Glyph*, 7 (1980); Stanley Fish, *Is There a Text in This Class?* (Cambridge, Massachusetts: Harvard University Press, 1980), chs 2 and 10; Jean-François Lyotard, *Driftworks*, edited by Roger McKeon (New York: Semiotext, 1984). Paul Hernadi's view of the usefulness of the conception of genre is ambivalent, but he at least suggests the likelihood of stylistic categories that will supersede those of genre: *Beyond Genre* (Ithaca: Cornell University Press, 1972), pp. 152–6. I do not mean to imply that the argument has been carried on only on one side. For strong defenses of the role of genre, see e.g., Tzvetan Todorov, *The Fantastic*, translated by Richard Howard (Cleveland: Case-Western Reserve University Press, 1977), ch. 3; and Adena Rosmarin, *The Power of Genre* (Minneapolis: University of Minnesota Press, 1985).
3 Richard Rorty, *Philosophy and the Mirror of Nature* (Princeton: Princeton University Press, 1979).
4 Martin Heidegger, "The End of Philosophy and the Task of Thinking," in *On Time and Being*, translated by Joan Stambough (New York: Harper and Row, 1972), pp. 55–73.
5 See, for statements on varieties of philosophical genre, Charles Schmitt, "Renaissance Aristotelianism," in *Aristotle and the Renaissance* (Cambridge, Massachusetts: Harvard University Press, 1983); Hannah Arendt, *Lectures on Kant's Political Philosophy* (Chicago: University of Chicago Press, 1982), pp. 31–3; Rosalie Colie, *The Resources of Kind* (Berkeley: University of California Press, 1973); Julian Marias, "Literary Genres in Philosophy," *Philosophy as Dramatic Theory*, translated by J. Parsons (University Park: Pennsylvania State University Press, 1971).
6 For a collection of views on this issue, see Berel Lang, ed., *Philosophical Style* (Chicago: Nelson-Hall, 1980).
7 For the lineage of the distinction, see Paul Hernadi, *op. cit.*, chs 2 and 3.
8 Thomas Hobbes, *Concerning Body*, I, 1, 2.
9 See Berel Lang, "Space, Time, and Philosophical Style," in *Philosophy and the Art of Writing* (Lewisburg: Bucknell University Press, 1983).
10 Northrop Frye, *Anatomy of Criticism* (Princeton: Princeton University Press, 1957), third essay: "Archetypal Criticism: Theory of Myths."
11 Mikhail Bakhtin, "The Problem of Speech Genres," in *Speech Genres and Other Late Essays*, translated by C. Emerson and M. Holquist,

(Austin: University of Texas Press, 1986), p. 78.

12 For the issues involved in the problem of synonymy and translatability, see W. V. O. Quine, "The Problem of Meaning in Linguistics," in *From a Logical Point of View* (Cambridge, Massachusetts: Harvard University Press, 1953).

13 *Consequences of Pragmatism* (Minneapolis: University of Minnesota Press, 1982), p. xiv; and in the same volume, the essay "Philosophy as a Kind of Writing." See also Rorty's "The Historiography of Philosophy: Four Genres," in Richard Rorty, Jerome Schneewind, and Quentin Skinner, eds, *Philosophy in History* (New York: Cambridge University Press, 1984).

3

Descartes between Method and Style

*Something, if all by itself, may rightfully appear very imperfect; but if it
is seen in its role as a part in the universe, it is most perfect.*
                                    Descartes, Fourth Meditation

The Style of Method

Before Descartes decided on the *Discourse on the Method for Rightly
Conducting the Reason and Seeking for Truth in the Sciences* as a
title, he had alluded to the test we now know by that name more
simply as the "History of My Mind (Esprit)" – and the structure
of the *Discourse* was indeed to remain that of an historical narrative
in which the authorial "I" recounts a sequence of experience and
thought leading to the formulation of a method and the conclusions
that followed from it. Descartes employs a conventional grammatical
form in this narrative: first-person singular, simple past tense. The
evident reason for his choice of this means of representation, as
unlikely philosophically as it is common for storytelling, is that the
"analytic" method which the *Discourse* is a discourse *on* has itself
the form of autobiographical narrative. It follows, according to
Descartes, the historical – and to *that* extent, the logical – progress of
perception and the thinking related to it, as they proceed moment by
moment and from cause to effect. Thus, the autobiographical narrative of the *Discourse* both recounts Descartes' discovery of a method
and affords a view of that method at work; and although it might be
argued that this doubling effect has no wider significance, that a
method can be "mentioned" without at the same time being "used" –

so, for example, that the *Discourse* could just as well have been written as a treatise: third person, present tense, passive voice – Descartes himself tells us that for *his* method, there is good reason why a connection between mention and use should be exhibited in his text. It had not been his intention, he writes to Mersenne (27 February 1637) explaining his choice of "Discourse" rather than "Treatise" in the title, to "*teach*" the method: the method is a "practice rather than a theory."[1]

The discussion here will focus on Descartes' conception of the analytic method in the *Meditations*; but for the moment, that focus is only foreshadowed by reference to a second, less obvious reason for Descartes' use of the first-person singular, past tense in the *Discourse*. This is the fact that this grammatical structure, describing the history of the person who is speaking – in particular, his thoughts or feelings – also serves to block or at least to defer objections or interruptions with which a reader might otherwise interrupt the narrative flow. If I say that yesterday I thought that I could fly, I am not inviting judgment either of a *present* claim that I can fly or of an assertion that I could indeed fly yesterday. I am reporting, usually as part of another and longer story, a thought that I *had* yesterday – and at least this much, that I had the thought yesterday, would ordinarily pass without objection since I am a privileged if not the only possible chronicler of my own thinking. Even the listener or reader who regarded this part of my account as a psychological symptom would be implying acknowledgement of the report itself as true. (If he viewed the report as a whole as a symptom, there would be no place for *any* discussion of truth, however long deferred.)

To be sure, any such narrative sequence may evoke silent reservations or questions on the part of the reader. Certainly, in the history he recounts in the *Discourse*, Descartes lays claim to "ideas" that are not self-evidently true and that might be and that since have been contested when they were judged to stand on their own, unsupported by the bracketing claim that they "truly" had been thought. Moreover, partly by omission – since he never suggests that the conclusions he cites in the course of this intellectual history had been subsequently (from the later vantage point of writer of the *Discourse*) rejected – and by commission, as he often suggests of the conclusions described in the *Discourse* that he not only found them true when he first came on them but continues to do so, Descartes seems to open the *Discourse* to objections directed beyond the incontestability of claims of past first-person experience.

Even with respect to the latter, moreover, the narrative structure within which *all* his assertions appear requires the sympathetic and even only the prudent reader to read to the end of the narration, in order to see if at any later time, within the narrative past or from the vantage point from which as writer he "now" looks back on it, Descartes might have reconsidered what he had earlier reported as his thoughts at the time. The reader, in other words, is impelled by the form of the work to reserve judgment until he sees how the narrative "comes out." This prescription is not, of course, for an indefinite deferral; short of trumpeting like Protagoras that he, Descartes, is the measure of all things (even if only of *his* things), a doctrine with which the *Discourse* itself is finally sharply at odds, the autobiographical narrative of the *Discourse* would have the effect only of temporarily deferring objections and counter-arguments, of urging that judgment be reserved until, as he would in the reading of other "fables" (one of Descartes' own designations for the *Discourse* (Part I)), the reader meets the narration in the actual present that they − the narration brought to conclusion, the reader at the end of his reading − eventually reach in common and at the same time. *Then*, the reader is in a position to judge, to affirm or to deny and in any event to question.

An issue that the *Discourse* skirts is whether this feature of deferral in the text is anything more than an incidental consequence of Descartes' impulse for dramatization − *self*-dramatization at that − or whether it makes no more than a rhetorical or ornamental (a "literary") difference in the presentation of an otherwise substantive philosophical argument. This question moves us abruptly away from the *Discourse* to the text of the *Meditations*. For there, even with the shift in narrative time from the historical past used by Descartes in the *Discourse* to the virtual present used by him in the *Meditations*, we find that the objections to the latter which he attempts to take into account are deliberately and explicitly deferred, to be formally acknowledged only as a later and distinct supplement to the text. Even without the access we have to Descartes' plans for the organization of the *Meditations* and his instructions to Mersenne about how the Objections and Replies are to be placed there, we might infer from their proportions − they are six times longer than the *Meditations* themselves, often repetitive − that Descartes had a specific purpose in mind, first in deciding to solicit and to include them, and then in placing them as he did, complete and separated from the body of the *Meditations* itself.

One side of the question of why Descartes would gather the objections in *one* place rather than have them interspersed topically in the text reflects his reason for soliciting and publishing responses to

the *Meditations* at all. This rationale was in part evidently prudential
and tactical – Descartes' concern to insulate his writings and himself
from social and religious criticism or persecution. He had before this
withheld publication of *Le Monde* when he learned of Galileo's trial
in 1633; and even the *Discourse* and the scientific essays which it
prefaced, purged of references to the "theological" issue of whether it
was the sun or the earth that moved, had stirred critical reactions that
Descartes was anxious to avoid in responses to the *Meditations*. One
means of avoiding unpredictable and possibly dangerous criticism
was to anticipate it by authoritative approval. Thus,

> The less [the ignorant contradiction-mongers] understand it, the more
> eloquent they will be unless they are restrained by the authority of a
> number of learned people . . . . If you agree, I would dedicate it to all
> the masters of the Sorbonne, asking them to be my protectors in God's
> cause. For I must confess that the quibbles of Father Bourdin have
> made me determine to fortify myself henceforth with the authority of
> others, as far as I can . . . . (Letter to Mersenne, 30 September 1640)

For this purpose, moreover, to have all the objections gathered in *one*
place, associated with their respective respondents, would allow
readers to see that the objections, however rigorous, did not carry
with them condemnation. The very absence of condemnation from
comments offered by eminences of the learned and clerical world
would itself be a protective hedge: even objections might serve as an
imprimatur in the absence of a more formal one.

But this, admittedly, is no intrinsic reason for the deferral of the
objections, and Descartes provides a cluster of such reasons as well.
He suggests, for one thing, that potential objections to the *Meditations* need to be formulated (published and then read together with
his replies) as following the order of the *Meditations*, since then the
order of the objections would, whatever their other merits or defects,
correspond to the order in which the assertions they were questioning
had been made. This insistence underscores the question of *what* in
the links that determine the sequence of the *Meditations* is so important for the reader's understanding. We find the answer to that
question by a process of detection that relates Descartes' own testimony about the need to defer readers' objections to his conception of
the method "practised" in the *Meditations*; this conjunction leads in
turn to a conception of the meditation as a distinctive medium of
philosophical expression. The line of argument here involves many
central themes of Cartesian metaphysics that have often been dis-

cussed independently – although it can be argued (as Descartes himself first claims) that such dissociation is often tendentious, that it introduces distortions into what these accounts then conclude to be Descartes' "position" in the *Meditations*. The latter objection, moreover, is not only a general comment about the importance of taking seriously the context in which a specific philosophical argument appears. For beyond this, Descartes' wish to defer objections reflects what he takes to be the *unusual* connections (and thus, the unusual context) established in the sequence of argument in the *Meditations*. The requirements embodied in those connections – historical, logical, metaphysical – lead Descartes to reflect deliberately and systematically on what otherwise might seem to be purely a formal or aesthetic matter: the question of what meditation – the practice, the literary genre, and finally, the specific character of *his Meditations* – is.

A direction is given to this line of interpretation in a striking statement written by Descartes to Mersenne (24 December 1640): "I do not think that it would be useful, or even possible, to insert into my meditations the answers to the objections that may be made to them. That would interrupt the flow and even destroy the force of my arguments." The claim that an "interruption" of the *Meditations* in order to respond to (and by implication, before that, to have stated) certain objections might "destroy" the force of his arguments must be startling to most modern readers. If the claim were true, of course, it undoubtedly would be a good reason (for Descartes, at least) for wanting to defer the objections. But how *could* it be true if we are here addressing the Descartes of "clear and distinct" ideas, those building blocks of knowledge which, attached to one another, constitute (on most interpretations) what Descartes takes to be the whole of the philosophical – and real – world? Would not the very notion of a *distinct* idea argue against a claim for the "flow" of an argument, one which could be "destroyed" by the interruption of objections?

The answers to these questions and to others implied by them are rooted in the connection between Descartes' conception and practice of method in the *Meditations*, on the one hand, and the genre of the meditation that Descartes in part inherits, in part creates, on the other. Viewed from one perspective, that connection is close, virtually an identity: the structures of philosophical method and philosophical style merge. From a second perspective, Descartes' interest in method and his concern with the dispositions of philosophical genre and style are not only distinct but at odds with each other, almost contradictory – method being held quite apart from the ornamental or aesthetic boundaries of genre and style. These two standpoints are more than only alternative ways of reading Descartes; they are, I shall be arguing, conflicting impulses in Descartes himself (one of them would become a dominant influence in the history of interpretations of *him*.) I am proposing, then, to consider these two versions of what amounts to *another* Cartesian dualism, less well known than the mind–body dualism, but for Descartes who would at once affirm and attempt to overcome the mind–body distinction, not much less fundamental or compelling. We might suspect, in fact, that the two dualisms – method/style, body/mind – are related conceptually and also in the task they leave to one side. For on Descartes' own account of the dualism of body and mind, he acknowledges, together with their difference, that there must be *some* way of fitting the two together. Insofar as Descartes is a dualist, he is clearly a penitent dualist; we might reasonably hope, then, for the equivalent of a pineal gland as an intermediary between style and method.

Descartes' method in the *Meditations* emerges both in what he says about it and in his practice. The fullest reference that Descartes makes to that method appears in his "Reply to the Second Set of Objections:"

> Analysis shows the true way by which a thing was methodically discovered and derived, as it were [to] effect from cause, so that if the reader care to follow it and give sufficient attention to everything, he understands the matter no less perfectly and makes it as much his own as if he had himself discovered it. But it contains nothing to incite belief in an inattentive or hostile reader; for if the very least thing brought forward escapes his notice the necessity of the conclusions is lost.... Synthesis contrariwise employs an opposite procedure, one in which the search goes as it were from effect to cause.... It does indeed clearly demonstrate its conclusion; and it employs a long series of definitions, postulates, axioms, theorems and problems, so that if one of the conclusions that follow is denied, it may at once be shown to be contained in what has gone before. Thus the reader, however hostile and obstinate, is compelled to render his assent. Yet this method is not so satisfactory.... [2]

This well-known comparison between the methods of analysis and synthesis contains a number of surprises for the modern reader, beginning with the contrast that Descartes finds between the "inattentive or hostile" reader and the more careful reader who gives "sufficient attention." The synthetic method that will "compel" the former reader would more usually be expected to emerge as the stronger of the two alternatives: an argument that can convince hostile readers would be likely also to serve for sympathetic readers. Conversely, the analytic method which persuades readers who are not hostile might well be judged to have limited force, to be tendentious, in fact, as it takes advantage of the reader's disposition to go along with the sequence of argument rather than to test it. Descartes anticipates the latter charge – that critics might claim that it was "unfair of me to want to have the truth of my contentions admitted before they have been fully scrutinized...." ("Reply to the Second Set of Objections"). Nonetheless, it *is* in this direction that he turns, defending the analytic method as the one more suitable for what he means to say and do in the *Meditations*.[3]

What is it, then, that marks the practice of the "hostile or inattentive" reader and his synthetic method, but is avoided by the sympathetic reader who follows the analytic method? In Descartes' statements that are quoted above, a principal difference between the two is that for the former, the sequence of argument opens itself to interruption by objections, that the reader there finds no reason to wait to see the whole of the argument before reacting to its individual assertions. To be sure, it might be objected that the latter response would hardly be extraordinary; it happens all the time. It would, in any event, be an unlikely basis for the selection or rejection of something as fundamental for philosophical discourse as a method. But it would matter, indeed it would be crucial, if the connectives in the sequence of argument were not only logical but actual, if the steps in the sequence corresponded to a development of history or experience and not only to a process of logical inference. For here an interruption by objections would have the effect of isolating a *part* of the sequence and of testing it by itself, when it was the cumulative sequence – what led the writer up to the present from which he writes and what was to lead beyond it – that was being "asserted."

This is, in fact, the issue on which Descartes' preference for the method of analysis turns. If – as the synthetic method presupposes – a philosophical argument is arranged not temporally but logically; if the conclusions of an argument are derived from a set of "definitions, axioms, postulates" that serve collectively as premises, then any of its logically possible conclusions can be inferred at any time. The order of discussion will thus be constrained only by the "order of topics" – that is, the order of whatever at a particular moment, on the temporal grid of what was logically possible, interested the writer; objections

to which he responded, then, would be "disjoined," and understandably so – since he could "say as much about one difficulty as about
another" (Letter to Mersenne, 24 December 1640). But the structure
of the *Meditations* requires a different manner of response. The
sequence of argument there does not depend on the interest of a
reader (or before him, the writer) but on its own terms – where it
perforce begins and then on the way in which it then continues; it is
the possibility of argument itself (and of the arguer) that is being
tested there. Thus the order of proof is inseparable from the historical
order: to break into the sequence by isolating one of its steps (even by
anticipating or skipping ahead) is to distort the line of argument by
altering its connectives or modalities. The interruption of mediation
is thus only incidentally a *psychological* phenomenon; the loss of
sequence affects the substance of the argument and not merely the
manner of its presentation. Thus when Descartes calls for patience
from his readers, when he quarrels with readers who do not take
ample time to formulate their objections to the *Meditations*, he
introduces more than only an author's plea for a conscientious and
sympathetic reading. The *character* of the argument is alleged to
require that sufficient time be taken by the reader with each step – and
then also that of judgment be deferred, if not necessarily the "two or
three years" that Descartes once suggests *he* would be prepared to
wait for likely objections, at least until the place of each step within
the whole has been adequately considered.

The reasons for this last, inclusive requirement become clear in
another aspect of the difference between what is now referred to as
the "hypothetico–deductive" method (of synthesis) and the analytic
method.[4] The former will not do – would *never* do, on Descartes'
account – as providing a foundation of knowledge because of its
starting point in hypothetical premises: definitions, axioms, postulates. We can, setting out from such premises, be certain that what
is alleged to follow from them does indeed follow, and this could
be assessed at each step of inference; but the truth of conclusions
reached in this way would be tested only so far as the premises had
first been tested – and *this* can not be assured by the synthetic method
itself. For Descartes, as James Collins writes, we are "held captive [by
the synthetic method] in a skeptical suspension of assent to the truth
of its principles and their inferred consequences."[5]

An important issue that was, in Descartes' view, decided by the
difference between the two methods appears in the dispute that
Descartes himself entered about the logical standing of the *Cogito* –
the charge directed at it almost immediately upon its appearance that
it was in fact no more than an abbreviated syllogism (an enthymeme)

with the major premise suppressed. Descartes' response to this is explicit: that the *Cogito* is *not* the question-begging syllogism it would be if the concluding "sum" were claimed to follow from the addition of a major premise (that "all thinking thing exist") to the explicit minor premise, "I think." Quite the contrary, in fact: we could not know that "All thinking things exist" except as we were initially assured that "*I* think, therefore I exist." "For it is certain," Descartes writes specifically about the *Cogito* in the "Reply to the Second Set of Objections," "that in order to discover the truth we should always start with particular notions, in order to arrive at general conceptions subsequently . . . . " (Cf. also the Letter to Clerselier, 12 January 1646, where Descartes directs much the same reply to Gassendi's similar objection.) To be sure, Descartes' dissent here does not resolve the question of what the logical status of the Cogito *is*. But if we assume that Descartes knew that the syllogism "All thinking things exist; I think; therefore I exist" was a valid argument, then his rejection of it as a reading of the *Cogito* indicates that in his view the *Cogito* represented a different argument – more than that, a different *kind* of argument.

One such alternative is that provided by the analytic method, and its reference to the actual order of events – that is, to a correspondence between the "virtual" time in a sequence of argument and the "real" time of history outside it. The plausibility of this basis for the analytic method is underscored because it is the possibility of knowledge as such that is at stake in the *Meditations*. That issue, furthermore, is not so much the question of where the Cartesian meditator can begin to rely on claims of knowledge but where the beginning of the meditator himself is. The same question of origins, moreover, persists in the successive stages of Descartes' argument, constantly forcing a relation among the later stages and between them and the starting point of the act of meditation. This is not to say that parts of the sequence of argument (including the *Cogito* itself) *cannot* be addressed by themselves, out of context, but that to do so entails an abstraction (both literally and metaphorically) from a sequence of argument whose function it is to constitute the actual world, not its abstracted parts – and a place for the thinker in it.

To be sure, according to Descartes, what exists discloses itself to the act of meditation, rather than, as one might expect from his emphasis on historical development, to the senses. The hard work that Descartes associates with the process of meditation (which turns out to be identical for the reader and the writer), requires more than anything else a disengagement from the senses. Interruptions in the sequence of meditation come, in fact, from critics who have not attempted (or if they have, have not succeeded in) this process of disengagement: "The majority of objections [to the *Meditations*] would be drawn from perceptible things, whereas my arguments get their force from the withdrawal of thought from objects of sense." (Letter to Mersenne, 24 December 1640).

Descartes may seem to move too quickly here in his assumption that the critic who breaks into his (Descartes') meditation *must* be at cross-purposes with that process; it might be objected here that he claims (circularly) that someone who interrupts the sequence of argument would *by that fact* be known not to have been meditating. But he might mean, more subtly, that objections likely to be obtruded would single out for criticism particular moments or items of evidence in what he had intended not as a series of distinguishable ideas, but as a cumulative sequence of steps at once possible and actual – *made* actual in the process of meditation as it had before that been actual in the order of things. Objections on refutations (themselves, after all, a "genre" of discourse) characteristically allege a conflict between evidence presented by the objector and individual claims in the original argument. Descartes is here contesting *both* these interventions. (A possible but much rarer objection might be directed to the *whole* of the original context; in the case of the *Meditations*, this would amount to "disproving" the existence of the meditator – a conclusion that Descartes might also welcome as proving what it had set out to disprove.)

Descartes' reference to the requirement of concentration in meditation, the need for disengagement by the meditator from the occasional and contingent moments that comprise sensible experience in order to follow the continuities of the analytic method, is an important clue in understanding Descartes' choice of the meditation as a distinctive genre of philosophical discourse. More will be said here about how the Cartesian meditation is shaped to take account of the continuities of the analytic method – but also this aspect of the meditation, we quickly see, is related to the denial of a philosophical role to the senses. One of the two intentions announced for the *Meditations* in Descartes' full title – to demonstrate the "distinction of the soul from the body" – is thus also held by him to be a *condition* for the practice of meditation.

The disengagement from the senses and its corollary in the process of systematic doubt of which the senses are the first and principal object do not by themselves account for Descartes' conception of the meditation either as practice or as a literary genre; still missing from that disengagement is the feature of temporality or sequence that turns out to be crucial in Descartes' preference for the analytic over the synthetic method. Indeed, the requirement of disengagement might seem to be at odds with this other feature. References to the writing and practice of meditation both prior and subsequent to Descartes have typically viewed the withdrawal from the senses as a means of eliminating or minimizing the effects of the temporal character of experience; and the literary tradition in which Descartes writes seems also to deny the requirement (or even the possibility) of sequentiality as a feature of the meditation. Montaigne is often cited as creator of the genre of the personal essay to which the *Meditations* is indebted. (He is also, on other grounds, an important figure in the Cartesian background, mainly as occasioning the contention that Descartes was as much interested in attacking skepticism as he was in dislodging scholastic dogmatism.[6] "All that is certain is that nothing is certain," Montaigne had inscribed on a beam in his study – certain grist for the Cartesian mill [as, for example, in Descartes' Second Rule: "He who doubts of many things is not more learned than he who has never thought about them."]) But the "I" encountered by the reader in Montaigne's *Essays*, even in the different settings through which Montaigne leads it, is nonetheless a constant that relates past events in its thought and experience to a present time from which it looks back, and that appears then not so much as a goal to be reached or even a consequence of the past as a distributor of equity, balancing and reconstituting the pieces of that past.

Descartes drew explicitly on the work of the Stoics for whom the meditation was also at once a literary genre and a mode of practice. But here again, in Seneca whom Descartes often cites, or in Epictetus and Marcus Aurelius, the internal structure of both the practice and the genre of the mediation is not sequential or cumulative. It is a notable feature in the meditative writings of these authors (for example, in Marcus Aurelius' *To Himself* or in Epictetus' *Manual*) that a reader can break into the text at almost any point and still be engaged by the directive towards detachment that animates the writing as read in sequence. This is entirely understandable, since if the Stoics hoped to encourage *apathia* or detachment in the reader, it would be inconsistent for them to require him to subordinate himself to anyone else (even to a writer offering instruction on the process of meditation). The meditation as a genre implies a freedom on the part of the reader to act on what the writer places before him, a freedom equal to that of the writer as *he* affirms or denies. Only so, moreover, is it possible to comprehend the clear and distinct ideas of knowledge: the compulsion that the latter carry with them presupposes the prior freedom of the understanding.[7] Almost always the evocation of freedom in the meditation is the more pointed because of the contrast it represents to a history of error and bondage: the requirement set by Descartes of disengagement from the senses is in this sense a variation on Epictetus' literal emancipation from slavery.

The literary genre that employs the feature of temporality which Descartes adds to the feature of disengagement in his own version of the meditation is not the traditional meditation at all but the autobiography. The latter genre[8] is built around a representation of authorial sequentiality in which the events of a life are traced within the life itself – from a stipulated beginning to the later point at which the autobiographer, writing, looks backward. To be sure, some autobiographies amount to little more than chronicles, with nothing more "inward" or reflective about them than is found in biographies; in those but also in other autobiographies as well, furthermore, the emphasis on chronological sequence might seem to work against the disengagement that I have suggested characterizes the meditation. But Descartes is deliberate not only in his choice of the meditation as a genre; he also revises the genre, shaping it to do *his* work – and it is in this light that the conjunction is to be understood of disengagement and sequentiality not otherwise characteristic of either the autobiography or the meditation by themselves.

This does not mean that there were no historical precedents to the *Meditations*. Just as Descartes, at the suggestion of a correspondent who had noticed their similarity, goes to the library in Leiden to read (so far as it known, for the first time) Augustine's version of the *Cogito* in *De Trinitate*, so he might also have looked back to Augustine's *Confessions* as making use of the feature of temporality that he employs in the *Meditations*.[9] Even that important precedent, however, often cited for its unusual joining of a spiritual history with the self-awareness of the mind writing the history, does not quite meet Descartes' requirements, since the sequence of Augustine's development does not have the logical force that Descartes ascribes to the development in his narrative. Augustine conceives the movement in the *Confessions* as a form of ascension, but the progression of the *Meditations* has a stronger necessity to it than that of an historical sequence reported as it occurred or even as willed. Descartes' autobiographical "I" is meant to leave enough space for the reader also to pronounce his own "I;" indeed, that pronouncement would be *required* of the careful and sympathetic reader.[10]

A similar distinction holds, with slightly different emphasis, between the *Meditations*, on the one hand, and Bonaventure's *Journey of the Mind into God* and Loyola's *Spiritual Exercises*, on the other – works sometimes cited as anticipations of Descartes. In both those accounts, the stages of development (Bonaventure's six "steps," Loyola's four weeks), although related to each other as it happens, are not internally related; they are also meant progressively to exclude certain thoughts rather than, as in Descartes' work, to achieve necessity by having cumulatively thought all of what can be doubted and what cannot.[11] (Derrida is undoubtedly correct in arguing against Foucault that madness, too, is regarded by Descartes as within the domain of thinking.)[12]

Although there is no evidence that Descartes conceived of his revision of the genre of the meditation as itself an issue, he was aware that the feature of sequentiality, of the cumulative and uninterrupted development of argument on which he insists in the *Meditations*, might seem at odds with the direct meeting – in the *present* – between mind and idea that the act of meditation had characteristically represented. Only in the light of this possible conflict does Descartes' reiteration that the *Meditations*, read in sequence, will nonetheless eventuate in clear and distinct ideas make sense; it is against that background, too, that we understand the escape route which Descartes assures himself (at least he believes he does) from the charge of circularity – a charge directed against the *Meditations* almost from the date of its composition (further discussed below).

Descartes' conception of the mediation as a genre thus directs his reader to the substantive purpose of his thinking in the *Meditations*. As I have been suggesting, it is virtually impossible to separate those two aspects of his work – and the objection that since (on the argument here) Descartes deliberately shaped the genre as a vehicle for his method, there should be nothing surprising in the discovery that they came to "fit" each other, argues as much *for* the claim of an intrinsic necessary connection as against it. The substantial evidence that Descartes deliberately turned to the meditation because of its features at once as a stylistic genre and as a representation of method also serves as evidence for a more general claim about philosophical writing – that the capacity, even the disposition of particular genres for realizing certain philosophical effects is a philosophical and not "only" a literary consideration. This last point is an important step in the direction of conceiving a general poetics of philosophical discourse,[13] and the irony that such a conclusion should be associated with Descartes – more often held up by both proponents and critics as a "purist," arguing for a disembodied method – only adds intensity to the issue itself.

For Descartes, moreover, the meditation is related in its literary features quite specifically to certain substantive issues of the *Meditations* often viewed as quite independent of the other. One group of these issues turns in common on the function that Descartes ascribes to memory – a function required at once in the mind of a knower, or, more immediately, in the mind of Descartes' reader; the importance of this function is due to the fact that it is mainly by way of it that Descartes thinks to escape the charge of methodological circularity, a charge that would be serious for any philosophical argument and fatal for a purportedly "foundationalist" theory of knowledge.

The alleged "Cartesian Circle" has appeared in a variety of formulations, all of which revolve around the relation between the *Cogito* and the proof of God's existence; it is in this relation, too, that a means of escape from the circle is provided. The progression moves in two steps: (1) It begins with the apparent contradiction between the claims, on the one hand, that the proof of the *Cogito* is indubitable, and, on the other hand, that only on the basis of proof of the existence of a God who is not a deceiver is certainty possible. The circularity apparently initiated by this contradiction – that certainty is required in the "proof" of God's existence in order that certainty, as sanctioned by God's existence, should be possible – gives way only as (2) the terms on which this objection rests are elaborated in such a way as to disclose the circle – and the prior contradiction – as only apparent. It is in respect to the latter point, I shall be suggesting, that the genre of the meditation is significant as an enabling medium for the distinctive sequence of argument that Descartes claims for it.

More fully formulated, the Cartesian Circle has the following form: The *Cogito* "proof," Descartes alleges at the beginning of the "Third Meditation," serves as a standard for all other truth: "Thus I now seem to be able to posit as a general rule that what I very clearly and distinctly perceive is true." But soon after that passage, *too* soon, one supposes, for an obvious contradiction, Descartes *also* interjects: " . . . I ought at the first opportunity to inquire if there is a God, and if there is, whether or not he can be a deceiver. If I am ignorant of these matters, I do not think I can be certain of anything else." Descartes then goes on to prove the existence of God – and the "circle" thus emerges: the premises in the proof of God's existence must be true and are judged so because they are seen clearly and distinctly (this includes the *Cogito* argument itself and then the criterion of truth based on it); but their (and any other) truth *depends* on the proof of

God's existence and its corollary that God is not a deceiver. Thus – the circle is here completed – God must be known to exist in order to be known to exist. *Circle*

In these terms, Descartes is apparently forced to choose between an apparent contradiction, on the one hand (that certainty is possible only with and only without proof of God's existence), and the menace of circularity, on the other, with the costly escape it would provide from the contradiction. A means of disrupting this circle, however, would be possible by showing that the criterion represented by clarity and distinctness and the criterion applied in the extended proof of the Meditations as a whole are not identical, but complementary – that they apply to two different contexts which, although not incompatible, are methodologically distinct.[14] The second of these is based finally on the limitations Descartes attributes to memory in holding together a long sequence of argument; it is the genre of the meditation which with God as guarantor overcomes those limitations. For less extensive ideas (like the proof of the *Cogito* itself), clarity and distinctness suffice by themselves as a criterion of certainty. Again, the key to this distinction – and thus to escaping from the circle – is the genre and practice of the meditation.

I have mentioned before that Descartes alludes on a number of occasions to the demanding nature of meditation, and in particular to the difficulty of keeping ideas meditated "before" the mind. So, for example, he writes to Chanut (1 February 1647) that his own mind, too, "is easily tired by them [ideas], and the . . . presence of sensible objects does not allow me to dwell on such thoughts for long." This difficulty would evidently be compounded when meditation had not one idea or object before it but was sequential, when the meditator was obliged to keep "in mind" a complex series of steps – like that in the *Meditations*. Descartes himself indicates that there are limits to what direct inspection by the mind can encompass – in other words, limits to what can at a moment be viewed "clearly and distinctly." At the lower limits, to be sure, there are numerous examples of ideas that can be viewed in that way, the *Cogito* argument being perhaps the most important but only one of them.[15] But *how much* of the sequence of argument in the *Meditations* – a sequence that, as we have seen, Descartes insists must be regarded as a single whole – can be comprehended by direct inspection of this sort?

A key text concerning this question appears in the *Conversation with Burman*, in response to Burman's formulation of the charge of circularity (Burman cites the standard objection – that the axioms in the proof of God's existence require a guarantee of certainty which only God himself would provide). Descartes' rejection of the charge of circularity is unequivocal: "He [the author of the *Meditations*; Burman represents Descartes' references to himself as given in the third person] knows that he is not deceived with regard to [the individual axioms][16] since he is actually paying attention to them.... Since our thought is able to grasp more than one item in this way.... it is clear that we are able to grasp the proof of God's existence in its entirety. As long as we are engaged in this process, we are certain that we are not being deceived, and every difficulty is thus removed."[17]

Descartes is not claiming here that the proof of God's existence is either the only or, more importantly, the most extensive proof that is based on a sequence of clear and distinct ideas viewed by themselves and without the *presupposition* of God's existence. Neither here nor elsewhere does he set a limit for the extent of ideas that can be known clearly and distinctly in a single viewing. But it becomes evident that there *is* such a limit – and it is at and beyond that point that the genre of the meditation and the role of God as the guarantor of memory become significant. Descartes' response to Burman, in any event, stops short of that point, and in this it corroborates other statements, principally in the "Reply to the Second Set of Objections," which also imply that at least *some* valid claims to knowledge do not presuppose God's existence (thus, an escape from the charge of circularity); and that God's existence does serve as a guarantee of knowledge in other contexts where it is the *memory* of clear and distinct ideas on which the claims of knowledge depend. The latter claim brings out the connection between Descartes' escape from the Cartesian Circle and the genre of the Cartesian meditation with its characteristic reliance on memory and God.

Exactly how God serves as guarantor for ideas not seen clearly and distinctly in themselves has been a matter of dispute. (This issue should be distinguished from the question of God's role as the guarantor of *existence*. Even God's power to have made everything different from what it is does not explain how the *knowledge* of God's existence serves man as an epistemological surrogate for clear and distinct ideas.) Cottingham, who focuses on this issue in the Introduction to his edition of the *Conversation with Burman*, argues that the guarantee provided by God's existence is a reaction to "the essential *disconnectedness* that would be a feature of knowledge without God" (p. xxxi), God's existence thus establishes the "possibility" that memory does not deceive us as we now recall having *had* a particular clear and distinct idea. But this explanation is not commensurate with the importance that Descartes attaches to God's role as guarantor, since in establishing only the *possibility* of knowledge, Cottingham does not, for any particular case of the memory of a clear and distinct idea (let alone for a sequence of such cases), show how that "possible" knowledge becomes "actual." And if God's existence (more specifically, his veracity) does not accomplish the latter, the meditator—reader would, for a progressively larger part of the *Meditations*, be left not with certainty and knowledge, but only with the fallible memory of what *might be* true and thus known. Where, still, would certainty come from?

A similar objection applies to Hacking's interpretation of the "circle," according to which God's existence and then his veracity are needed for reassurance in those cases when we remember having been certain of an idea but also feel (because the proof is not immediately before us) that we might have been "wrongly convinced."[18] Here again: if – against Descartes' position – the original certainty (of clear and distinct ideas) carried over to our memory of them, then God's veracity would not be required, any more than it had been in order to certify the original clarity and distinctness; if the original certainty does not carry over to memory, then (on Hacking's account) God's veracity could be appealed to for certifying *any* memory of certainty, those which were in fact mistaken in their remembered claims of certainty as well as those which were correct. And Descartes nowhere claims the infallibility of memory for *all* ideas. (If he did, there would be no need for God in the role of guarantor.)

Descartes does not, in thus responding to the charge of circularity, assign a role to memory in general, even to that of the person for whose *particular* memories God's existence serves as a guarantee. Descartes explicitly avoids offering any such general endorsement in the *Conversation with Burman* shortly after rejecting the charges of circularity: "I have nothing to say on the subject of memory. Everyone should test himself to see whether he is good at remembering. If he has any doubts, then he should make use of written notes and so forth to help him." (p. 5) In order to reconcile this bland denial with the explicit references Descartes *does* make to the role of God as guarantor of memory (an odd inversion of this role is Descartes' appeal to the hypothesis of the "evil genius": without bearing in mind the possibility of that demon's capacity to deceive, Descartes might *forget to doubt* the "longstanding opinions [that] keep coming back again and again"); and in order to avoid the difficulties identified in explanations such as those of Cottingham and Hacking of what God is a guarantor *of* – we ought, it seems, to distinguish: (1) the function of memory in general (here we can take Descartes at his own explicit word); (2) the memory of a *kind* of idea that would *itself* guarantee memory (in which case God's role as guarantor would be redundant); and lastly, (3) a sequence of argument that because of its complexity requires the use of memory and therefore requires a guarantor for it (which then would become the guarantor of the argument and its conclusion.) It is true that in the *Meditations* Descartes repeats assertions and arguments he has sometimes made elsewhere, in texts organized quite differently; but his formulation of those ideas in the *Meditations* is distinctive in respect to the order in which they are presented, the tightness of the relation among them, and the extent of the whole which they then constitute and which requires the aid of memory. Since memory is not guaranteed as a function of individual clear and distinct ideas or of groups of ideas as such, there must be something about the arrangement or order of the ideas in the *Meditations* on which the certainty that Descartes claims for it is based – and it is just such an order, with God as its guarantor, that Descartes finds in the genre of the meditation. The specific order that *he* follows may not be required for meditation as such (although Descartes seems to imply that one cannot meditate simply about *anything*, that the object of meditation is linked to the possibility of meditation. So, for example, it is clear that one could not meditate at all, in Descartes' terms, if the existence of the meditator remained in question). But the order of the *Meditations*, at any rate, is regarded by Descartes as necessary and one that can only be sustained as God guarantees the memory on which a view of the whole as clear and distinct is made possible. The clear and distinct ideas of the *Meditations* form a sequence. This – both the clarity and distinctness, and the fact of the sequence – can be known at any point in the sequence (since it is always known how the "I" has reached that point); thus, too, if one of them is in doubt, they are all in doubt.

The proof of God's existence – more specifically of his veracity – provides assurance that they could not *all* be in doubt, that the sequence is indeed a sequence of proof. Single ideas or even, up to a point, complex arguments, can be perceived clearly and distinctly – and directly; God's veracity, on the other hand, makes possible certainty about a sequence of clear and distinct ideas when the sequence is too extensive to be itself perceived directly. God is thus guarantor of the practice, and then of the genre, of the meditation. It is not too strong to claim, moreover, that He serves in this rôle *because* the power of clear and distinct ideas, at least as they may be related to each other in a chain of argument, is limited. Consider the analogy of a runner on a track. On the first lap, the runner counts "one," seeing "clearly and distinctly" that nothing has come before that lap. By the eighth or ninth lap (perhaps earlier), he can no longer distinguish in memory among the laps he has run – but he may be quite clear in his mind about the *number* of laps run because of the connection between each one of them and its successor which he designates by a number. The effect is that of a clear and distinct idea, although not every part of that idea can itself be known clearly and distinctly.

Would not this contention imply a role for God as the guarantor of *any* clear and distinct ideas that memory (which we know to be fallible) might look back to? And again, if this *were* the case, either God's role would be redundant, or all instances of memory (and certainly any particular one) could be claimed as infallible. But it is not just *any* idea that God is guarantor of; it is the possibility that *all* the ideas in the meditative sequence (because they are so closely tied to each other, it would be all or none) might turn out to be false that Descartes guards against: the possibility, in other words, that knowledge as such is impossible. It is the practice of meditation itself, of establishing a ground of certainty for the self of the meditator, that is at once tested and asserted in the *Meditations*; thus also the process of meditation, as it assumes the possibility of certainty, is dependent in Descartes' account on the remembered (and guaranteed) conclusions of the *Meditations*.

It is in reference to this last point that we can understand Descartes' otherwise puzzling emphasis on the conclusions reached in the process of meditation. He repeatedly encourages readers of the *Meditations* to rely on the conclusions reached there rather than to keep repeating the process by which those conclusions are reached. So he reassures Elizabeth (28 June 1643): "I think the best thing is to content oneself with keeping in one's memory and one's belief the conclusions which one has once drawn from [meditation] and then employ the rest of one's study time to thoughts in which the intellect cooperates with the imagination and the senses." Again, in the *Conversation with Burman*: "You should not devote so much effort to the *Meditations* and to metaphysical questions. . . . It is sufficient to have grasped them once in a general way and then to remember the conclusions."[19] There is some irony in the fact that precisely because of the distinctive character of the Cartesian meditation – the close bond between its temporal and its logical character – the meditator (and so for Descartes, also the reader of his *Meditations*) is obliged to take them either all or nothing: they do not come in pieces. Understood properly, even the conclusions of the *Medita-tions* – the elements of the world restored – are mnemonic devices for recalling the process of meditation. Thus, in the non-meditative (and greater) part of the life of a Cartesian meditator, it is memory and habit that recall the force of the meditation, although they do not, of course, substitute for it. But this is possible only because of the role of memory – based on God's warrant in the act of meditation itself.

The genre or literary form of the meditation thus solves an epistemo-logical problem for Descartes. By its means, he is able to show how the effect of "clear and distinct" ideas perceived directly and in the present can be maintained over the course of a sequence of ideas that would *not* be clear and distinct if they were viewed as individual ideas. In the end (so I have been arguing), these two functions of the meditation, the genre and the practice, are for Descartes hardly distinguishable; the reader who meditates with him, that is, who *reads* him, will be committed to the steps and then to the conclusions of the process of meditation. Descartes insists again and again on the practice of his work *as* meditation – not only as thinking (as that applies to *all* mental activity) and not only as demonstration or argument. In the "Reply to the Second Set of Objections," he writes, "Hence . . . I rightly require singular attention on the part of my readers and have especially selected the style of writing which I thought would best secure it . . . . My writing took the form of meditations rather than that of philosophical disputations so that I might by this very fact testify that I had no dealings except with those who will not shrink from joining me in giving the matter attentive care and meditation." Or again, in a remark to Silhon (Letter, May, 1637): "But as for intelligent people like yourself, Sir, if they take the trouble not only to read but to meditate in order the things I say meditated . . . I trust that they will come to the same conclusions as I did."

   To be sure, there is no possibility of demonstrating that the genre of the meditation conceived by Descartes was (or is) unique in its capacity as a medium for the kind of argument that Descartes envisioned for it; nor is it possible, aside from the *Meditations* itself, to show that he succeeded in his design even there. But the deliberate-ness of his choice and the reasons for it are clear – as are the reasons also for his rejection of the alternative genres available to him. The philosophical treatise, as Descartes himself suggests, represents a logical and temporal structure; it requires the commitment of narrator or reader to the implications of its premises – but in no necessary order so far as the conclusions are concerned and not at all to the premises which remain always assumptions. This objection applies as well, in slightly variant form, to the geometric method (Descartes takes the trouble in his "Reply to the Second Set of Objections" to show that he could have used this method had he chosen to: "I append here something [!] in the synthetic style that may I hope be somewhat to my reader's profit"). Although Descartes does not seem to have commented specifically on the dialogue form,[20] this too, it seems, works to defer the determination and certainty that Descartes was seeking and believed possible in the meditation. The objections and counterarguments characteristic of the medieval *summa* as a genre would have defined a means not much different from the objections and replies that Descartes placed only as an appendage to his own *Meditations*.

It might be objected that the claims thus implied for the relation between style and method in the *Meditations* do not demonstrate either that the form of the Cartesian meditation is intrinsically tied to its method or that the meditation as a genre is unique in its capacity for philosophical expression. And again, it is difficult to know how any such claims *could* be argued except as the nominalist argument might be made (on a priori grounds) for a deep distinction – that is, uniqueness – not only among genres but among all individual philosophical works. On the other hand, the likely objection that what Descartes "says" or "argues" in the *Meditations* could just as well have been said or argued by other means has itself to be treated with suspicion as a priori or stipulative (and notwithstanding his *own* use of other genres, as I have argued in chapter 2). For that apparently modest appeal to common sense typically begs an important question in its use of "says" or "argues" – terms which are themselves embedded in a tacit but quite specific conception of knowledge. One characteristic assumption in this conception regards philosophical discourse as a propositional structure that has the properties of its parts, that is, of the independent – and independently verifiable – propositions. But on the account given here of Descartes' intentions in the *Meditations*, precisely this conception of philosophical assertion is in dispute. The genre of the meditation, like the act of meditation, turns out to be a doing as well as a saying, and the doing is in fact broader than saying, *much* broader if saying is limited to asserting and connecting a series of independent propositions, like beads on a string. The difficulty of demonstrating that the meditation is a necessary means for Descartes' project, in fact, cuts two ways. For if it is not a necessary or exclusive means, we should be able to identify other possible ones; but none, in fact, seemed evident to Descartes, and if we take seriously the requirements that Descartes set himself, it is arguable that none seems more evident even now.

Even if objections persist to the claim for an intrinsic or necessary connection between method and style in the *Meditations*, the more limited claim of a *de facto* connection between them seems undeniable: that in the *Meditations*, Descartes was concerned not only to say what he had to say but, by means of the saying, to *establish* what was proposed or believed first in his own life and then in the life of the reader who was thus to be no mere observer but an agent in the same process. The medium of expression was frankly intended to make provision for an unusual second party in the standard contract between writer and reader – not only the "implied" reader that all texts provide for but an active participant whose role, in the end, was to be identical with that of the implied author. Reader, in effect, becomes writer – since to read a Cartesian meditation with understanding of what meditation is, *is* to meditate. ("He [the reader] understands the matter no less perfectly and makes it as much his own as if he had himself discovered it" ["Reply to Second Set of Objections"].) The genre of the Cartesian meditation, moreover, clearly is intended to match its form to that of the objects or issues at stake: if the possibility of radical doubt is truly to be tested, then the possibility of reconstruction must be available in the same medium; both possibilities will carry conviction if either one does. Descartes' writing, in his claims for the act of meditation and the role there of memory, thus at once recognizes the threat to the existence of the writer and finds a means for turning that threat aside.

To be sure, the *Meditations* has as its subject the "demonstrations" that Descartes maintains in them: the existence of God and the distinction between mind and body. It also has as its subject the method which Descartes had identified in his earlier *Discourse* and which in the *Meditations* he then displays and acts on more fully. As an essential part of the latter step, Descartes has before him, and so also before his reader, the practice of meditation, the role of the meditator, and the method and art of the *Meditations* as his subjects. Even if he had referred to these topics less often or less self-consciously than he does, their importance would be evident. As Descartes himself, the "I" meditating, is every place present in the *Meditations*, so too is the act of writing.

Descartes Looking Backward

Even if Descartes' detailed concern with the art of meditation – and then with the art of *his Meditations* – were admitted, it might still be argued that measured against his own metaphysical assertions and conclusions, this other aspect of his work remains insignificant philosophically. Notwithstanding his own attentiveness to these claims (and their intimate connection with his philosophical life), they might still be construed as evidence only that Descartes took seriously the rehetorical or pedagogical effects of his writing – as we recognize that he also took seriously the question of its political standing. And all of these, it might be concluded, singly or together, are instrumental considerations for the writer or the reader that contrast sharply in importance with the assertions of philosophical or scientific truth – Descartes' or anyone's – that invite judgment outside any particular literary and even historical context. Descartes had, after all, committed himself to just such a search for truth, one and universal in its appearances; and even if *he* had not done so, the philosophical reader might *now* be justified in holding him to that standard and measuring him by it.

This objection frames the perspective from which most contemporary readings of Descartes set out. The statement by Margaret Wilson that "while perhaps the order of arguments presented in the *Meditations* does reflect Descartes' own progress in philosophical inquiry, it is not obvious that this is so, and not in the least relevant to the philosophical purpose of the *Meditations* whether or not it is so" only says forthrightly what many other writers do not trouble to articulate at all.[21] Wilson conceives of reading Descartes ("interpreting Descartes" suggests too contingent a relation for Wilson's conception, too much a subordination of the reader to the authority of the text) as an act by which the reader intends to see through the *Meditations* to the elements of argument assembled there, to examine those pieces in an order established by the individual reader who may have a more informal and informative view of them than Descartes himself, and then to assess the relations between those elements of argument and the conclusions which are alleged by Descartes to come from them. Did not Descartes himself support this possibility by writing the *Regulae* on one side of the *Meditations* and the *Principles* on the other – thus implying that the constraints of genre in the immediate setting of the *Meditations* do not limit the formulations of truth or knowledge there?

A variety of issues are raised by this objection, one of them a quite general point concerning the role of the "hermeneutic circle" in the explication of philosophical texts. Like other readers, readers of philosophy bring to bear a set of expectations and dispositions which affect the meaning and other "readerly" conclusions drawn from those texts. As in other settings, moreover, the "meaning" of the philosophical text is not to be deduced from the reader's dispositions alone; text and reader – here the hermeneutic circle emerges – interact in a way that yields textual meaning as the product of them both. This does not imply (for philosophical or other texts) that all or any meanings are possible; the variant interpretations historically of individual philosophical texts attest at once to a variety of possible interpretations and to an exclusionary perimeter within which they appear.

Philosophical readers, however, typically attach to this general "index" of interpretation an additional disposition or expectation in the form of a conception of philosophy – its intention, form, and protocol of argument. The imposition of this expectation situates the text and proposes to derive from it answers to questions which have priority in the reader's, if not necessarily in the writer's philosophical perspective. This imposition, furthermore, is not only a matter of association on the part of the reader. As the question of "what philosophy is" persists as an issue in all philosophical discourse, readers characteristically assess (and before this, understand) a text in terms of the conception of philosophy held by the reader – not necessarily out of dogmatism (although this may occur) but because the issue of what philosophy is is continually being tested by the texts themselves (this is an important point of difference between philosophy and other fields of inquiry).

Although this imposition of a framework is in some measure unavoidable, the different ways in which this is done can lead to various results. Two sets of philosophical assertions and the conceptions of philosophy which they represent from the respective sides of reader and text may fully coincide; or, two sets of questions (and also the responses to them) may coincide in a single area of genuine agreement or disagreement between two otherwise quite different frameworks; or again, *apparent* agreement between two sets of questions or answers may turn out to be quite different, even at odds with each other, because of different meanings (in respect to presuppositions, requirements of evidence, etc.) attached to them in the process of their formulation. It is this last alternative, I should hold, that appears in accounts like Wilson's which identify in Descartes' *Meditations* answers to questions based on what he refers to (and

rejects) as the synthetic and/or geometric method. Individual statements made within those frameworks may *seem* to be identical with
those that he makes on the basis of the analytic method: "I exist,"
"God exists," "I know that I have a body," etc. But insofar as the
settings and thus the questions to which those claims are responses
vary, their own significance also varies; Descartes' contention that
the abstraction of a single proposition or sequence of propositions
from the flow of an argument may obscure their meaning is an
important formulation of this point, but only one such item of
evidence among many. As such inconsistencies may occur among the
works of a single philosopher, they are still more likely a possibility in
judging apparently identical statements set within quite different
philosophical frameworks. Pascal and Kant both affirm that "God
exists" – but to interpret this as fundamental agreement between
them (and then between them and Descartes) is evidence of misreading and misunderstanding more than anything else. Each of the three
might reasonably insist that for the sense in which the others hold
that God exists, God *does not* exist.

Assertions made within one framework or "paradigm" of philosophical system can sometimes be translated into assertions in other
frameworks (if not for *all* assertions or systems). But where the
differences between frameworks are fundamental, then a reader who
assumes that statements or arguments from one of them are identical
to statements or arguments in a second one (typically, his own) and
assesses it in the terms provided by the latter, begs the question: it is a
version of *his own* meaning, not that of the first author, that has been
identified. He is here caught doubly by the hermeneutic circle of
interpretation – one, in the reader's construction of meaning in a
non-philosophical text, built around an ascribed intentionality of
which the reader is an agent; and secondly, as a specifically *philosophical* set of rules of interpretation obtrudes on that construction.

It might be objected, to be sure, that to reject Descartes' stylistic
prescriptions in the *Meditations* by transposing the assertions or
arguments he presents there into an alternative framework (e.g. of the
synthetic method) is not a violation of the kind just described (even if
such violations *may* occur elsewhere). For, again, the Descartes of the
Meditations is also the Descartes of the *Regulae* and the *Principles* –
texts in which he himself writes in a non-meditative form, eschewing
the analytic method. If *he* sees no inconsistency in this, moving from
one genre and method to another in addressing apparently identical
questions, and if, moreover, the arguments in the non-meditative
works appear to be consistent with, even inferrible from what he says

in the *Meditations*, then why should any other reader, even a sometime "meditator," doubt the effectiveness of this translation?

In chapter 2, I have anticipated a response to this question in
relation specifically to Descartes' writings; for the moment, I focus
on a more general aspect of the issue of translation among systems
(one that is also anticipated there). This is the fact that even if it
were conceded that philosophical doctrine or method set initially in
one genre can be formulated with *some* degree of adequacy in
others, this does not imply that such translations are even in principle capable of being complete, or that one or another of the forms
of philosophical discourse is philosophically privileged over the
others. There can be little doubt in fact that a measure of adequacy is
possible in translations among various genres, tropes, and figures of
writing – even (to go outside philosophy) in the extreme case of a
highly figurative poem rendered in discursive and non-figurative
prose. But this is not evidence that a full translation (of cognitive
content or any other) is possible, still less that the translation into a
supposedly neutral and discursive – propositional – prose has epistemic priority over the original expression. The fragmentary, often
misleading character of such translations in practice argues in fact to
the opposite effect. The common insistence on reading philosophy
through the medium of a "neutral" translation amounts in itself only
to the claim that for the group of readers so engaged, certain
conventions of discourse are more inviting than others – a preference
that reflects a psychological source more immediately than a philosophical one. Accounts of the history of philosophy may be unable to
avoid such an homogenizing effect; it is often a specific purpose of
those accounts to describe the individual characters in that history as
arrayed along a single chronological and in some sense progressive
line. The dangers of this historical homogenization are more serious
still when they are understood – as they are usually intended to be –
as also reflecting substantive or philosophical homogenization.

The contention (as in Wilson's comment) that for reading
Descartes, considerations of genre or style are philosophically
irrelevant conflicts with a number of extrinsic, historical aspects of
the *Meditations* as well as with the internal and systematic ones cited
so far. These historical facets have sometimes later become systematic in philosophical discourse, even, in a peculiar sense, in reading
Descartes' own work retrospectively; but it is important to view
them first *as* historical if only because Descartes is most commonly
credited by the modern reader with having effected a radical break in
the history of philosophy, one which successfully denied the hold of
that history on him. To base a reading of Descartes on this premise,

disregarding the relation between Descartes and his past in favor of his anticipation of the future (*our* past), is, however, at least half a mistake: so far as concerns the reading and writing of philosophy, Descartes is heavy with his past hardly less than he is with the future. For even if a contemporary reader *now* concludes that Descartes' attentiveness to rhetorical or literary detail is philosophically insignificant, it is true nonetheless that in *his* mind the philosophical relevance of those considerations was not in doubt, that they were not "merely" aesthetic features of discourse – and thus, that far from breaking here with his medieval predecessors whom he otherwise sharply criticized, on this question of the substantive importance of philosophical writing, he placed himself in their midst.

The evidence cited earlier of the contrivance by Descartes of the form of the meditation by itself supports these claims, but additional, more fundamental testimony about the principles involved appears in the disjunction he finds between the order of knowing – of *human* knowing – and the order of being. If anything is clear in the *Meditations* about the process of coming to know – meditating – it is that knowledge is acquired sequentially, in steps which have an order of their own, and that this sequence is not necessarily coordinate with the order of being. In the latter order, Descartes emphasizes repeatedly, God's existence is first, prior to other existence not only in time but as cause; for the foundation of human knowledge, on the other hand, of *learning* what the order of being is, it is the *Cogito* that marks the point of origin. God is responsible for what knowledge is *of*: thus, for example, Descartes' account of the origins of mathematical and geometric relations as aspects of God's efficacy more generally – "We must not say that if God did not exist nonetheless these truths would be true" (Letter to Mersenne, 6 May 1630). But the order of *knowing*, of the way in which the knower comes to grasp "these" or other truths – to know them – is a human matter, turning on human capacities and limitations. As I have argued here earlier, it is the latter order, based on the constraints on memory for sustaining "clear and distinct" ideas, that is the basis equally for the method and style of the *Meditations*. Admittedly, another side of Descartes balks at the constraints under which the "all-too-human" knower labors, and he *sometimes* conceives of reason, even human reason, as limited only by the constraints of logic itself; this is the ground for Maritain's charge against Descartes of "angelism" – that is, conceiving of the self as *more* than human.[22] Where Descartes writes about the historical process of writing or learning, however, this emphasis is absent.

Knowing how to read Descartes means at least in part knowing how Descartes *would have* us read him, and it is from this perspective that the historical and external factors referred to take on their main significance. One of these factors is the distinction to which Descartes repeatedly calls attention, between his use of the French vernacular in writing the *Discourse* and his reversion to Latin for the *Meditations*. He was, we know, far from the first learned author to write in the vernacular (Ramus' *Dialectique* was published in 1555, long before the *Meditations*); and we know, moreover, that both the *Discourse* and the *Meditations* were translated into the language of the other not long after their original publication. But neither was the use of the vernacular such a commonplace that the decision to write in it would have been a matter of course. (The more skeptical and less conservative Montaigne, although he himself wrote in French, had also argued about the Bible that there would be "much more danger than profit" in having it translated into the vernacular.) Descartes, beyond the general issues of social class that attended the invention of printing and the emergence of a reading "public," explicitly associates the difference in language in these two of his works with substantive differences in the texts – alleging that certain questions taken up in the *Meditations* had been excluded from the earlier work at least in part *just because* of the difference between them of accessibility: "I could not [in the *Discourse*] deal any better with this topic [the soul as a distinct substance] without explaining in detail the falsehood or uncertainty to be found in all the judgments that depend on the sense and the imagination . . . . I left this out on purpose and after deliberation, mainly because I wrote in the vernacular. I was afraid that weak minds might avidly embrace the doubts and scruples which I would have had to propound, and afterwards been unable to follow as fully the arguments by which I would have endeavoured to remove them" (Letter to Mersenne, 27 February 1637). And again, writing to Vatier (22 Febrary 1638): "The certainty and evidence of my kind of argument for the existence of God cannot really be known without a distinct memory [!] of the arguments which display the uncertainty of all our knowledge of material things; and these thoughts did not seem to me suitable for inclusion in a book which I wished to be intelligible even to women while providing matter for thought for the finest minds."

Descartes is not always a "reliable narrator" even in his ostensibly historical references in the *Discourse* and the *Meditations*, and this reservation almost certainly applies also to the "I" of his correspondence. (Letter-writing was in any event a highly conventionalized genre in the seventeenth century; we are not far in advance here of the appearance of the epistolary novel.) Since his private claims to have avoided certain themes in the vernacular *Discourse* appear *after* it was published, mainly in anticipation of the appearance of the *Meditations*, they evidently are his reaction to the contentious role as author of the *Discourse* in which he then found himself. (He had, again, for a time attempted to maintain anonymity in that role.) But even if we admit such reservations – also acknowledging that a translation soon appeared (1647) of the *Meditations* into French – Descartes' appeal to the differences between Latin and the vernacular suggests a rhetorical and finally also a philosophical principle about the relation between writer and reader. One aspect of this relation is undoubtedly prudential: Descartes' biography attests that he knew well the power – and capriciousness – of social authority. But there is also another description of the relation in which a theory of reading and finally a theory of knowledge are at issue. This includes a claim first of differences in individual capacities of understanding – and then of an implication drawn from this, that this variable capacity is itself a legitimate or even a necessary consideration for the philosophical author. In these terms, it is not only the conception of an argument as the author himself would construe it that is properly the author's concern, but *also* the way in which it is likely to be construed by the reader. The author has a responsibility in these terms not only for his own understanding, but for that of the reader as well. (Dr Johnson's quip provides the antithesis: "I have found you an argument; I am not obliged to find you an understanding.") Descartes seems clearly to recognize that the two sets of capacities and intentions in any transaction between writer and reader may conflict. He is also prepared to say that in some such instances, the author's own conception of the argument must be if not sacrificed, at least modified or reshaped; that the author cannot simply demand that the reader conform in his understanding to the requirements of the text – not, at least, if the writer wants to convey to the reader as much of the argument as the latter is capable of understanding.

The suspicion may arise that Descartes is here enlisting in his conception of writing the same final cause that he had excluded from his metaphysics and criticized in the thought of his predecessors. (So, for example, in the *Conversation with Burman*: "This constant practice of arguing from ends is Aristotle's greatest fault." [p. 19]; cf. also the reply to Gassendi, in the "Fifth Set of Objections.") A *textual* role for final causality has already been noted in connection with the *Meditations*, as the reader was required there to understand that only by anticipating a meaning for the work as a whole – by deferral – would its parts become intelligible. But Descartes' concern with the phenomenon of "reader-response" is tied more thoroughly to a role for final cause than even this might suggest. That begins to become clear as Descartes explained why his writing may pose more than only a "difficulty" for the understanding; readers might be left in a state of doubting or skepticism – "on a false path" (Letter to Mersenne, 27 February 1637) – with consequences for them (and then also perhaps for Descartes) that did not need to be spelled out. This concern, whether only prudential or also, as it seems, conceptual and moral, means that it is not sufficient that a philosophical writer should be concerned only about persuading himself; he must also take into account what his readers will be persuaded of. This does not mean that a writer is entitled to falsify (the "evil demon" which is as close as Descartes comes to incorporating a version of Plato's "noble lie," is soon overcome); but silence – that is, the avoidance of issues – and difficulty – for example, the use of Latin rather than the vernacular – are themselves means of expression which supplement the more obvious possibility of aiming at different registers in the course of an argument. Descartes does not claim that variant appearances of truth would be equal in their force (quite the contrary, in fact); but his acknowledgement that truth may emerge from variant forms or genres of expression establishes the reader as a quasi-creator of the text: the author writes always with the reader's shadow filtering his light. Thus, for example, Descartes writes in the "Reply to the Second Set of Objections," about Biblical anthropomorphism: "Everyone knows the distinction between those modes of speaking of God that are suited to the vulgar understanding, and do indeed contain some truth, a truth, however, relative to the human point of view ... and those other expressions that give us the more base and rigorous truth though not that accommodated to the human mind." The argument here cuts two ways; for although Descartes undoubtedly gives preference to truth that is *not* "vulgar," he is nonetheless willing to justify vulgarity – *epistemological* vulgarity, it turns out – for those to whom access to truth is otherwise impossible. It is, finally, the life and not only the mind of the reader that occupies Descartes.

   A second, more philosophically substantive item of evidence for the claim that discourse is not a transparent and neutral medium, simply a vehicle of method, is Descartes' acknowledgement of a causally connected relation between discourse and its object. With this additional step, the elements of a theory of philosophical style, although appearing episodically in Descartes' thought, constitute a whole. For not only now must a writer in his discourse and its form take account of the understanding of the reader and thus of variations *among* readers; and not only (as suggested earlier) does the object of writing affect its representation in the manner of discourse; but potential objects of knowledge turn out to have various capacities *to be represented*. There could, on this account, be objects that human discourse and reason cannot comprehend, however complex or elaborate its form – and a predictable instance of such incommensurability is evident for Descartes in man's inability to comprehend God. "But though we conceive God only inadequately, or, if you prefer to put it thus, in an utterly inadequate manner, this does not prevent its being certain that his nature is possible or not contradictory; nor does it prevent our affirming truly that we have examined it with sufficient precision (i.e., with as much as is required in order to attain to this knowledge..." ("Reply to Second Set of Objections").

To be sure, Descartes refers in this statement to the *conception* of God, not the adequacy of language in relation to that conception; moreover, a limitation on the knowledge of God does not entail a more general disproportionality between knowledge (or language) and its objects. But although something that cannot be adequately expressed *might* be conceivable, it is impossible that something inconceivable could be adequately represented in discourse (how, in any event, would one *know* this?). Descartes' forthright statement here, moreover, has echoes elsewhere of the importance he attaches to the relation between language and human comprehension, on the one hand, and the specific objects they represent, on the other. Understanding itself is not a shapeless or indeterminate medium, Descartes emphasizes in a very strong statement in the *Conversation with Burman*: "But understanding depends on its object and cannot be separated from it; so it is not the case that understanding is understanding" (p. 20). This is, it will be noted, a broader claim than the one (which Descartes also makes) that "truth, in the strict sense, denotes the conformity of thought with its object: (Letter to Mersenne, 16 October 1639). In the latter formulation, thought is regarded as capable of conforming to an object – and then of doing that in fact when truth is realized; in the statement to Burman, Descartes implies more strongly (as in an intentional theory of consciousness) that there is no thought (let alone truth) independent of an object – and even beyond this, that the kind or degree of understanding achievable is also a function of the object. The connection asserted here, moreover, is not between the object and a particular genre of representation, but a function of discourse in general and thus as cutting across genres: understanding thus takes *something* of its character from its individual objects.

These considerations, added to the more specific claim of a connection between the genre and the method of the *Meditations*, suggest a general aspect of Descartes' thinking that is often overlooked: the moral tendency of even his ostensively metaphysical or scientific writings. It is perhaps trivial (although nonetheless true for all) to claim that the "disinterested search for knowledge" has itself a moral ground, in the presumed status of knowledge as a value. But Descartes' search for certainty and truth has a more explicitly moral design to it than this, one that is evident in his conception of the meditation itself. If may be impossible fully to understand (or credit) Descartes' statement to the Marquess of Newcastle (Letter, October, 1645) that "The preservation of health has always been the principal end of my studies," but there are numerous other references in his writings and correspondence to the relation between ideas as meditated and the conduct of life – a relation cited in justification of the practice of meditation (cf. e.g., Letters to Christine, 20 November 1647 and to Huygens, 10 October 1647). Like the Stoics, knowledge (or the lack of it) determine conduct for Descartes – and this means in turn that the principles that underlie or guide conduct cannot be dissociated from the search for knowledge or the means of its representations.

That these two aspects of Descartes' thought are closely linked can be seen from the relation claimed by Descartes between the will and the understanding – that is, for the connection in the meditator between ethical conduct and knowledge. Much of the traditional analysis of this relation in Descartes has called attention to the "Fifth Meditation" in which Descartes' account of the dissonance between will and understanding as an explanation of error is construed as arguing for their independence from each other, for their status as virtually separate "faculties." The latter conclusion is then taken as a basis for the further inference that Descartes' *own* metaphysical or logical arguments can be reconstructed and assessed without reference to conative or evaluative elements (those which figure either in *his* system or in that of the interpreters). But there is surely an irony in the fact that this design for interpretation is based on Descartes' account of *error*, not of truth. Even in that context, moreover,

Descartes does not deny the potential connection of the will and the understanding when they function fully; and when he does speak elsewhere specifically of understanding or knowledge, he often quite explicitly refers to the conative power found in them, to their direct consequences for moral practice. Modern proponents of the fact–value distinction may look to Descartes as an ancestor, but in these terms Descartes himself was no Cartesian and hardly a dualist at all; if anything, he comes closer here to upholding a straightforward Platonism in which the will is subordinate to the understanding. So he writes to Mesland (2 May 1644): "For it seems to me certain that a great light in the intellect is followed by a strong inclination in the will; so that if we see very clearly that a thing is good for us, it is very difficult – and on my view, impossible, as long as one continues in the same thought – to stop the course of our desire." Even while maintaining the formal independence of the will and the intellect, Descartes speaks differently about the relation between them when they act at fully force; at that time, the will is no match for reason.[23]

To be sure, people act in the *absence* of knowledge or understanding, and both for and (presumably) against them when they are less than complete: "So far am I from thinking that assent must be given only to what is clearly seen, that on the contrary I believe that we need not always expect to find even probable truths there" ("Reply to Second Set of Objections"). The disparity between understanding and the will – between the incompleteness or error of the one and the "wilfulness' of the other – accounts for moral "errors" when they occur. But far from implying a sharp distinction between the will and the understanding (like that asserted by Kant), this dissonance underscores the connection between them. If knowledge, even if only in its highest or ideal form, compels action, then *some* correlation is implied even in more diminished appearances of knowledge; one property of an idea, then, *whatever* its clarity or distinctness, will be its implication for action or practice. If this relation holds for formulations or writings by which ideas are transmitted – a step which returns us to the connection asserted between method and style in the Cartesian meditation and the more general implications suggested by that. If the very structure of an idea, its status *as* an idea, is linked to the form of its articulation; and if, moreover, the truth of an idea characteristically has conative effects, then to weigh ideas and their representations in terms of the way in which they engage their audience is not at all arbitrary. At the very least, it can be justified as prudent (on *all* sides – for writer, reader, critic); at most, it is warranted on a combination of theoretical and moral grounds. Writing is here conceived as a deliberate form of action, with the agent responsible (as he would be in others) for its consequences.

As Descartes' acknowledgement of this doctrine (in part explicit, in part tacit) influences his practice, to read Descartes requires that we look backward to his predecessors rather than forward to the view of philosophical reading dominant in modern philosophy and science. For Descartes' conception of the text stands in this respect in a tradition of philosophical discourse that had been fully elaborated in medieval philosophy and in the scholasticism that he otherwise determinedly rejected (in figures like Averroes, Maimonides, and Thomas), and that even in these writers represented an inheritance whose origins extended back to Plato. The presence of the Platonic tradition in this background, in fact, is consistent as it is evident – presaged in Plato's own view of philosophical discourse. It is not only that in choosing the dialogue form from such alternatives as "linear" discourse, on the one hand, or philosophical poetry (as in Empedocles), on the other, Plato would have been arguing by implication that the means to philosophical knowledge is a function of the *object* of knowledge – but more specifically that within the genre he chooses, the means is attuned and readjusted to the substance of what is being conveyed. The movement among several levels of argument within (most) Platonic dialogues is constant; there is no single discursive line to which that movement can be reduced, where a reader can with assurance conclude that "Plato asserts that . . . " The conversations within the dialogues invariably disclose, and thus finally represent, not only arguments but distinctions of character in the speakers. And unless the reader simply decides to deny these distinctions, to contract them into a single structure of argument, he will acknowledge that the always various *dramatis personae* make distinguishable claims of their own in the discourse – and that Plato, addressing them not in a neutral or universal idiom but at their own respective levels, means also to seek out the reader in his terms. The fate – present and future – of both the objects of knowledge and the knowers become the responsibility of the writer and so, then, of Plato himself. Even the Platonic myths, it seems, reflect this intention, as they address the reader as well as the figures in the dialogues who either can find their way by no other means or who, if they can, nonetheless require confirmation of reason at the level of the senses or imagination engaged by mythical discourse. For Plato, the act of writing thus constantly anticipates the act of reading – not primarily as a matter of etiquette or of convenience, but because the meaning and justification of the former are linked to the outcome of the latter. Truth in itself does not depend for Plato on the knower – but truth *as known* does; despite his disclaimers in the Phaedrus about the status of the written word in general, Plato, when he did write, was writing for readers, for potential knowers.

Such comments touch only superficially on the Platonic conception of discourse, and this is not the place to examine that conception at length. But its features that stretch into the medieval tradition and then, on the argument presented here, into Descartes' work are readily summarized: firstly, that the means of philosophical discourse, if the ends of the latter are to be realized, will be shaped by a combination of the writer's views of the expectations and capacity of the audience, on the one hand, and his sense of the capacity for representation in the object of discourse, on the other; and secondly, that the balance struck by an author among these variables is not a mechanical means to some other end (like adjusting the temperature in a room) but is itself an aspect of the metaphysical and moral representation that the author hopes to realize. Discourse here is a form of action – in contrast to the more standard conception of discourse as representational and transparent, with the reader seeing through it to the objects beyond. Here discourse (and finally, also, meaning and truth) are contextually opaque, themselves shaping and coloring whatever the discourse is *of*. The force of the latter claim is perhaps most noticeable when contrasted with the standard view of scientific writing as affording access to – revealing – independent facts or events of nature. One does not need to be unduly suspicious to doubt that the characteristic devices – the style – of scientific discourse (impersonality, passive voice, use of neologisms, etc.) would be as obtrusive as they are if the "facts" of nature were simply speaking through it for themselves. And hardly less obviously for philosophical writing: As philosophy pushes at the limits of both discourse and world, the recognition that it cannot escape the constraints which they impose on each other amounts finally to acknowledgement that philosophers, like all other writers, cannot hope to find a place outside that world from which to write about it. They may talk more than other writers about the dualism between body and mind – but no less than the others they are bound by the former whatever hopes they may have for the latter.

Other figures might be cited among Descartes' predecessors, but Maimonides is perhaps the surest example in the entire history of philosophy of an author who conceived of the relation between text and reader as a decisive factor in the author's conceptualization of the text, indeed as part of his moral responsibility. The constraints that Maimonides acknowledged as writer – the social existence of the Jewish community added to the severe requirements of reconciling religious and philosophical doctrine – weighed more heavily on him than would analogous constraints for a secular philosopher or for the quasi-secular Descartes who wrote under the threat of censorship, or even for the explicitly Christian thinker, like Augustine or Anselm, themselves committed to a richer theological tradition. Thus Maimonides carefully encodes *The Guide for the Perplexed*, apprising the reader of the existence of the code in which he writes and the reasons for it, addressed at once to the tendencies and capacities of potential readers, and to the nature of what is being written about. His concern with the act of reading as part of his own act of writing takes the form of statements ranging from general caveats to quite specific instructions. So (as an instance of the former):

> You who study my Treatise, know that something similar to what happens to sensory apprehensions happens likewise to intellectual apprehensions in so far as they are attached to matter. For when you see with your eye, you apprehend something that is within the power of your sight to apprehend. If, however, your eyes are forced to do something they are reluctant to do – if they are made to gaze fixedly and are set the task of looking over a great distance, too great for you to see, or if you contemplate very minute writing or a minute drawing that is not within your power to apprehend – and if you force your eye, in spite of its reluctance, to find out the true reality of the thing, your eye shall not only be too weak to apprehend that which you are unable to apprehend, but also too weak to apprehend that which is within your power to apprehend." (I: 32)

Or again, a more specific prescription, as he selects two reasons (from a list of seven that together explain the appearance of contradictions in any text) why a reader might (mistakenly) think that he had discovered contradictions in the *Guide*:

> [One such cause] arises from the necessity of teaching and making someone understand. For there may be a certain obscure matter that is difficult to conceive. One has to mention it or to take it as a premise in explaining something that is easy to conceive and that by rights ought to be taught before the former, since one always begins with what is easier.... [The second such cause is that] in speaking about very obscure matters it is necessary to conceal some parts and to disclose others. Sometimes in the case of certain dicta this necessity requires

that the discussion proceed on the basis of a certain premise, whereas in another place necessity requires that the discussion proceed on the basis of another premise contradicting the first one. In such cases the vulgar must in no way be aware of the contradiction; the author accordingly uses some device to conceal it by all means. (Introduction to I).

Such statements bring out more clearly what has been attributed to Descartes earlier in this discussion as a conception of reading within a context of authority. The latter includes both the authority of the writer – the "author's authority" – in shaping his work to the needs and capacities of his audience; and a conception of the authority of the object of discourse which determines what it is that the writer can say about it (including whether he can say anything at all). Two points are suggested by this "authoritative" conception of writing that may serve as a general summary of the specific issues that have been raised in relation to Descartes as author. The first of these is that the conception of authority described – at once originating in the objects of discourse and in the readers' capacity for understanding – is almost entirely absent from the work of modern philosophers and from the consciousness of their readers. (To the extent that they are conscious of this absence, an irony is inescapable: Descartes is viewed as an authoritative source for it.) The second point is one toward and around which the second part of this chapter has been directed – that however later history might (now) choose to view him, Descartes himself conceived of writing and philosophical discourse on the model of what was even for him philosophy's past, not its future, with a connection firmly established between philosophy and rhetoric, between method and style. Descartes was in this sense not a modern at all.

There is a history to the requirements Descartes sets (and accepts) for himself as a writer that clearly marks the connections that link him to the past. The lineage that begins with Plato, that extends in the tradition of Latin rhetoric (as in Seneca) and through Augustine, whose *De Magistro* remains a firm and explicit statement on this theme, into the medieval ties with Islamic (as in Averroes), Jewish, and Christian thought (as for example, in Thomas' doctrine of analogy) dominates the background out of which Descartes came: they *are* the background. And although as commentators have emphasized (overemphasized, it may now seem), Descartes vigorously rejects parts of that background – parts which loom so large in his own sense of the proportions of his background that he appears in speaking out against them to be attacking the whole of it – he either could not or would not put it *all* aside. I have been suggesting that at least his conception of discourse discloses a likeness to the past that did not occur accidentally – and that even if it might have been accidental, it would still now have to be acknowledged in its own terms, as resembling an earlier tradition of philosophical discourse in which writing and reading were functions of the author, reader, and the objects of discourse, not simply of the medium of language itself. To deny that learning how to read Descartes is essential to understanding Descartes – a requirement that we see to have been willed by Descartes himself – is to deny or to ignore or (most probably) to beg the question of what there *is* for a reader to understand in Descartes' writings. Descartes here stands with what was even for him the past of philosophy; what has been lost to modern philosophy from that past in its own conception of writing and reading has also been lost to it in its understanding of Descartes. How to repair those losses – both of them a combination of history and theory – is an important question for contemporary critical and philosophical understanding.

Notes to Chapter Three

1   References to the correspondence are taken from Descartes' *Philosophical Letters*, translated and edited by Anthony Kenny (Oxford: Clarendon Press, 1970).

2   Unless otherwise indicated, the text of Descartes cited is that edited by Elizabeth S. Haldane and G. R. T. Ross (Cambridge: Cambridge University Press, 1970).

3   Descartes uses "analytic" and "synthetic" in the context cited here in a different (although related) sense from both the then standard usage of the terms and his own usage elsewhere (which is close to that of the standard usage, e.g., in the *Regulae*). In that standard usage, "analysis" refers to breaking down the objects or elements of an argument to their least knowable parts, "synthesis," to the process by which those least parts are put together. (See for a discussion of the standard distinction, P. A. Schouls, *The Imposition of Method* (Oxford: The Clarendon Press, 1980), ch. 1). The emphasis in the "Reply", as cited here, is on the difference between the respective *orders* of argument in the two methods, corresponding to their development in experience, a difference between them that seems a distinctively Cartesian addition to the standard notion.

4   Descartes' objections to the synthetic method apply equally to the syllogistic form of demonstration of the Schoolmen and to the *modus*

geometricus which he took as the more serious rival to his own method. Although for both of these, the premises *need* not be hypothetical – i.e., they may independently be known to be true – there is no requirement of this within the method itself.

5 *Interpreting Modern Philosophy* (Princeton: Princeton University Press, 1972), p. 65.

6 See on this topic Alexander Koyre, *Entretiens sur Descartes* (New York: Brentano's, 1944) p. 33.

7 Although it also seems at odds with the *radical* freedom that Sartre finds and approves in Descartes. See the volume on Descartes in *Les Classiques de la Liberte* , with Sartre's "Introduction" (Genevre-Paris: Trois Collines, 1946).

8 As Momigliano points out (*The Development of Greek Biography* [Cambridge, Massachusetts: Harvard University Press, 1971]), the genre was not named until the nineteenth century and before then had always been a marginal follower of biography – itself, from its origins in the Greeks until the nineteenth century, a problematic genre.

9 Cf. Etienne Gilson, *Etudes sur le Role de la Pensee Medievale dans la Fonction du Systeme Cartesien* (Paris, 1930) p. 193.

10 See Dalia Judovitz, "Autobiographical Discourse and Critical Praxis in Descartes," *Philosophy and Literature*, 5 (1981), pp. 102–3, and *Subjectivity and Representation in Descartes* (New York: Cambridge University Press, 1988), ch. 4. For an account of Descartes' emphasis on the writing of philosophy in reference to the *Discourse*, see Andrew E. Benjamin, "Descartes' Fable," in Andrew E. Benjamin, Geoffrey N. Cantor, and John R. R. Christie, ed, *The Figural and the Literal* (Manchester: Manchester University Press, 1987), pp. 10–30.

11 J. L. Beck (*The Metaphysics of Descartes* (Oxford: Oxford University Press, 1965) p. 31 notes also that retreats at la Fleche, Descartes' school, were organized on the basis of Loyola's exercises, suggesting a likely influence on the structure of the *Meditations*. But again, it is the structural frame at most for which Descartes is thus indebted, not for the content or the activity of meditation. Like any exercises, Loyola's are *preparations* for something else, a set of instructions; one could hardly be said to have *done* Loyola's exercises by having read his book in the way that one could have meditated by reading Descartes. Again, in contrast to Descartes' *Meditations*, the *Spiritual Exercises* constantly invite the use of the senses and the imagination. So, e.g., "the Fifth Exercise of the First Week" requires the reader "to see with the eyes of the imagination those great fires [of Hell], and the souls as it were in bodies of fire." For an account that claims a closer likeness in these works to Descartes, see Amelie Rorty, "Experiments in Philosophical Genre: Descartes' *Meditations*" *Critical Inquiry*, IX (1983).

12 Jacques Derrida, "Cogito and the History of Madness," in *Writing and Difference*, translated by Alan Bass (Chicago: University of Chicago Press, 1978).

13   For a more systematic account of the question of a "poetics" of philosophical discourse, see Berel Lang, "Towards a Poetics of Philosophical Discourse," *The Monist*, 63 (1980), pp. 445–64.

14   In the "Third Meditation," Descartes seems to subordinate the claims of clear and distinct ideas to the power of God. Without knowing that God is not a deceiver, he writes "I do not see that I can ever be certain of anything." It is not altogether a satisfactory solution, but the likeliest means of judging the apparent contradiction between this statement and those in which clear and distinct ideas are alleged to provide knowledge not guaranteed by knowledge of God's existence is by attending to the passages in which Descartes is actually responding to *charges* of contradiction.

15   See on this point Hartman and Schwartz, "Translators' Introduction," to Kant's *Logic*, pp. lx–lxv.

16   Descartes, in Bruman's account of his reply, uses the term "axiom" in this context, evidently without believing that doing so would take him back to the synthetic method. The alternate explanation that Schouls gives (*op. cit.*, p. 17) – that the analytic method *includes* the synthetic method – seems to me groundless. Descartes himself, in the "Reply to the Fourth Set of Objections," makes room for "provisional" assumptions in the analytic method.

17   *Conversation with Burman*, translated and edited by John Cottingham (Oxford: Clarendon Press, 1976), pp. 6–7. In *Descartes* (Oxford: Basil Blackwell, 1986), Cottingham suggests that God serves as a guarantor even within a "systematic body of knowledge" of individual ideas, if (for example, p. 71) "when my attention wanders from some proposition, I am assailed by . . . nagging doubt." This, too, seems to me to underestimate the importance of the *actual* connections asserted in the *Meditations* which, taken together, require memory and its guarantee. (For a broader conception of memory as a means of breaking the circle, see Willis Doney, "The Cartesian Circle," in Willis Doney, ed., *Eternal Truths and the Cartesian Circle* (New York: Garland, 1987), and also the criticism of that account by Harry Frankfurt, "Memory and the Cartesian Circle," in Doney, ed., *op. cit.*, pp. 72–9.

18   Ian Hacking, "Proof and Eternal Truths," in S. Gaukroger, ed., *Descartes* (London: Harvester, 1980), p. 173.

19   J. L. Beck explains such statements in terms of Descartes' wariness of the censor (*op. cit.*, p. 4). This may well be a side of Descartes' concern here, but it seems unlikely to have been the whole of it. His concern with the issue, in any event, goes back to the *Regulae* (cf. Rule 8), written before Galileo's trial and the other encounters with public reaction that were later to contribute to Descartes' wariness.

20   In specific references of Plato, Descartes ignores the generic role of the dialogue altogether (cf. Rule III in the *Regulae* where he addresses as one the "arguments" of Plato and Aristotle). Of his own dialogue (*The*

Search After Truth), Descartes writes in his prefatory comments that it is meant to make the arguments he advances "equally useful to all men." But in the fragment of his dialogue that survives, Descartes' purpose, through his spokesman, Eudoxus, is discursive in a way that places it closer to the form of the treatise than to the dialogue.

21 Margaret Wilson, *Descartes* (Boston: Routledge and Kegan Paul, 1978), p. 4.

22 Jacques Maritain, *Three Reformers* (Port Washington, New York: Kennikat Press, 1970), p. 54.

23 Sartre seems to invert this order in Descartes, subordinating reason to will, in effect making Descartes a proto-existentialist. (See Sartre's "Introduction" in *Descartes* (*op. cit.*).) On the relation of will to reason, see David M. Rosenthal, "Will and the Theory of Judgment," in Amelie Rorty, ed., *Essays on Descartes' Meditations* (Berkeley: University of California Press, 1986), pp. 405–34.

4

Philosophy in Its History: Two Views

I: Irresolute Empiricism

After a hiatus that dates from the post-World War II advent of "analytic" philosophy, American philosphers have again begun writing about literary topics and even about the literary status of philosophy itself. Slightly earlier, literary critics and theorists, reacting against the anti-speculative New Critics, had again begun to admit philosophical methods and concepts to the work of criticism; as Richetti does in *Philosophical Writing: Locke, Berkeley, Hume,*[1] they also turned their attention to discursive texts which, in the purist tradition, would hardly have been acknowledged as literary at all. The potential benefits from such crossing of disciplinary boundaries are obvious, and one might expect any possible loss of rigor to be outweighed as the converging disciplines forced a fuller disclosure in the work of each. There are illuminating moments of the latter sort in Richetti's study, and surely it is important to have the point made – again and again – that philosophical texts will reward a literary reading. But as these apercus occur in his book, they neither emerge from nor point toward a recognizable systematic structure. This lack imposes a considerable strain even though Richetti is usefully showing at the same time that writing itself was one common element that the writings of Locke, Berkeley, and Hume were "about".

For Richetti, the problem of the literary reading of philosophy requires striking a balance between the view (as in Frye) that all "structures in words" are literary, and the narrower, more traditional view that philosophical texts (for one) are of marginal literary relevance. The problem of reconciling these, Richetti suggests, is more than an issue just for the literary readers; it seems, in fact, to be embedded in philosophical discourse as such, and at least for Locke, Berkeley, and Hume, "the search for a suitable rhetorical mode for philosophy is at the center of their thought." Whatever they may do beyond that point, then, those writers first face the challenge of balancing "logic and rational demonstration against rhetoric or persuasion of any kind" (pp. 2–3).

Limited to these terms, the premises of Richetti's account are straightforward: Locke's description of figurative language as a "sweet cheat" is familiar, as is Berkeley's deeper skepticism about the distorting effect of language as such. What we might expect then to follow is a discussion of the ideal of "plain language" applied to philosophical writing and thought as it ran parallel, for example – and encountered the same difficulties, internal as well as external – in the then developing scientific ideal of language as a neutral, non-figurative, and purely instrumental medium. But things, it turns out, are not to be that simple. For skeptics though they were about the usual medium of philosophical expression, Locke, Berkeley, and Hume also stood opposed to the supposed "aloofness" of the philosopher in the posture often ascribed to him of detached spectator. "Their writing habitually stages a turn from logic and demonstration to anecdote and example, thus placing them and their readers in the center of a reality fraguht with uncertainty and confusion" (p. 27). The ideals of discursive generality and transparency are thus subverted by another current in which those ideals are seen as impossible to realize and (for that and other reasons) not even as ideals. Thus, Locke's "defining and notorious ambiguity as a thinker" is a central feature of Locke's own writing as he goes about "dramatizing the difficulties of knowing a plentitude whose stability is consistently interrupted . . . by a 'signifier' that is shifting and uncertain" (pp. 34–5). Philosophy for Locke – and then in different ways, for Berkeley and Hume as well – means living life or at least discourse always on the edge, calling attention to its own problematic as writing, exposing its "own (and others') delusions of centrality" (p. 35).

It remains a question whether Richetti means that the writers whom he discusses had themselves thus anticipated Derrida's grammatology or only that their writing can be deconstructed to show its intrinsic instability. Richetti's account in fact leaves open the possibility that for him these two may amount to the same thing, but this looseness matters less than it might since the evidence on which he draws seems either to apply to *all* writing or to hold for the writers he specifically addresses only in the loosest sense. His finding – in varying combinations – of ambiguity or uncertainty and an ironic reflexivity as themes in the writing of Locke, Berkeley, and Hume is the main item of evidence he provides, and it also raises the most serious questions. For even if those *were* significant features of the work of those writers, and even if such features could be distinguished stylistically from the philosophical claims they accompanied – Richetti provides debatable evidence for the first of these and no evidence at all for the second – nowhere here would his reader find an indication of what it is that has associated the texts discussed with what remains to this day the noticeably singleminded epistemological commitment of the empiricist tradition. The Logical Empiricists of the Vienna Circle in 1920s and 1930s undoubtedly exaggerated aspects of Hume's analysis of verification that they claimed as precedent – but they did not make up their reading of whole cloth. Even if they and other commentators were finally mistaken in the emphasis of their interpretation, moreover, Richetti offers no explanation of how such a persistent misreading of the history of philosophy might have occurred; quite specific evidence would be required even before this to demonstrate that Hume, for example, as he consigned books of metaphysics to the flames, regarded that gesture as ironical (on this response, it seems, Hume and Derrida *would* agree).

Richetti himself seems not entirely serious about the theoretical framework in which the instability of the text plays a central role. This is most evident when he comes to address the three writers individually in the single chapters he respectively devotes to them; he reverts here to the more traditional and quite different distinction between rhetoric and logic as basic to understanding their intensions. At the conclusion of his introductory chapter (titled "Rhetoric, Style, and Philosophical Writing"), he suggests that he will be providing a "gloss upon the literary surfaces and rhetorical movements of the texts as they promote philosophical issues," thus addressing what he accepts as – to quote Altieri – "the specific literary mode of the text." (p. 47). To take this formulation at its word is to suppose the existence of a literary appearance or surface under which philosophical content is to be found: a version, in effect, of the form – content distinction openly at odds with the Derridean conception of discourse and style that Richetti also invokes.

The distinction between literariness and philosophical assertion has, of course, recurred in literary studies of philosophy (as well as of literature) and in philosophers' views of their own work; but if poststructuralism has proved anything at all, it is precisely the dubiousness of this bifurcated version of essentialism. Admittedly, on the premises that "philosophical writing does not have the overt formal ordering of literary genres" (p. 31), and consequently, that it was, for example – because it could not be otherwise – part of Locke's intention "to establish a new way of writing philosophy" (p. 32), the literary critic might hope to analyze philosophical writing piecemeal, characterizing individual tropes or figures and interpreting meaning without reference to the "final cause" (generic or otherwise) of what the discourse intended. But the value of any such conclusions would be seriously limited if, as seems to be the case, a schematism *were* possible of the development of genres in the history of philosophy and of the pressure they had exerted there. Richetti acknowledges Colie's association of Locke's *Essay* with the tradition of Montaigne and the personal essay, but there, except for occasional allusions to its specifically literary appearances, his analysis of genre begins and ends. The literary allusions, moreover, are themselves impressionistic, leading mainly to *obiter dicta*: thus, Locke, a writer of "urbanity and wit" (p. 56), assumes "an amused relation to the lower world, where his philosophical opponents are busy with the childish games he has rejected" (p. 57), appearing as a "sly questioner and disposer of error" (p. 111) – an anticipation, in short, of the "Shandeyan parody" (p. 116). Richetti makes the useful suggestion that the philosophical subject or thesis sometimes surfaces in the character of the discourse itself (thus, about a passage in the *Essay*: "Just as revelation is beyond analysis and commands immediate assent, the rhetoric appropriate to revelation features those compelling gnomic structures that call for acceptance (or rejection)" [p. 64]. But such connections, too, can be only accidental so long as an impassable distinction is maintained between rhetoric and philosophical method.

In part, Richetti defends the latter distinction as Locke's own ("There are moments in Locke's writing when he seems to aspire to a purely nonassertive mode" [p. 65]); but more often he simply leaves to one side the question of what position Locke is at any moment taking *qua* thinker in favor of a focus on his writerly stance. Thus, the way to deal with apparent inconsistencies in Locke's work is to infer that Locke was writing *about* or even extolling inconsistency. The many disparities claimed by Locke's commentators – between the conception of mind as a blank tablet or as active in imagination or memory; between the denial of a Cartesian self and the assertion of personal identity; between the characterization of primary qualities as independent of the observer and a conception of reality as subjective (Richetti's own doubtful attribution to Locke) – all these become elements, then, of Locke's own espousal of an unstable "narrative" form intended to "replace static philosophical entities such as 'essence'" (p. 95). That Locke might have been *caught by* inconsistency rather than celebrating it is a possibility that Richetti effectively dismisses (along with the many readers who have read Locke that way). It is no doubt true that the conception of philosophical truth has figurative and rhetorical elements, and it would be important to have this pointed out, especially for the empiricist writers who have claimed and too often been conceded to establish a place for truth beyond rhetoric or ideology. Nonetheless, it is also clear that each of the writers whom Richetti discusses thought of himself as providing a logically coherent and verifiable representation of the world and the human mind, and that this was one, if not the exclusive, motive for their writing. How else are we to understand a statement as forceful as Locke's proposal to do for the human mind what Newton had done for nature? This element of the empiricist tradition, however, carries little influence in Richetti's account, a proportion that would be warranted, it seems, only if he had also shown (at least if he had argued) that philosophical writing reduces to nothing more than a series of tropes upon tropes.

The focus of these comments first on the framework of Richetti's book and then on its practice mainly as he applies it to Locke are representative, beyond the book itself, of its relation to the current discussion of those topics. (Richetti himself pays only incidental attention to the other work in the area: one bibliography – "*Philosophy as an Art Form*," compiled by Ben-Zvi, Garvey, and kiefer[2] lists over 600 entries in English alone for the period 1960–80.) Much more might be said about questionable details that bear on the philosophical background to which he looks for support. To cite Adorno of the Frankfurt School as an "anti-Cartesian" and thus as an ally of Locke, Berkeley, and Hume might be only a lapse of philosophical tact; but to infer that Collingwood is "anti-systematic" from his assertion that philosophers are always confessing their "difficulties" is to misconstrue the assertion itself as well as the systematic bulk of Collingwood's own work. Hacking is supposed to support Richetti's claim of an intrinsic ambiguity and uncertainty in Locke, Berkeley, and Hume, when all that Hacking says (on Richetti's own account) is that those figures are inconsistent in their use of the term "idea". Evidence for the conclusion that Bennett and Ayer are "unimaginative" (p. 25) amounts mainly to citing their contentions that the imagination is less significant a faculty than Richetti himself believes it to be. These historical misconstructions would be relatively unimportant if, beyond them, Richetti had provided, against the background of rhetorical practice in the eighteenth century, a serious account of the ways in which Locke, Berkeley, and Hume figure in that history and its aftermath. But although he writes about texts of a single historical period, his account is basically ahistorical, moving between the individual figures of Locke, Berkeley, and Hume and more recent – still individual – theorists like Derrida and de Man. Thus, too, the justification is missing for singling out (and then combining) Locke, Berkeley, and Hume as his subjects – as is a response to the important literary and philosophical question of how, more generally, they came to be canonized in the first place (at a cost, obviously, to other philosophers: Reid, for example, with his strong critique of Hume that Richetti himself simply writes off as "vulgar").

Such appeals for method and fact may in the end seem no more than a plea for restoring the same disciplinary walls which it is evidently a purpose of such work as Richetti's to subvert. But the latter effort is unlikely to succeed unless what is put in question is judged, at one level at least, in its own terms. This requirement has the admittedly difficult consequence that antitheoretical perspectives may themselves be obliged to speak theoretically, with all the unwanted baggage that that carries. But the alternative would open discourse (even when, like Richetti's, it affirms an ostensive object) only to the agreement or conflict of individual intuitions. And although that is undoubtedly part of what literary analysis can supply for the reading of philosophical texts, it is impossible to know even how much of a part that is without an account of the method and history to which also intuition may be bound.

II: Spinning in the Kantian Revolution

It has often been pointed out that the great artists are not usually the radical artistic innovators. Bach, Rembrandt, and Tolstoy all worked within well-marked generic forms, and an economical theory of creativity might argue that this was – *is* – necessary; that to touch bottom in his own creations, the maker of art cannot afford to be diverted by efforts to test or revise its boundaries. The analogy that holds between philosophy and art in some respects (as for their claims on the possibility of historical progress) may not find exact parallels between the structure of philosophical texts and the stylistic features of art, but it is demonstrable that the patterns of convention and idiolect – of "constant form" – associated with artistic style also affect philosophical discourse. Thus, to speak of Gotshalk's *Art and the Social Order* as belonging to a style of aesthetic inquiry which has its source in Kant's *Critique of Aesthetic Judgment* and a nearer anticipation in the line of American aesthetics joining Santayana's *The Sense of Beauty* (1896) and Dewey's *Art of Experience* (1934) is to raise a question about the intentions and content of that one moment of stylistic continuity against the background of the continuity itself.[3] Gotshalk did not, it seems to me, initiate a program of his own: his work was that of consolidation, reflecting, together with the usual virtues of consolidation – clarity, assurance – also its characteristic liabilities: mainly, a diminished sense of history, both of where the issues addressed come from and of what they might turn into in the future. Much like the appearance of style itself, these features of Gotshalk's book become clearer – perhaps they become visible at all – as the book is seen retrospectively. Even what I shall be objecting to as the ahistorical design of *Art and the Social Order* hardly impedes a stylistic view of that work, since that design itself, I suggest, is part of the book's history.

Any such emphasis on continuity and historical location may seem to patronize the individual text by putting it (or its author) in their places – in effect, encouraging critics and their audience to believe that they see more than their predecessors did simply by virtue of living after them. But a greater danger than this is the belief that the thinking and writing of philosophy occur independently of a physical or historical context – and the myth of individualism, with the philosopher in solitude reconstructing the world, has no more realistic a grip on philosophical truth than its *laissez-faire* counterpart has in economics. The idea of periodicity or style applied to the writing of philosophy discloses, in fact, what is otherwise easily ignored: namely, the corporate nature of much philosophical work, the enacting of a project whose collective features outweigh the obvious fact that writing is physically the work of a single hand.

To be sure, philosophical writing is sometimes derivative rather than simply corporate (and no philosopher is entirely underivative, after all). But often the writing is part of a common effort in which the corporate members are so linked by affinities in impulse, conceptualization, and idiom – in what turns out to be a common *form* – that they appear finally to be working with each other even if members of the group do not conspire or even meet. The analogy between philosophy and art makes a further point here. Painters do not set out to be members of a "school," yet they are often viewed retrospectively as comprising such groups; in assigning them membership, we refer not only to direct historical encounters, but to the fact that they have addressed artistic questions and problems in common and have applied to them a common means. This is, I suggest, as much as the conditions for corporate membership require, and it is in this sense that Godshalk's book is usefully seen, looked at backwards now from a distance of 35 years, as a member of the much older Kantian Corporation, spinning still in the revolution for which Kant himself claimed pride of authorship and which extended its Copernican turn to aesthetics as well as to epistemology and to ethics.

I wish to emphasize in this claim for a style of aesthetic discourse two central (and related) features of *Art and the Social Order* – the roles there of the concept of aesthetic experience and of Gotshalk's methodological ahistoricism. But it will be useful before analyzing them to have available an outline of the book's structure. Part I, titled "The Basic Processes," allots separate chapters to "The Aesthetic Experience," "Fine Art," and "The Creative Process." Part II is titled, "The Public Object," and here Gotshalk, again in separate chapters, distinguishes four "dimensions" of the public object: the materials; the form; the expression; and its functions. ("Public" thus seems to be redundant with "object," and the phrase as a whole, to be a manner of speaking about the conditions for aesthetic experience.) Gotshalk calls Part III, "Implications," referring with this to the context in which art and aesthetic experience appear and act: he devotes one chapter to a discussion of art-criticism and two chapters (the last two of the book) to "Art and the Social Life" and "Art and Social Living."

The book, then, has the pattern of a two- rather than three-dimensional dialectic. It starts out from aesthetic experience as an (allegedly) distinctive moment of experience, then steps sideways to the art object as a likely ground for that moment, and finally moves sideways again (on a different side) to discuss the social consequences of art. The principal line of argument claims that aesthetic experience is distinctive among the varieties of experience, mainly in contrast to instrumental and theoretical moments. This contrast is based on both intrinsic and extrinsic grounds – intrinsically, for the sense of freedom and "heightening of the self" (p. 26) which emerge from aesthetic experience; and extrinsically, for the social importance of aesthetic experience, beyond the individual, as a civilizing force. Such claims are quite broad, but it is clear nonetheless that they stand in the recognizable Kantian tradition of aesthetic inquiry, with strong echoes (although no mention) of Schiller's *Letters on the Aesthetic*

Education and, as I shall be arguing, with even more explicit reflections of Kant's *Third Critique*.

The "final cause" of art as represented in Gotshalk's view by these intrinsic and extrinsic consequences of art requires further discussion; but the means which lead to those consequences afford a more immediate entree to *Art and the Social Order*, and it is here also that the two factors mentioned above are pertinent. Together, these factors – the concept of aesthetic experience itself and its ahistorical derivation – shape the book, internally, with respect to its content, and externally, with respect to its form. Indeed they provide evidence for what I take to be true more generally – that the substantive and formal elements of philosophical texts are often indistinguishable, their assertions or arguments also figuring in their representation. The style, in other words, is also the philosophy.

In his "Introduction", Gotshalk proposes to "begin with aesthetic experience" (p. xvi). There is little self-consciousness about this opening; the reader is meant to regard it as natural, even necessary, for the philosophy of art ("*fine art*," as Gotshalk insists). Gotshalk nowhere acknowledges that his choice of a starting point in aesthetic experience makes contestable assumptions about aesthetics, about metaphysics, and (obviously) about experience – or that the "point-zero" for aesthetics could be and at times has been other than this (for one major example, as in Aristotle's *Poetics*). The question becomes significant, then, of *why* the role of aesthetic experience in aesthetics assumes this role of nature itself; and it is in answer to that question that the Kantian source seems to me most directly pertinent, filtered though it had been for Gotshalk through the post-Kantians and annealed as it was with empiricism before its appearance in the American pragmatists who are Gotshalk's most immediate companions.

My thesis about this can then be put simply: that it was Kant who first defined the form for aesthetic inquiry that Gotshalk, 150 years later, invokes as a matter of course. Admittedly, that metonymic relation does not in itself prove historical continuity or even piecemeal indebtedness. But the genealogy can be supplied, and the circumstantial evidence of the connection is evident. Kant sets out from the "fact" of aesthetic judgment: "The judgment of taste," the first line in the *Critique* reads, "is aesthetical." And this starting point has two direct consequences – first, that the distinction between aesthetic and other types of judgment is a principle that the subsequent analysis is compelled continuously to justify; secondly, that the aesthetic object, what the judgment or experience is "*of*", becomes a function – both as aesthetic and as object – of the judge or perceiver. The work of art, in other words, is subordinated to the experience, and the experience itself to a more general distinction among types of experience.

These consequences reappear in virtually identical form in Gotshalk's account. Thus, he equates aesthetic experience with a *kind* of perception. This is not (and here a momentary divergence) perception of the beautiful, since much aesthetic experience does not involve beauty at all (p. 4); the more basic, and Kantian, reason for the equation is that aesthetic experience turns out not to have a distinctive *object*. What marks off aesthetic experience for Gotshalk is rather its modality, its functional difference both from perception *simpliciter* and its variety. Perception by itself, for Gotshalk, is sensory experience without cognitive content: *intrinsic* perception then adds to noncognitive sensation a requirement that the viewer subordinate himself to the view, excluding purpose or reference. Gotshalk thus relates the distinctiveness of aesthetic perception to a conceptual equivalent of Kant's "disinterestedness" or "purposiveness without purpose." One important effect of the latter concepts (and so, for Gotshalk's work as well) is to bracket the art object, to make its manner of appropriation crucial for its status as art and thus to leave the object *as object* – in its history, reference, or purpose – irrelevant to the experience. Pure tones and flowers, for example, serve Kant no less well than paintings or poems as occasions of aesthetic judgment, and although Gotshalk must be skeptical of those examples (he speaks of nature as "aesthetically deficient" (p. 34)), there seems little basis in the objects of art themselves for his preference for them.

The shift that Kant initiated for aesthetics from object to experience, from cognition to feeling, was part of the larger movement that has since been addressed by generations of cultural historians under the disputed title of "Romanticism." One aspect of that shift in particular figures in Gotshalk's *Art and the Social Order*, namely, an impulse for transcendence or escape in which aesthetic experience is raised to equality, even to superiority to other modes of experience, and where the person who "has" the experience is also elevated. Undoubtedly, the nature of art itself has something to do with these changes, but more notable is the process: why, we ask, all the elevation?

I understand this question as a version of "cui bono?" – the search for interest or profit being as usefully directed to moments of philosophical revision as it is to any other institutional actions. In these terms, the move from object to experience suggests mainly the advantage of the consumer, the aggrandizement of the individual user of art who benefits first by a new power to determine and to enjoy the location of art and then the grander status also accorded that experience. The impulse expressed here is towards privatization and individualism, where even the related doctrines of social theory speak of multiplying individuals rather than of evolving the common structure intrinsic to them. For aesthetics, the extreme conclusion of this shift comes when Croce, and Collingwood following him, place both the creation and the work of art in the mind of the artist, with no essential role assigned either to *his* body or to the body of art itself. Gotshalk does not himself join in this view – but that is not because it would be inconsistent with the premises from which he sets out; indeed it would be less *ad hoc* a conclusion than the one he does propose with its gesture to the "public objects" of art.

The choice of the aesthetic for this mode of experience seems almost incidental. Prior to the nineteenth century, religion served as an easy representative of individual and social ecstasy, but the post-Enlightenment suspicions of religious claims hinder its continuation in that role. Better, then, to turn to art which anybody with taste can appreciate in general and which may serve as a means of individual enlargement even when particular judgments are disputed. The issue in this turn towards experience is not so much *what* particular modality should be selected as that there should be *some* means by which the individual could escape from material and collective constraints, where he could become truly an individual without the hindrance of theoretical or ethical generalization. Let it then be art that does this – and let everyone have access to art through the feelings they claim individually as persons. Let everyone, in effect, *be* an artist; let everyone go his own way with aesthetic experience; let everyone, in the end, be *his own* art work. "'He becomes a masterpiece himself,'" – Gotshalk approvingly quotes Nietzsche (p. 215).

There are two ways in which a philosopher who is not writing specifically about history can yet take history seriously. One of these is by attending to the history of his own discourse, locating himself and the concepts he employs in respect to the past of his discipline.

The second way is by applying history as a category to the objects he studies. Gotshalk follows neither of these alternatives, and the avoidance is evidently deliberate. Perhaps he might have quarreled with the characterization of his work as still Kantian, but he himself offers no alternate description; reflected in his own lights, his book would have no history at all. It is not, moreover, that Gotshalk avoids only the philosophical *past*; he is as much distant from his contemporaries – and this conjunction deepens the sense that the reader faces here a general representation of philosophy and its objects as ahistorical. Gotshalk does acknowledge the "materials" of art as an essential dimension; but his analysis of even that historical element cuts no more deeply than the near-tautology that "for certain purposes certain materials are definitely superior [to others] . . . " (p. 95). The title of Gotshalk's book suggests that the "Social Order" is to be coordinate with "Art" – but this, too, turns out to be more an aspiration than a measure of proportion. Even in his last two chapters where he does relate art to the social order – attacking twentieth-century art for its anti-social and finally anti-humanistic character (he explains that failure by the absence from the culture generally of a "unity of belief") – his analysis is notably ahistorical; one looks in vain for evidence of similar correlations between art and the social order in the past. Moreover, he cites few of the writers on the social consequences of art whose arguments he might have used to advantage (he looks hopefully to the art of the new Russia and its Socialist Realism, but Marx is not mentioned in the book). The *features* of the material dimension of art thus remain obscure. Gotshalk says nothing about the impact of technology on the development of specific arts or of aesthetic concepts; nothing about the actual difference that variations in the medium make in aesthetic experience. It is as if the concept of "intrinsic perception" is assumed to have such explanatory power for the mechanism of aesthetic experience and for the structure of what is experienced, that it requires no further analysis.

This judgment seems to me mistaken, but more to the point, the exclusions are characteristic of the form of Gotshalk's work and of the way in which the concept of aesthetic experience determines – and joins – the substance of his work to its external form. Is the "way" a philosopher writes related to the choice of what he writes about and what he writes about it? I have been suggesting that for important elements of Gotshalk's book, the "way" may itself *be* the "what" that the philosopher writes. Style in this sense is broader than method and inclusive of it, if only because method cannot be fully self-conscious.

The incompleteness which is a defect in method is, in other words, a characteristic ingredient of style as it *requires* omission in expression: a complete statement or "instance" of expression would be like any other and thus not in a style at all. Admittedly, the omissions thus intrinsic to style raise other, extra-stylistic questions (for example, about truth-claims in the text); but where the omissions are acknowledged, also these other questions find a basis of response. The assignment of *Art and the Social Order* to the Kantian Corporation thus brings into focus the appearance of *a* philosophical style against the background of the concept of philosophical style as such. And although the test of seeing this in any particular case is unavoidably in the eye of the beholder, the features of continuity in Gotshalk's work, are if not unmistakeable, at least as evident as they are in the more standard examples of philosophical style.

It might be objected to this line of interpretation that even if it accurately represents certain aspects of *Art and the Social Order*, those aspects seem accidental or procedural, not substantive; that because a writer on aesthetic theory starts, for example, from the experience rather than from the work of art, this means only that he will get to the work later rather than earlier – and that this is what happens in Gotshalk's book. This response resembles the one sometimes proposed for the broader split between idealism and realism: that the worlds which those doctrines constitute turn out remarkably alike, with the differences between them verbal or even (merely) aesthetic. There is surely some force to this claim of redundancy; but as the metaphysical differences initially claimed are not simply thought into existence, they cannot simply be willed away later – and this is true as well for the conceptual starting point of Gotshalk's analysis.

Thus, philosophical inquiry which begins with experience (aesthetic or other) may yet disclose a related object; but the structure ascribed to that "inferred" object will unavoidably reflect its history as inferred, and nowhere is this more noticeable than for the relation between aesthetic experience and the objects of art. There, with aesthetic experience first in the order of analysis, almost invariably the object of art appears later as an occasion of the experience, not ingredient in it. The object thus claims for its properties only what the constraints of an aesthetic surface – a thin and formal surface – leave them, systematically excluding reference or purpose as those would figure in cognitive or ethical judgment. In effect, aesthetic experience is defined negatively, by what it is not.

With such significant exclusions, aesthetic experience also becomes strangely unproblematic; only a half-step more is required – and often taken – to join aesthetic experience fully to the will. I do not mean here that at the end of this sequence, the observer is able simply to translate himself into aesthetic experience, but that the power of the will to effect that translation grows in proportion to the remoteness of the object. A striking feature of Gotshalk's – and before him of Dewey's – rendering of aesthetic experience is how easy it seems; it depends almost on how a viewer or listener *decides* to look at the world – the objects of experience and their social context, we suppose, then falling into place. Such optimism about the malleability of aesthetic or of *any* kind of experience is, to be sure, often denied by the message of art itself – but that testimony, too, might be expected to have little effect where the shape of experience is abstracted from its context and where it is the former aside from the latter or even as opposed to it which counts as evidence.

One additional thread runs through this texture of ahistoricism, less subtle than the others but in a restricted sense still more basic to the pattern. This is the fact that for most theories in which aesthetic experience serves as a starting point – here again I span the distance between Kant and Gotshalk – the phenomenon of aesthetic experience is viewed as an historical constant. Thus, Gotshalk never asks whether what *he* recognizes as aesthetic experience would have been present or even available (for example) to the audience in Sophocles' Athens or to Rembrandt's patrons in Amsterdam. He simply assumes this to be the case – that reflecting a human capacity, the experience accompanies man wherever he is or has been. That assumption may, of course, be true; but it is far from self-evident, and the available evidence is equivocal at best. Thus, once again, the question for Gotshalk's reader as he identifies the omission and its place in a pattern, is how to understand the representation of which the omission is part.

That the continuities I have described link *Art and the Social Order* to a style of aesthetic inquiry in itself carries no value judgment, and although I have also indicated what seems to me the liabilities of that connection, the direction of my criticism is hardly original. It figures, in varying proportions, among many recent movements of aesthetics: among the Marxists, for example – e.g., Lukács, Goldmann, Benjamin – for whom consideration of the historical status of both aesthetics and its objects is a requirement for understanding either: in the work of "analytic" aesthetics (Danto, Goodman, Wollheim) where, as the conceptual status of aesthetics itself is placed in question, the role of aesthetic experience is also dependent on the prior

discrimination of the individual artwork; in Heidegger's phenomeno-
logical aesthetics where althogh a version of aesthetic experience is
still fundamental, its relation to other modes of experience is so
altered as to make those modes cognate forms rather than separate or
even derivative.

The history of philosophy is long enough for prudence alone to
suggest that even a widespread critical reaction may not persist. This
is not to say that philosophy is committed to make the *same* mistakes
it has made before, but that there are always new ones to be made.
One way of understanding this, in fact, is as the lesson of style itself:
that as style always involves omission or repression, any objects
represented stylistically will be only partially represented, with that
limited perspective stamped on whatever is expressed – even the
supposedly impersonal expressions of philosophy – with its own
personal and historical character. There seems no way that the
individual text can escape this constraint, since even the effort of an
author to deny it also becomes part of the pattern: art conceals
philosophy no more than it does art. I do not mean by this claim of
intrinsic incompleteness – a stylistic version of Godel's Theorem –
that the individual text of philosophy or aesthetics is outside the reach
of criticism, but that more is at stake in such criticism than only the
individual assertions bound together between the covers of a book.
We could not address those assertions singly or in isolation even if we
chose to.

The same point is made on a larger scale, in the relation between
philosophy and its objects, in what continues to be a valuable part of
Gotshalk's book; the relation betweem aesthetics and *its* objects as
well as between philosophy and aesthetics are also parts of this
conception. For as Gotshalk suggests that aesthetics is linked to
philosophy not as part to whole but as microcosm to macrocosm, so
philosophy itself is not seen as something separate from or in addition
to the things of the world, but as a reconstruction – in the event, a
criticism – of those things. The objections I have been raising address
Gotshalk's specific concept of the artworld; but the general relation
between philosophy or aesthetics and that world is separable from
what he asserts specifically about the latter. Like Dewey, to whom he
is indebted here, Gotshalk moves sharply away from the deductive
and representational role assigned to philosophy in the Kantian
tradition which in other ways leaves its mark on his work so clearly.
The conception of philosophy as consummatory or "visionary" –
"Philosophy," Gotshalk writes, "is merely life ... organized into
vision" – has itself been disputed (and in the conditions sometimes

attached to it, is arguably mistaken; so, for example, the optimism which Gotshalk shares with Dewey that philosophy will find happiness without metaphysics); but it is clearly an important view of the nature of philosophy and thus of aesthetics – especially important at a time when philosophy persists in regarding science as a model by which its aspiration to be a "mirror of nature" may be realized.

The critical reception to *Art and the Social Order* when it first appeared was positive, mainly as his reviewers responded to Gotshalk's view of the humanizing importance of art. But the reviews were also too brief to develop fully the reasons for this approval, and it is worth nothing that even when they disagreed with Gotshalk, his reviewers accepted the issues on the terms presented by Gotshalk. Their dissent is never with his formulation of those issues or with the *kind* of evidence he adduces. Tomas, for example, in the *Philosophical Review* (LVII [1948], pp. 196–8) after agreeing with Gotshalk's claim of the hostile environment to art in the *laissez-faire* economic structure in the United States, questions his finding of the "unity of belief" as a basis for artistic development in Russia. Aiken is sharper on the same point (*Journal of Philosophy*, XLVI [1949], pp. 204–7); "There is no evidence whatever that social unit produces artistic excellence." Gotshalk's contention that the modern artist has turned his back on society is, Aiken concludes, "just *silly*. [Mann, Joyce, T.S. Eliot, Auden] have been obsessed with the spiritual plight of modern society." And Van Meter Ames, in his brief review of the book (*Journal of Aesthetics and Art Criticism*, VII [1948] pp. 167–8) thinks mainly to hoist Gotshalk on his own petard, arguing that Gotshalk both impugns didacticism in art and "assumes [that same principle] in hoping that the present tendency towards general-welfare states . . . will foster art of the caliber to promote the social good."

These comments do not question or diverge significantly from Gotshalk's own *principal* thesis that the potential social consequences of art follow directly as the sum of moments of aesthetic experience in the lives of individuals who "have" those moments. His reviewers object principally to the examples which Gotshalk cites (his optimism about the Russian "experiment" and about a future "international language of art," his criticism of capitalism as a home for artistic development). They do not dispute or even question what appears now, retrospectively, as the use of such evidence to support a thesis which, against itself, is fundamentally anti-historical. The idea of a national or even an international aesthetic experience can hardly be stronger than the basis from which Gotshalk infers it – aesthetic experience, free-floating and self-warranting in the life of all individuals. In this sense, the reviews are firmly bound to the same philosophical continuities which *Art and the Social Order* exemplifies. But it is hardly surprising to find such contemporary reiterations of the continuities on which Gotshalk drew, when now, more than a generation later, we recognize that the Corporation responsible for them is still open for business.

Notes to Chapter Four

1   (Cambridge, Massachustts: Harvard University Press, 1983).
2   *Style*, 16 (1982), pp. 273–364.
3   D. W. Gotshalk, *Art and the Social Order* (Chicago: University of Chicago Press, 1947; 2 edn, 1962).

5

Philosophical Humors

All men who are outstanding in philosophy, poetry or the arts are melancholic, and some to such an extent that they are infected by diseases arising from black bile.

Aristotle

If laughter, or their reputations as philosophers, depended on the jokes that philosophers tell, we should pretty quickly reach the end of both. So, for example, the magisterial Kant, who like a number of other Enlightenment figures had a soft spot for ethnic jokes, uses the American Indian to demonstrate – he thinks – how funny it is for anyone to mistake aesthetic pleasure for the satisfaction of an appetite: "[It would be] like that Iroquois Sachem who was pleased in Paris by nothing more than the restaurants." And then. the spiritual Bergson, writing about laughter in his book by that name and arguing that it is the mechanization of nature which produces it, appeals for proof to the lady "whom Cassini, the astronomer, had invited to see an eclipse of the moon. Arriving too late, she said, 'M. de Cassini, I know, will have the goodness to begin it over again, to please me.'"

Some greater appreciation may attach to the jokes of which philosophers themselves are the subject. However we may distrust Diogenes Laertius, for example, we are still reluctant to forgo his portrait of Thales, in which Thales, laboring to earn his future title as the First Philosopher, stuns his tough-minded contemporaries with the declaration that the innumerable solid and earthly things that they thought they saw were really, underneath it all, water – and then, one evening, his eyes fixed on the stars (perhaps attempting to strong-arm them too into his thesis about water), tumbles into a well.

But then, such jokes are in the eye of the beholder – and often, we might suspect, in his mind as well. "Which way was I walking when I stopped to talk to you?" asks the practical Dewey, standing on Broadway (or perhaps it was the clerical Whitehead on Massachusetts Avenue). "That way," replies the puzzled graduate student, pointing in the direction of Columbia (or perhaps in the direction of the Widener). "Ah, then I've had my lunch," the philosopher (Dewey or Whitehead, or perhaps even Thales) replies. And our interest in such anecdotes is in reassuring ourselves that the mighty are sometimes fallen, not in recalling that (or how) they are also sometimes great philosophers.

Is there anything more to be said about philosophical humor – something to demonstrate that, whatever the advantages of brevity, longevity, that evidently necessary condition of both philosophers and philosophy, is no barrier to wit? This is, I believe, a serious and unsmiling question, the answer to which – an anatomy of philosophical humor – turns out also, I believe, to be serious and unsmiling. But if talk about humor had a special obligation to be funny, talk about tragedy would in fairness have to be tragic, about war, martial, and about love, amorous. And it is clear that we should do what we can to avoid such invidious requirements.

I shall then be arguing, or at least exhibiting, two theses, one of which is conventional enough to pass without notice, the second of which is unlikely enough to be questionable even with notice – although it is the second one that, if true, has the larger consequences for a conception of literary philosophy. Thus:

Thesis I: Irony is the characteristic literary form or trope of philosophical humor.

Thesis II: Irony is the characteristic literary form or trope of philosophy as such.

First, Thesis I. Humor or the comic may finally be indivisible, but provisional distinctions are obviously useful, and I shall be depending here on a traditional distinction among four types of humor: *irony, satire, romance,* and *farce.* The points of difference among these comic forms – those features which control all generic or subgenre distinctions in literature – are differences in the types of action that they represent. So, for example, it is essential to farce that it should leave things (and people) at the end of the farce exactly where they were at the beginning (the repetition which this entails being a large part of its attraction); romance brings a transforming resolution and harmony, often in the form of marriage or reconciliation, to the scene of a conflict; the satire is aimed to produce conflict or separation where at first there seemed none; and irony both incites conflict and discloses the subordination of one side to the other in that conflict without, however, reconciling them.

In terms of the power motivating these actions, irony contrasts with the other forms in the kind of its efficacy; namely, the power of seeing or knowing. The original character of the *"eiron"* – the stock character in Greek comedy from whom the term *irony* comes – assumed a role of weakness and self-deprecation. But that weakness was also allied with awareness and a strength of consciousness – on this point Socrates' role as *eiron* remains a paradigm – and the same balance of power appears in different combinations in the other comic forms: in satire, for example, where the end to be realized is practical rather than conceptual; in farce, with its emphasis on the physical role of power (as in slapstick); in romance where the power that acts is the power of hope or expectation that follows reconciliation.

The feature of irony which is central to this very rough map of contrasts is its peculiar doubling effect, the combination of apparent surface and more real depth, initial weakness and eventual strength, affirmation and subsequent denial – all held together in the single view of the ironist. There is something of this bifocal effect, to be sure, also in the other comic forms, and there may be no general theory of the comic in which a version of the doubling and then reversal of consciousness does not play a role. The distinctiveness of irony is that this doubling is forced on the viewer with its two parts as cotemporal or synchronic; the fact that we also, at the *same* time, recognize that they are not equals, that one of them – the part which is unspoken – is a base or ground. At no moment in irony is the agent or his audience permitted to lose sight of the immediate object of irony or, on the other side, of the ground by whose presence the object is put at a distance, made into an object. It is this sense of juxtaposition that is emphasized in the common definition of irony as "the use of a word to express its antonym" (Ducrot and Todorov, *Encyclopedic Diction-ary of the Sciences of language*). What is essential in this definition is the reference to opposition, where an opposed and stronger truth is clearly present even in absence, where what *is* said is said under constraint to such an extent that it need not be expressed directly – indeed, where if it *were* expressed directly, it would be *less* present.[1]

The field of vision in irony – again, for both author and reader – is thus literally binocular in a way that the other comic forms do not require or equal. Irony is, moreover, disclosed in a single view – much as physically binocular vision brings together the independent perceptions of the two eyes. To put this in terms of the literary concept of point-of-view: the perspective of the ironist is unified and constant to a degree that makes the perspective readily transferrable. The latter feature is significant in explaining the unusual intersubjectivity of irony, the fact that the reader or audience of irony takes up exactly the position of the ironist himself.. "Beautiful day," I say, as we drive out to the country together in torrential rain – and there is little chance that you will quarrel with the implied opposite: we see the same rain, we were going on the same picnic; we know equally well that it is *not* a beautiful day. There is even less room here for dissonance or for "creative interpretation" on the part of the audience than occurs in other forms of humor – and humor is altogether less a creature of criticism than are other literary forms. Perhaps the only thing more difficult than teaching or arguing someone into laughter is teaching or arguing someone out of it. In all literary genres or figures, some correlation is indicated between the roles of implied author and implied reader, but irony seems the clearest, if not the only, case in which those roles are directly superimposed one on the other.

Such comments only anticipate a theory of irony, but they serve to frame the evidence for the thesis that irony is the principal form of humor to be found in philosophical discourse. Socratic irony is, again, the source from which the career of philosophical irony sets out, although I mean with this first thesis to refer not only to philosophers whose work is comprehensively ironic but also to the many more local and isolated appearances of irony which populate philosophical texts.

Thus, there is nothing startling in adding a claim here for the strongly ironical character of the writings of Kierkegaard and Nietzsche to the one more usually made for Plato, and one common aspect of the work of these three figures in particular affords a useful entrance to certain of the intentions of philosophical irony. For as these authors are among the most self-conscious writers in the history of philosophy, the most constant object of their irony, it turns out, is the history of philosophical discourse itself. So, for example, Nietzsche launches himself against the tradition: "[Philosophy's] systematic form attempts to evade the necessity of death in the life of the mind as of the body; it has immortal longings on it, and so it remains dead. The rigor is rigor mortis; systems are wooden crosses, Proscrustean beds on which the living mind is primed." Or again, Kierkegaard, also on the attack: "What the philosophers say about Reality is often as disappointing as a sign you see in a shop window, which reads: Pressing Done Here. If you brought your clothes to be pressed, you would be fooled; for it is only the sign that is for sale." And in Plato we find this irony turned not only against the conventions of philosophical writing, but against writing as such and surely against his own writing as well: "No intelligent man," the author of the Platonic dialogues writes, "will ever be so bold as to put into language those things which his reason has contemplated, especially not into a form which is unalterable – which must be the case with what is expressed in written symbols."

The ironic reversals invited by these writers are not, to be sure, directed only at past history. They are more explicitly pointed at their own conceptions of what the work of philosophy is; and the key function here, I believe, is displacement – that same displacement by which, at the level of individual statement, irony is in effect the assertion of its opposite. Socrates in this sense does not only practice irony, he *is* irony – combining in his own person the two stock figures of Greek comedy; the *eiron* and the *alazon* (the self-deprecator and the imposter). "I do not know," Socrates repeats to the politicians, the poets, the generals, the Sophists whom he confronts – although he also acknowledges that he does at least know *that*. With this confession, he discloses his imposture, his strength, and the ideal of knowledge that, as a final cause, continually feeds the Platonic irony; the assertion of ignorance implies it opposite, knowledge. Socrates' own person, it may thus be said, represents the literary figure of irony, implying *its* opposite, motivating the tensions in the dialogues between Appearance and Reality and the work of dialectic which is intended to unmask the one to the other. Not to know is to start from where we are, as we are. That place is the world as given and apparent, where politicians make laws, generals give commands, Sophists sell their knackeries. Is there anything beyond or more real than those practices? Well, let the practitioners drive themselves to the denial which is indeed more real than the practices are. So Thrasymachus shows how power can make mistakes by making one. He contradicts himself: "Of course not, Socrates; only when they do even fools can see – that justice is nothing other than power. "Even when those who have power make mistakes?" – Socrates asks – and Thrasymachus shows how power can make mistakes by making one. he contradicts himself: "Of course not, Socrates; only when they do not make mistakes." Is Socrates unfair to take advantage of Thrasymachus' blunder? Not if we understand the irony which the blunder makes possible, and the fact that the ironist then uses it to displace one piece of the apparent world with a patch of the real one. Thrasymachus himself also implies his opposite – and Plato adds Platonic irony to the Socratic variety. So we understand, too, something more about that peculiar doctrine of anamnesis – knowledge as recollection which is, after all, always and everywhere available. Error and ignorance thus can never justly claim for themselves that they are the best their possessor can do, whoever he is and however incorrigible or invincible his mistakes may seem. The dialogues move through the disclosure by appearance itself of a reality behind it; the *eiron* – Socrates – provides the motive force by upholding the possibility of knowledge itself – the innate and thus truly constant possibility by means of which ignorance may and, logically if not historically, *will* become its opposite, knowledge. Even where it is not actual, irony is always possible; the truth is always present, lurking, waiting for the reversal that will disclose it.

Kierkegaard speaks more explicitly about his use of ironical method in *The Point of View for My Work as an Author*: "An illusion can never be destroyed directly," he writes there – thus justifying the systematically oblique attacks in his other works on the aesthete, the ethicist, the normal Christian – each of whom is, must be, driven from within, by *his own* works, to the reversal based on despair. The author's view here is two-fold, and not only as the writer who is in control of his characters, but as consciousness itself. "In order to help another effectively," Kierkegaard writes, "I must understand more than he – yet first of all surely I must understand what he understands." The philosopher then, Kierkegaard as writer, will start not from where *he* is but from where his audience is; his task is the task of subversion, of showing to its holder from the terms of his starting point both its own inadequacy and its implication of an opposite – what we saw before to be conditions for the definition of irony. The person at the median stages of life's way affirms its opposite (in this sense consciousness itself is ironical) – and so we come back to that two-fold division by which individuals may yet go beyond themselves and which Kierkegaard as author attempts to infuse in both his writings and his readers. Why did Kierkegaard sign his pseudonymous works pseudonymously? The author too must be aligned with the creation, not apart from it; it is the means by which the reader is made to feel so at home that he will not doubt his own later discovery of the inadequacy of that identity – as he undoubtedly would if an author simply told him that that was the case. Even at this last point, moreover, where the leap of faith takes over, Kierkegaard's irony does not stop. Without that leap, irony would lose its power to mere skepticism which is, for Kierkegaard, a feature of the aesthetic life, itself a cause of despair.

The claim for the importance of irony in the work of these several writers is hardly novel, and as I have mentioned, my first thesis is directed not only to such broad examples, but to the appearances of philosophy at the level of individual statement as well.[2] Here, too, in fact, we find ready and many examples, an insistent use. One would not, for example, usually think first of Aristotle as an ironist, although that surely has something to do with the sheer bulk of his work: what, we ask, did he leave out or *not* speak about which might then be implied by what he did say? But this, nonetheless, is the case, at least in individual statements or arguments. The concept of the mean, for example, is central for Aristotle to the science of ethics. By it, we learn, reason enters practice; striking between the extremes, the moral agent finds in the mean the right act for the right occasion. But, the reader is asked to consider, is the mean *always* to be consulted? Consider, Aristotle suggests, the actions of robbery, or of adultery. Would the doctrine of the mean commit us to adultery "at the right time, at the right place, with the right woman?" And so the reader is driven in the opposite direction by a view of how misleading even the mean can be.

Again, the medieval tradition takes seriously the role of the philosopher as educator, and nowhere is this more evident than in Maimonides' *Guide of the Perplexed* where irony, again, turns out to be a principal one of the educator's devices. Anthropomorphism, Maimonides recognizes, is a threat to the idea as well as to the ideal of monotheism. This danger includes, of course, the ascription to God of emotions; and after recalling for the reader that the anthropomorphic features of anger or jealousy are attributed to God in the Bible only where he reacts to idolatry, Maimonides concludes: "Know accordingly that when you believe in the doctrine of the corporeality of God or believe that one of the states of the body belongs to him, you provoke his jealousy and anger" (pt. I, ch. 36). God does not become anthropomorphically jealous – except as idolaters conceive of Him as becoming angry or jealous.

And so, also – skipping rapidly forward – the stern and unforgiving Kant, sometimes represented as so far separating morality from pleasure as to leave them not only distinct but opposed, himself yet takes pleasure in ironies at once ornate and deep. "The light dove, cleaving the air in free flight, and feeling its resistance, might imagine that its flight would be still easier in empty space," he writes in the

"Introduction" to the *First Critique*; and we see in that turn a capsule history of the philosophical dogmatism which the *Critique* as a whole is intended to subvert: the claim for an unmediated or immaculate grasp of reality – the makers of which claim, like the dove if *it* acted on its beliefs, fall, Kant believes, flat on their faces.

Or again, consider Ryle's use of travesty, those imagined examples with respect to which Ryle invites his readers to supply from their own world the more cogent counterexamples. Arguing in *Dilemmas* against reductionism, for example, Ryle confronts a hypothetical undergraduate with a hypothetical college auditor who explains to the undergraduate that "all the activities of the college are represented in these [the auditor's] columns" of financial assets and debits. Should not the undergraduate be persuaded, then, Ryle writes, "that this expert's way [is] perhaps, the right way in which to think of the life of the college . . . ?" That *that* is what the college is? This imaginary proposal gains its power from the reader's recognition both that it is false and that it is not imaginary at all. The irony here forces its way through, leaving scientific reductionism more real an object – and more objectionable – as the reader himself supplies a refutation for its economic analogy.

Such examples could be multiplied, but short of gathering them *all*, of course, there is no way of showing that they do outnumber other types or instances of philosophical humor. Indeed, although I have been claiming that this *is* the case, it should be clear that the philosophical comic *in general* is a recognizable phenomenon and that it also includes the other parts of the four-fold distinction among comic forms that were cited earlier.

More's *Utopia*, for example, is inconsistent in various ways, including that of its form, but certainly one of its basic impulses is to satirize the society that was not nowhere but immediately present. So, in political relations with other countries, the Utopians, we learn, never make treaties:

> In their part of the world, which is diametrically opposed to ours
> . . . you can't rely on treaties at all. The more solemnly they're made,
> the sooner they're violated, by the simple process of discovering some
> loophole in the wording . . . . That, as I was saying, is presumably why
> Utopians make no treaties. Perhaps if they lived in Europe, they'd
> change their mind.

There seems, in fact, a natural, or at least literary, affinity between many of the great futurist visions of philosophers and an impulse for satire. Certainly we miss much of the vividness (and some of the argument) in Plato's *Republic* if we do not see that he wrote with one eye, mocking, constantly on the Athens whose citizens had become so accustomed ot life in their caves that they would take the shadows cast on the wall before them for creatures of the real world: who chose their political leaders on the basis of favors done or promised, not on the favors bestowed by nature; who accepted as literal models for their own actions the poets' descriptions of the gods lying to (or with) each other.

The romantic comedy, too, has a place, although its characteristic "green world" comes in mottled hues.[3] Readers have often found Leibniz's *Monadology* amusing, but they have usually understood this amusement simply as a reaction to what is, on any reading, a philosophical oddity. But as we watch Leibniz's transformation of the fragmented and disjointed world of common experience, mixed as it is with wrong-doing, evil, and incoherence, into a harmonious collective of monads each one of them at once realizing its own nature and mirroring and supporting every other one, we do well to recall the standard version of romance in which conflict is transformed to reveal affinities, reconciliation, marriage – a world where pleasure is a natural expectation. The *Monadology*, we may well conclude, amuses not, because it is odd, but because it is, in the manner of romance, funny.

A more serious if more literal-minded version of the romance appears in the classical statements in political philosophy of the Social Contract theory. Admittedly, if that theory is understood as designating a single historical moment at which the Social Contract was signed, one moment which then governs the political future of the members of a society, the dramatic impulse in such accounts will be viewed rather as tragic than as comic: a falling off from origins which evokes inevitably frustrated efforts to recapture that first moment of reason and compliance. But if on the other hand, the Social Contract is seen as a- or transhistorical (and there is evidence for such interpretation even in Hobbes and Locke), then we have the prospect not only of a single eventual moment of resolution, but of reconciliation and communal celebration at *every* moment of apparent disharmony or conflict. That citizens should think of themselves, whatever their reservations, as continuously giving "tacit consent" (Locke's phrase) to both the policies and authority of the government, is surely, from the points-of-view of the government and even of the citizen, an idyllic picture. (Insofar as democracy presupposes a Social Contract theory, it shows, we infer, how romantic comedy extends to political practice as well as to theory.)

Farce, with its characteristic emphasis on physical and nonverbal mechanisms (typified by the literal "slapstick"), is a rarer form in philosophical discourse than the others, but even here instances are available – predictably in the genre of the philosophical dialogue where the individual characters inject a bodily presence. Diderot's *D'Alembert's Dream* and *Rameau's Nephew* have strong elements of slapstick and farce; the same elements are notable in a number of the Platonic dialogues – for example, with Alcibiades' riotous entrance to the *Symposium* (in which we have already heard Aristophanes' explanation of love as the longing of our half-bodies – all that we have left – for the other halves from which they have been split off). Or in the opening of the *Protagoras* where Socrates, dragged from sleep at the crack of dawn by a young friend to listen to the master Sophist, arrives at the appointed house only to have the door slammed in his face – and then, grudgingly admitted, discovers Protagoras already pacing and holding forth in the portico, a line of luminaries flanking him, a band of lesser lights behind. "As I looked at the party," Socrates reports, "I was delighted to notice what special care they took never to get in Protagoras' way. When he turned round to walk back, the listeners divided in perfect order, and circling round took their place each time in the rear. It was beautiful." Beautiful enough, we recognize, to be repeated later, many times and to good effect, by the Marx Brothers.

Such examples, however, do not, I believe, tip the balance; the main part of philosophical humor is still and nonetheless ironic, even though the counting required to make good that claim is here left incomplete. And the question then, if we are unwilling – as we ought to be – to conclude simply that the occurrence is accidental or arbitrary, is why this should be the case. It is in response to this question that my second thesis becomes pertinent – and even before addressing that thesis head on, we can see something of the direction it takes from the notion of philosophical system itself and the clear disposition in favor of systematic thought in the history of philosophy, even from the history of very different philosophies. For irony, I suggest, is not only compatible with a formal adherence to system, but requires it – in the sense mentioned before, that the doubling vision with which the ironist sees is not a doubling of equals. There is nothing ironical in the duck/rabbit example of "seeing as" which Wittgenstein borrowed from the Viennese "funny papers," and the reason for this is that nothing in the figure itself suggests priority for either the duck or the rabbit (although the figure *as a whole* suggests a priority for a world in which ducks do not appear as rabbits or vice versa). Such equality is clearly absent from the instances already cited of philosophical irony; the binocular vision represented there has in each case one eye fixed on a ground that Kierkegaard himself, in *The Concept of Irony*, names an *Urgrund*, and it is only because of this ground that what is then seen by the other eye – the appearance – becomes exchangeable or problematic and is shown, i.e., demonstrated, to be so. Irony, in other words, is at odds with skepticism (here I am at odds myself with other accounts of irony, for example, that of de Man[4]) – and at least some of its own force comes from the possibility of a system that skepticism, for example, would preclude. It is precisely the ground that system provides which irony requires in order to demonstrate that the incongruities, gaps, or extraneous items of appearance – the first side of the two-fold vision – can be overcome, ironized. Lukacs refers to its role in the novel when he describes irony as "the highest freedom that one can attain in a world without God." Even when the philosopher admits God to his world, and certainly when he does not, that world is also the world of the philosopher's making, one in which *he* is the Prime Mover and thus where *he* realizes that "highest freedom" of irony.

Thesis II: Irony is the characteristic trope of philosophy. The very dimensions of this claim may seem strained. The thesis requires first that we think of philosophy and philosophers as a single whole, without setting up fiats of exclusion and inclusion. It requires, secondly, that we think of philosophy as a unified or at least recognizable set of literary artifacts, subject to analysis of the kind applied to standard "genres" of literature like poetry or drama. Neither of these premises will pass easily through the eye of the philosopher's needle, but for the moment, in any event, they can be viewed through the filter of the willing suspension of disbelief. My own way here is motivated once again by Hayden White's proposal in *Metahistory* that the writing of history is hardly the straightforward compounding of events and facts, that in fact the varied structures of written history – his examples are the works of nineteenth-century historians: Michelet; Ranke; Tocqueville; Burckhardt – disclose significant connections with one or another of the four main literary tropes distinguished in medieval rhetoric and later, more substantively, by Vico: metaphor; metonymy; synecdoche; irony. Against this background, the possibility presents itself of moving up a level – advancing from varieties *within* historical writing, for example, to varieties of writing of which the writing of history *as a whole* would then be one. Is it possible to draw analogous distinctions *there*, to view entire disciplines or areas of study as modeled on the literary tropes? If the tropes are more than just techniques or accidental devices, would they not represent systematic modes of thought?

The difficulties that such questions must surmount before they can win conviction are only too evident. The tropes, themselves, even historically, have been problematic in form and in number. On another side, the fields of discourse are vague at the perimeters and unruly within them. Is there, for example, a formal distinction between history and the study of literature? Between history as such and the history of literature? Are such differences proportionate to the differences between philosophy and social science? If philosophy is, as a whole, tropic, are these other disciplines as well? And if so, what figures do *they* emobody?

The latter two questions in particular are crucial for any general theory in which the thesis argued here would have a place, and I have only a preliminary view of what might constitute such a theory: the physical sciences, for example, as a sustained version of synecdoche and then of the romance, as they look ceaselessly for a least and common unit (the atom, the gene) which would then neutralize the many more apparent natural differences; the writing of history, with its metonymic particularity – the single events standing in for the whole – as tragic, irretrievable (unless, as Marx suggests, history should in fact repeat itself – when we would be back, as he himself adds, to farce). But it would be more than enough if something useful could be said along these lines only about philosophy and the claim that philosophy is natively, characteristically ironical; that it is this trope that fundamentally shapes the otherwise various literary forms of philosophy and whatever else this substantively implies about its text.

This proposal depends once again on the concept of doubling and reversal that I have referred to in the examples already given of philosophical irony. Those examples came mainly from *within* philosophical texts, where the philosopher draws a circle around single items to be seen through; I am suggesting now that the frequency in philosophy of such examples is not accidental, that irony is not only a manner of speaking adopted by philosophy, but a manner of being; that what individual ironies attempt piecemeal – disclosing its opposite by way of affirmation – philosophical systems characteristically do as corporate wholes, the surface of experience serving the philosopher as a foil for deeper intelligibility. This is, simply put, a claim that the Appearance-Reality distinction is as essential to philosophy as it is to irony – that as irony posits a state of affairs the more sharply to emphasize the opposed truth, so philosophy characteristically posits a surface "given" (given by reason or by experience or by the philosophical tradition, or more likely, by a combination of these) which is then taken to disclose the less apparent reality. Heraclitus finds in any apparent instances of stasis evidence of motion, as Parmenides finds in apparent plurality and motion evidence of the One which has neither of those qualities. Those examples are clearly opposed to each other in *what* they say, but they are much alike in the saying itself; and the formulations of that saying are recurrent in the history of philosophy, in the voices of the individual philosophers: "You (or others, or the tradition) ascribe to appearance this character – but if you look harder, admit the evidence that the appearance itself provides, you will see that reality is in fact the other way round." The dualism here is not between falsehood and truth or between inadequacy and adequacy, but rather an opposition in which the second term is implied by the first, as reality is implied by appearance in the many specific mements from which the philosophical systems that most openly name those concepts.

Bradley's heavily ironical *Appearance and Reality* is the most forthright modern confrontation of the distinction celebrated in its title; but we understand something more in the character even of that work, and of the distinction more generally, when we place them both against the background of Hegel, who lays fair claim to title as the supreme philosophical ironist. It was Hegel, after all, who argued that the least likely of texts, an encyclopedia, could also be ironical. Look, he suggests there, at the pieces of world history: Egyptian painting, the Chinese invention of gunpowder, the rise of monarchy in Europe, the Indian *Upanishads*, the shape of the human figure. At first blush, one might be inclined to say that such diverse items must be unrelated, that they *could* have nothing to do with each other, in themlves or historically. But at second blush, they turn out to represent not only an order, but a necessary order – in the single and tightly woven plot of world history in which a protagonist named Absolute Spirit struggles past an array of obstacles, diversions, and temptations until finally, whipping them all into one shape, he (it?) triumphs. Was there ever, we ask ourselves, reflecting on these adventrues, a *Bildungsroman*, the triumph of consciousness over experience, that was *not* ironical? "The logic called dialectical," Loewenberg writes about Hegel's method, "is the logic of comedy par excellence." It is no *deus ex machina* that here discloses the reality behind the appearance; the machinery of appearance *itself* does so, always pointing out the fragmentary or partial character of what had gone before. "In Hegel," Kierkegaard concludes, "each moment contains within itself the seeds of its own dissolution."

Even where the Appearance-Reality distinction is less openly cited, moreover, the tension between concepts that feed into them is often unmistakable – and this in a broad range of philosophical accounts that may otherwise seem to share almost nothing more than this common subversion of appearance. This is, quite clearly, a strong factor in the heady career of Hume's scandalous claim that causes and effects are, *in reality,* no more than what they *seem* to be (a double irony, in the terms I have been proposing) – namely, constant conjunctions; it surely is the only way we can account for the fact that Moore's otherwise quite unremarkable two hands remain joined in philosophical memory to the existence of an external world.

Point Two: In these varied instances, it is not only the Appearance–Reality distinction that gives a shape to the arguments – the Appearance being addressed first, the Reality then allegedly forcing its own way out of the Appearance. The overcoming is always here a function of mind or vision; it is a domination by understanding, not by action, not by feeling or taste, only provisionally even by experience, since for empiricism, too, it is understanding that gives a name and shape to experience. This again, as I have suggested, is native to the figure of irony, where first the ironist and then his audience see or understand their way through appearances at the same time that they hold them in view *as* appearances. This claim is not diminished, I believe, even by the classical ideal (Plato's for example) of philosophy, as the *love* of wisdom rather than as an abstracted seeing that we might associate with *theoria* – for the love that sustains Plato's *philosophia* is the love of mind for itself. Nor is the claim constrained even by Marx's attempt to turn Hegel right side up. For there too – "Philosophers have only interpreted the world in various ways, the point, however, is to change it" – the action is the action of *praxis* in which the mind is conceived as instrumental, where thinking takes place in the hand more than in the head. Indeed, Marx honors that same confidence in the rationality of history that was represented by Hegel, the same keen eye – albeit with a different lens – for finding reason in the dispersion of historical event: "The truth is always present," Marx notes, "but not always in truthful form" – as fundamental a faith in the power of irony as has ever been openly (i.e., non-ironically) professed. In each of these instances, the philosophical starting point at once reveals its own inadequacies and at the same time poses the corrective that would make for adequacy; it implies – or at least is *intended* to imply – its opposite.

It may be objected that the ironical elements I have been pointing to are hardly peculiar to philosophy; that there is perhaps no organized intellectual discipline from which such elements are absent; that described in this way, irony itself is so equitably distributed – in the projects of history, sociology, or even physics – that if *that* is what is supposed to be distinctive about philosophy, philosophy (as numerous detractors and even some proponents have claimed) has no character of its own, is nothing apart from any of them. But there are differences here, I believe, that nonetheless warrant the claim for the distinction. The writing of history, for example, takes the reality of its own discourse for granted; moreover, as it reorders or makes sense of events or objects, it moves only from one sequence to another – from Appearance, in effect, to Appearance, leaving the way always open to historical revision. But philosophy benefits from neither of these vantage points: For it, Appearance, is radically in question – in the first instance, its own Appearance, since the nature of philosophy is itself one, even the principal one, of its own questions. And this is the more heavily underscored because that Appearance contrasts not with another Appearance but with a putative Reality to which the Appearance attests even if it does so negatively, offering "one word to express its antonym." That is, ironically.

Does this emphasis on the trope of irony mean that the other tropes do not "figure" in philosophical texts? The obvious answer to that question is no – that as there are plentiful examples in philosophy of comic forms other than irony, so the tropes other than irony also affect philosophical writing. Metaphor, for example, as analyzed in the history of philosophy by such writers as Stephen Pepper or McKeon, is demonstrably an important factor in shaping philosophical texts, even in writers like Locke or Hobbes who explicitly criticize the use of metaphorical figures. Thus, my contention is not that the other tropes do not affect philosophical writing, but that their roles are subordinate to the more basic turn of irony – that they begin (and indeed take their specific content) at a source that irony provides.

But what, it may be objected to this general claim, of philosophical writers who seem not in the slighest ironical, even in the perhaps too generous sense of that term I have been using? Here a distinction might be made between philosophers whose work is deliberately and openly directed against the partial or bifocal vision essential to irony, and those philosophers who escape irony because they never, perhaps even to themselves, acknowledge it as a possibility. About the latter – the naive realists and naive skeptics, in their assorted contemporary guises: positivists, ordinary-language philosophers, those phenomenologists whose only act is to bracket reality, the deconstructionists, even, I suppose, Rorty's "conversationalists" – there is little to be said that they do not say themselves. They eschew irony in effect only to become its objects, incongruously split in the view of any onlooker more willing than they are themselves to notice the difference between what they say and what they do. The image that comes to mind here is again the figure of Protagoras (through a surrogate, Theaetetus), this time pursued by Socrates for his doctrine that knowledge is perception.

> *Socrates*   Can a person know something and also not know that which he knows?
>
> *Theaetetus* It is impossible, I suppose.
>
> *Socrates*   Not if you say that seeing is knowing.... Consider: a gentleman puts his hand over one of your eyes and asks you whether you see his coat, etc., etc....

The other case is stronger and more difficult, bringing out again the fact that although irony is not only in the eye of the beholder, there is no irony without that eye – and that the eye itself, for the reader of philosophy as well as for the philosopher, may have various impulses. It might be conceded, for example, that Aristotle sometimes wrote or spoke ironically, but it could still be asked how with a project that sets itself to the study of being *qua being*, we are to find irony in such a system? So, Aristotle opens the *Metaphysics* by asserting that "All men by nature desire to know"; and we can even appreciate the ironical reflection – half an objection – by which a commentator (John Herman Randall, Jr.) reacts to that assertion: "Aristotle never had the privilege of teaching in an American university." But what, we ask, of Aristotle's initial statement itself?

I can only return here to the general form of the argument so far presented, suggesting in fact that if Randall's objection were taken as ground rather than figure, then it is Aristotle's original statement (against the backdrop, to be sure, of students or faculty in Athenian, not American universities) that represents the ironic turn I have been speaking about. Certainly one would have had to look well, and vigorously, beyond the political and social *appearances* of even fifth-century BC Athens to discover that the common impulse of its entrepreneurs, soldiers, politicians, courtesans, and Sophists was indeed toward knowledge. It is not, here, Aristotle's single statement (or the immediate context of which it is part) that is ironical, implying or at least evoking its opposite; it is the evidence that speaks through the philosopher and which his statement then consummates. In this sense the irony is at one remove, mediated – but the remove does not itself affect the ironic turn that continues to be represented. The point here is that even with being *qua being* as his object, the role of the philosopher is that of disclosing, of unveiling, of catching his reader looking in one direction or at one set of surfaces when it is in another direction, toward another set of surfaces, that the reader is in fact committed, whether he knows it or (more likely) not. I cannot, again, show this to be the case for all the instances that might be brought up – and so I close with what seems at once an unlikely instance and thus a likelier piece of evidence.

There is, we would be inclined to say, nothing funny about the *ordo geometricus* or Spinoza's application of it: not irony, not satire, not farce, not even, as far as I have been able to discover, a solitary or accidental joke that slipped past the author's passion for regularity and order – a *single* order. Spinoza, the most conscientious of monists, would never, could *never*, see double; that is in fact what the method is intended, not only to reflect, but to demonstrate. Well, perhaps. For he only succeeds in this to the extent that we accept him – that "gottertrunkenes Mensch" – as indeed part of his own system, as living within it as well as talking about it. But can we, his readers, do that? Perhaps we could if he did so himself – but there, it seems, is the rub. So Spinoza writes in the *Ethics*: "I will analyze the actions and appetites of men as if it were a question of lines, of planes, and of solids." That "I," we recognize, his or his reader's, is not itself a line or a plane, not even, geometrically speaking, a solid – and the disparity here, the wedge through which irony pushes its way, is framed for the ages in an epic misreading which Spinoza, we may reasonably conclude, invited. "I would call attention," the respectful and supportive Henry Oldenbury, Secretary of the British Royal Society, writes to Spinoza, "to the ambiguities in your treatment of God and Nature: a great many people think you have confused one with the other."[5] Spinoza, of course, had wanted to do nothing else; Oldenburg reports the sort of mistake that invites laughter not just because pratfalls are funny, but because when it is a missed irony that causes the pratfall, the sound of the thud is especially loud. What Oldenburg reports as confusion not only was deliberate but was the most forceful turn that Spinoza had intended to give to the view of reality he was proposing – a turn which Oldenburg's statement also discloses as ironical. For irony asks us to see double; when we do not understand that request, we do not see even once.

Notes to Chapter Five

1 Fowler, in *Modern English Usage*, anthropomorphizes this doubling effect into a requirement for irony of an audience of two persons – "one party that hearing shall hear and not understand, and another party that, when more is meant that meets the ear, is aware both of that more and of the outsider's incomprehension." But although irony may often be thus used as a weapon, the more fundamental – and philosophical – account it means to settle is with the audience of a Single One.

2 I refer here to the claim that irony is methodological only (as in the alleged interchangeability of Socratic Irony and Socratic Method), that finally, at the point where Plato or Kierkegaard open their systems to an element which is non–ironical (as in the theory of forms or in the leap of faith), they leave their roles as ironists. This is, I should argue, a confusion of irony with skepticism. Since irony occurs as a figure only so far as one part of its double vision serves as a base, this is also true for the trope of irony as a whole.

3 Northrop Frye discusses the place of a "green world" in the geography of New Comedy in "The Argument of Comedy," in D.A. Robertson, Jr., ed., *English Institute Essays, 1948* (New York: Columbia University Press, 1949).

4 P. de Man, "The Rhetoric of Temporality," in C. Singleton, ed., *Interpretation* (Baltimore: Johns Hopkins University Press, 1969). Irony is also, I believe, at odds with allegory which has sometimes been held to be one of its forms; the difference there is that allegory begins when the dialectic of irony ends.

5 Letter from Oldenburg to Spinoza, 15 November 1675.

6

Rorty Scrivener

"I would prefer not to," said Bartleby.

In November, 1979, Rorty's *Philosophy and the Mirror of Nature*[1]
was published; a month later, at the annual meeting of the Eastern
Division of the American Philosophical Association in New York
City, Rorty, who had been elected to office the year before, delivered
the presidential address, titled, "Pragmatism, Relativism, and
Irrationalism."[2]

In retrospect, these three events – the election, the publication of
the book, the presidential address – take on significance that was
much less evident when they occurred. The office, for example,
preceded the publication of the book by almost a year – an honor that
would not have been accorded Rorty without support from the
linguistic or "analytic" philosophers then dominant in the political
structure of the Association and many of whom, *after* the book's
appearance, would have voted differently[3]. Even before that, in fact,
there could have been doubts and doubters. Rorty received his
doctorate at Yale at a time (1956) when Yale was still a home to
traditional metaphysics; in the several years prior to 1979, he had
published essays in (philosophically) wayward journals like the *Geor-
gia Review* and *New Literary History* and oddly skeptical articles
even in mainstream periodicals like the *Journal of Philosophy*. But the
credentials based on his earlier writings and other accomplishments
were strong, and his ideological commitments seemed at least strong
enough – if only through the circular argument that if they were not,

he would not have been in Princeton's Department of Philosophy which had guarded itself watchfully against the trespasses of non-analytic or "soft" philosophy.

But not, as events now suggested, against subversion from within – which is more or less the way that Rorty's role in the events of 1979 was construed at Princeton and by analytic philosophers more generally. This reaction added heat to the more substantive reaction directed by the same audience against the radical views expressed in *Philosophy and the Mirror of Nature* and in the presidential address. In both these formulations, Rorty declared an end to philosophy as it had been practised, not only in its longer "metaphysical" tradition but also in analytic philosophy which had itself reacted against the metaphysical past. But the scientific ideal espoused in much analytic writing of a distinctively philosophical method and subject matter joined to determinate criteria of truth was, for Rorty, of a piece with the grander metaphysical speculations that had preceded it. In one as in the other, Rorty diagnosed the futile attempt "to escape from history . . . to find nonhistorical conditions of any possible historical development." (*Philosophy and the Mirror of Nature*, 9) That attempt was not only futile in fact; it proposed to do the impossible – and its failure had thus been assured from the beginning.

That Rorty exempted a number of twentieth-century "greats" (Dewey, Wittgenstein, Heidegger) and certain more immediately contemporary figures like Quine and Sellars from the sweep of his objections did little to blunt the edge of his criticism or the reaction against it. Rorty, it was evident, had produced – or, more simply, *was* – a philosophical scandal; "traitor" was among the labels attached to him, albeit more revealing of his critics' conception of the allegiances of philosophy than of Rorty's. In retrospect, it seems certain that had *Philosophy and the Mirror of Nature* been published *before* his election, Rorty would not have had the opportunity, at least not in 1979, to address his colleagues *ex cathedra* on the "neurotic Cartesian quest for certainty" that motivated modern philosophy, or the "watered-down Kantianism" by which analytic philosophy disputed the claims of the "watered-down Platonism"[4] of continental philosophy – each oblivious to the sound of the bell that had already tolled for them both.

Nor would be have been making this address at the moment that a revolt was breaking out in the ranks of the American Philosophical Association against the alleged abuse of power in the Association by the analytic establishment. Ideological orthodoxy rather than philosophical commitment, the instigators of the revolt claimed, had

become a condition for awarding places and privileges in the Assoca-
tion – in shaping the programs of Association conventions, in determining nominations and membership for committees, and in making
recommendations from the Association to foundations and granting
agencies. Those responsible for this prejudice, the charge went, had
also assumed for themselves the authority to say officially both what
philosophy was and (more to the point) what it was not. The group of
"pluralist" philosophers initiating this protest were related to each
other more by what they opposed than by common philosophical
ground; they included phenomenologists, Whiteheadians, pragmatists, Thomists. And they certainly had neither counted Rorty in their
informal membership nor foreseen the confluence of the events mentioned in planning to speak out at the 1979 meetings.[5] It was as it
happened, then – but it nonetheless *happened* – that Rorty was
presiding over the Association when a severe ideological conflict in
the organization surfaced at its convention – a split reflected as well in
the division between old and new in his own philosophical work.

As for many narratives, the plot-development in this one was more
concise and dramatic than its denouement which still, 10 years later,
continues. At the 1979 convention itself, Rorty assumed the role of
mediator; in part through his office as President, in part through his
own history, he had access (even if increasingly grudging) to both
sides. The resolution devised in those hectic days opened up the
committee structure of the Association, including that of the Program
Committee – a change subsequently reflected in other organizational
arrangements and decisions and in more directly philosophical ones
as well. The proliferation of specialized philosophical societies meeting in conjunction which the Association but autonomous organizationally would no doubt have occurred anyway; but this, too, was
given a strong impetus by the confrontation at the 1979 meetings. By
1989, the Association convention drew more sessions from this
source – the Nietzsche Society, Society for Women in Philosophy,
Society for Value Inquiry, the Marxist Caucus, *et al.* – than appeared
on the official program, although a careful distinction continued to be
made between the sessions approved by the Association's Program
Committee and those which were not. In 1979, the still more scandalous Derrida would have been unlikely to find a place in the building;
in 1989, he addressed, by invitation, a plenary session of the convention. It may be too much or even yet too early to claim that the
landscape of American philosophy, institutionally but to an extent
also substantively, would not be the same after the events of 1979; as
with most stirrings in the history of ideas, Rorty's revisionism was

undoubtedly symptomatic as well as causal. But there is no question that in the decade between 1979 and 1989 significant changes occurred in the profession of American philosophy – and that Rorty was and remains a central figure in this process. His decision to leave Princeton (in 1982) for a chair as "Professor of Humanities" at Virginia was emblematic of the terms of the conflict over which he presided organizationally in 1979 and also, although less formally, in his writings.

Rorty's book, *Contingency, irony, and solidarity*[6], is usefully understood against the background of this brief excursus into the sociology of knowledge, on the one hand, and the progression in his own thinking since 1979, on the other. *Philosophy and the Mirror of Nature* was primarily a critical work, posed against the entire post-Cartesian history of philosophy and, although less systematically, against classical and medieval philosophy as well. With the exceptions noted, analytic and linguistic philosophy found itself tarred with the same brush – as perpetuating a conception of philosophy which aimed for a description (as in a "mirror") of reality more general and fundamental than anything provided by the non-philosophical "sciences". This search for foundations, Rorty contended, was misbegotten in its origins, not only a failure in fact: every claim historically on behalf of a metaphysical starting point – Descartes' *Cogito*, Kant's categories, Plato's forms – had been, because it could only be, circular. The search itself would thus best be viewed now as an historical curiosity, much like the varieties of religious orthodoxy with which it had often been associated.

Rorty's second book, *Consequences of Pragmatism* (1982) was a collection of essays with much the same critical design. A number of the essays had appeared prior to *Philosophy and the Mirror of Nature*; those written afterwards served to consolidate the conclusions reached there, rehearsing Rorty's attack on the tradition as dogmatic, ahistorical, and most of all, fruitless – conscious, it seemed, of every self except its own. As in *Philosophy and the Mirror of Nature*, the enemy here was unmistakable: metaphysics, foundationalism, transcendentalism, representationalism – the entire clutch of efforts to improve on the "apparent" world by evoking the "real" one, to locate a fulcrum for philosophical understanding in fixed criteria of knowledge and ethical principles. By contrast, for the new "post-Philosophical" culture which now supersedes the other, the criteria applied to questions about truth and conduct provide at best "temporary resting places" (*Consequences of Pragmatism*, xlii); they are valuable *because* they do not claim permanence and are thus able to respond to new – live – contexts. On the deep questions of traditional philosophy, the pragmatists, Rorty claims had it right (with a small "r"): "Everything is up for grabs at once."

A thesis with claims as radical as those of Rorty's indictment of philosophy's past could hardly avoid an adversarial edge – and this edge, muted to some extent in *Philosophy and the Mirror of Nature* by the detail of philosophy's history, becomes sharper in the occasional essays collected in *Consequences of Pragmatism* and, still more so, in his latest book. In his sub-title to *The Genealogy of Morals*, Nietzsche designated it a "polemic" ("Streitschrift"); and although Rorty's new book retains some of the even-handedness of liberal discourse ("they belive 'this', but we believe 'that'"), an often strident tone and occasional nastiness seem designed, polemically, to place the reader under attack, whether guilty or (less likely) not. Even at his harshest, however, Rorty's own inheritance of systematic philosophy mediates; notwithstanding the distinction in *Philosophy and the Mirror of Nature* where he comes down on the side of "edifying" as opposed to "systematic" philosophy, he seems in fact to remain of both minds. There is no doubt in all Rorty's books of the moral conviction that moves them and is meant to move the reader; but there is also no doubt about his continuing attentiveness, as it were despite himself, to the systematic argument. Rorty sustains the two forms of discourse at once – one explicit and hortatory (and edifying); the other tacit and systematic, making certain that the guns of the first are well-aimed. Whatever objections may in the end be directed against Rorty's work, they will be evoked by what he has committed himself to, not by what he has failed to register.

This underlying sense of system also bears on the direction he takes in his latest book. For as *Philosophy and the Mirror of Nature* criticized the philosophical tradition in its (alleged) foundations, and as *Consequences of Pragmatism* elaborated on this criticism – for one, by arguing its affinities with the claims of such figures as Derrida, Foucault, and Bloom – the pressure increases on Rorty himself to respond to the issues so unsatisfactorily addressed by the tradition. Having rejected the longstanding foundations of epistemology, ethics, and political theory, what would *he* make of the questions which those foundations had been relied on to answer? Some of these questions might be supposed to disappear with the foundations themselves – but at least some of them seem bound to survive, if only because the most general question motivating ethics and politics and at least by implication, epistemology as well will not go away: What, after all, *is to be done?*

This challenge to Rorty, at times sharpened by charges against him of political conservatism or reaction, had already made itself felt in a general way at the edges of literary deconstruction with which his work is associated. The furor set off by the surfacing in the Fall, 1987, of Paul de Man's collaborationist writings and subsequent silence about them,[7] and the renewed attention called to Heidegger's moral and political culpability by Farias' *Heidegger et le nazisme,*[8] brought into the open a long-standing suspicion that there was in poststructuralism a soft spot for moral quietism or epistemic intuitionism (or both) – features which if they do not entail, at least open the door to political reaction and to varieties of totalitarianism. The different, albeit related philosophical challenge to Rorty on the status of truth or meaning had been present from the beginning: what could those concepts or properties hope for, if there was, in Derrida's words, "nothing outside the text" – that is, in the absence of a correspondence *in some sense* between word and world?

In the three parts of *Contingency, irony, and solidarity,* Rorty relates what can, in his view, still be said about the traditional questions of epistemology and, with still more emphasis, of ethics and social theory. In the first part, "Contingency," Rorty maps the whole, with chapters on "language," "selfhood," and "liberal community"; in Part II, "Ironism and theory," he focuses mainly on the "private" domain of morality, and in Part III, "Cruelty and solidarity," on politics and the means of community.[9] The distinctions among the parts are quite rough, with questions and issues running into and over each other and often repeating themselves; the effect resembles the "pastiche" proposed by Jameson as the distinctively postmodern genre. So far as allusion or reference are concerned, this is entirely deliberate; against the usual taboos of academic writing, nothing is in principle irrelevant: Proust, Larkin, Nabokov, and Orwell appear side by side, line by line, with Davidson, Hegel, and Heidegger.

That the account given in the book is intended *not* to provide an "argument" but to appear, to afford a "look," is itself one of its recurrent themes. The epistemic and moral perspectives that Rorty holds up for viewing are not meant to refute other "descriptions," because descriptions do not contend with each other in that way: there is no external or neutral criterion to move the process of rejection or assent. What occurs is at most a comparison among alternatives and then, possibly, the supersession of one by another – not because the "world outside" dictates this but because the relations among the alternatives themselves somehow turn out this way.

Rorty's own "argument" in presenting this view is concise and rapid. Truth is a property of sentences, not of things or facts or the correspondence between them (or anything else). Furthermore, since "sentences are elements of human languages, and... human languages are human creations," (5) truth is itself made rather than found. All that we have to work with, then – here Rorty applies the Wittgensteinian analogy between language and tools – is a "vocabulary" that enables us to describe (more accurately, since there is no bottom to stand on, to *redescribe*) whatever it is we are attending to. Such redescriptions are not themselves true or false but alternatives: "... Rebutting objections to one's redescriptions of some things will be largely a matter of redescribing other things, trying to outflank the objections by enlarging the scope of one's favorite metaphors." (44) The basis for judging between seemingly conflicting accounts is not by appeal to a neutral ground, but by a competition among the accounts on grounds other than truth. Thus he writes about his own position in *Contingency, irony, and solidarity*: "I am not going to offer arguments against the vocabulary I want to replace. Instead, I am going to try to make the vocabuary I favor look attractive by showing how it may be used to describe a variety of topics." (9) One way of accomplishing this goal will be by urging invidious comparisons: "... My strategy will be to try to make the vocabulary in which... objections [to my redescriptions] are phrased look bad...." (44) This project is well worth pursuing, moreover, since "anything can be made to look good or bad by being redescribed." (73)

The broad strokes of this view emerge from a more nuanced discussion of the "contingency" of language – its historicity and thus its constantly provisional character. Rorty recognizes that his reference to the contingency of language applies more readily to "vocabularies as wholes" than to "single sentences" – e.g., 'The butler did it' or 'The doctor did it' – where the appeal to *some* fixed criterion of truth seems unavoidable. Moreover, his attempts to replace the language of argument by one of presentation and comparison – instead of invoking premises and conclusions, inference, consistency, or refutation, he "urges," "recommends," "offers," "suggests" – are attended by such numerous lapses into "claims," "reasons," objections of "circularity," that the discrepancy itself becomes significant. He does not go so far, moreover, as to assert that truth bears *no* relation to the world (so, for example, he acknowledges "the fact that the world contains the causes of our being justified in holding a belief" (5). But he does not admit that these apparent deviations have implications for his general position – and since what makes a redescription "look bad" or "look good" is a matter of the "look," not of reference beyond it, this is in a way consistent. But only to restate the claim does not help in determining when or – still more basically – *why* a particular redescription "looks good" or "looks better than another;" and *that* issue, it will be suggested below, casts a long shadow on much else that Rorty proposes.

The aesthetic connotations of the concept of the "look" are significant here – insofar as a look is all surface (there is no place else to look). This implication also accounts for Rorty's reliance on "literary" texts for evidence and example, and one of these examples in particular underscores both the extent and limitations of his account of truth. In chapter 8, titled "Orwell on cruelty," Rorty considers two alternative interpretations of *Animal Farm* – his own being contrasted with the more common one which identifies Orwell as a "realist philosopher" who proposes to 'see things as they are, to find out true facts' [Orwell's words, quoted by Rorty] – "a defender of common sense against its cultured, ironist despisers."[10] On the common sense view, *Animal Farm* is intent on "stripping away appearance and revealing reality" (173), showing what the Russian Revolution had *actually* produced in contrast to the tendentious accounts which apologists, inside Russia or out, had concocted. But this second interpretation becomes less plausible if one denies – as Rorty does – that "there are any plain moral facts out there in the world . . . . It [in this case, *Animal Farm*] is better thought of as a redescription of what may happen or has been happening – to be compared not with reality, but with alternative descriptions of the same events . . . an alternative perspective from which we liberals . . . could describe the political history of our century." (173)

The implication is evident here that if Orwell did not himself conceive his work in these terms, he should have. It thus seems fair to ask in response to Rorty's reading what *Animal Farm* would amount to *without* an assumption of the existence of "plain facts" – a question with a special point here, since in conventional terms, *Animal Farm* combines the genres of allegory and satire, each of them based on a representational ground or object – what serves the text as a foundation from which it pushes off. It is no doubt possible to *imagine* the relations between these two genres and their respective objects as open or symmetrical (e.g., the butt of satire as itself a satire, the Russian Revolution as a satire on *Animal Farm*). But the strain of any such interpretation is obvious, and it is hardly mitigated by

Rorty's reiterating that within the text as outside of it, there *is* no ground. On his own reading, *Animal Farm* offers the reader an apparently indefinite number of alternative views, with that offer itself, reflexively, part of the text's own assertion and with no possible reason for choosing among the views offered even when they conflict. One supposes that Rorty would agree that whatever else it is or is not, *Animal Farm* is undeniably anti-totalitarian in its implications; but having categorically renounced the category of "plain facts," it is not clear where even this one could come from for Rorty.

The theory of interpretation that Rorty makes part of the understanding of *Animal Farm* indicates the importance he attaches to "vocabularies" or (again drawing on Wittgenstein) "language games." These contexts of discourse are intended to subvert the traditional concept of truth as based on a theory of correspondence or representation. In language games or vocabularies, individual statements can be made and assessed; but in contrast to the traditional view, they cannot themselves be assessed, or at least not in the same way. There is no neutral or "first" vocabulary or language game, and this implies that even within a particular vocabulary or language game, all criteria of truth are fated (strictly speaking, immediately) to acquire the quotations marks of obsolescence (that is, as "truth"). It is evident historically that language games come and go, and that both the coming and going in some sense require the concurrence of their speakers. But none of this involves a criterion by which one vocabulary is found "false," and indeed there is hardly a decision to be made here at all. What occurs, Rorty proposes, shows only that a culture and its members have "gradually lost the habit of using certain words and gradually acquired the habit of using others." (6)

This account has the advantage of providing a non-invidious description of historical displacements such as that of Aristotelian by Newtonian physics or of the impasse between apparently conflicting moral claims. Since there is no neutral vocabulary by which to choose among such differences, their resolution depends not on an appeal to objective features of the world "outside," but by acknowledging the history of which they are part. We ought, in fact, to stop thinking of the apparent conflicts between vocabularies as a theoretical problem and get on with the business of using them (or, in the event, of finding that they have outlived their usefulness). Rorty is aware of the likely charge of relativism against a view in which "redescription" replaces "truth"; but this charge itself, in his view, reflects a worn-out opposition. Both relativism and its absolutist opponent assume that a reasoned choice leads to the acceptance of one or the other – and it is this assumption that ought now to be discarded. Where "decisions" are sought about adopting or rejecting vocabularies (even for the individual), the choice is more apparent than real. Reasons in effect merge with causes, and about causes *non disputandum est* – at least in the sense that we do not, cannot *deliberate* about them as a condition for getting on with the work of the present.

To ask how one knows when one is "in" one vocabulary or language game and not in another may seem itself a gesture to the metaphysical past, and Rorty's objection here is explicit: "I have no criterion of individuation for distinct languages or vocabularies to offer, but I am not sure that we need one." (7) And indeed, if the only role of vocabularies or language games is as *past* redescription, the need for criteria would be slight: it hardly affects the distinction between Aristotelian and Newtonian physics if we cannot say exactly when the shift from one to the other occurred. But for deciding how to proceed in the present, an appeal to history as *eventually* settling the matter is not very helpful – although it is this that Rorty seems obliged (and willing) to rely on. To think of a decision in the present as a "redescription" suggests a detached form of narration on the part of the agent – a self telling a story about a decision which is being made, as it happens, by the same self.

One way to make *this* redescription more plausible, Rorty seems to suggest, is by appealing to the usage of the "dominant" vocabulary. Such an appeal is apparently unhindered by any difficulty in deciding *which* vocabulary is dominant – an assumption which suggests that something like the process of history, rather than individual agents, points the direction. To be sure, Rorty never invokes anything as metaphysically loaded as the notion of a determinant historical process. There seem instead to be numerous small-scale processes, although the fact that they are small does not in the end seem to make them any less impervious to human intervention: "Most of reality," he writes, "is indifferent to our descriptions of it . . . . " This condition holds, moreover, not only for broad cultural or social change but even for shifts in personal commitment – as from theism to atheism, from "one spouse or circle of friends to another . . . . We should not look within ourselves for criteria of decision . . . . any more than we should look to the world." (6) And with the two likeliest sources of agency – in the self and world – excluded, what seem to be left are the language games themselves, developing and changing if not haphazardly, certainly not by choice or reason. "'Language speaks man,'" he quotes

Heidegger approvingly (50), on the basis of what for Rorty appears to be very much like a fundation.

Against this apparently deterministic conception of language, both the need and the possibility of introducing choice and discrimination among language games are implied by Rorty himself in two related examples. The first of these is in the distinction between the private and the public domains which he cites early on as a central thesis of *Contingency, irony, and solidarity* but which appears thereafter as only a sporadic and muted presence. A common mistake of traditional metaphysics, Rorty suggests, is in the attempt to "fuse the public and the private," to bring the process of "self-creation together with justice at the level of theory." (xiv) Not only have such attempts failed in fact, Rorty claims, but they were bound to fail: " . . . The vocabulary of self-creation is necessarily private, unshared . . . . The vocabulary of justice is necessarily public and shared . . . . " (xiv) The only means of bringing them together is by a theory of human nature which cites certain features as common to all persons and thus as the common basis for a conception of the private and the public domains. But, he objects, theories of human nature are by *their* nature either circular – repeating in their conclusions only what their premises have invented – or so general as to be vacuous: "platitudes." (Rorty's application of this label to Aristotle's opening line in the *Metaphysics* – that "All men by nature desire to know" – has something of the flavor of the objection to *Hamlet* because of all the clichés that Shakespeare quoted in it.)

Rorty's argument here (and here there surely is an argument) does not deny that attempts have been made to join the private and the public domains – in Plato, in the Christian tradition and Marxism, even in figures whom he otherwise cites with approval on one side or the other of the dichotomy (Nietzsche, for example, on the side of self-creation, Mill, on the side of public justice). But the price paid for connecting the two realms – that is, a theory of human nature – is too high, especially since accounts can be given of each of the sides without joining them. Rorty himself thus proposes two vocabularies – one of "private irony," the other of "liberal hope;" these are "largely irrelevant" (83) to each other, and we should in fact "stop trying to combine self-creation and politics . . . . " (120)

It can be argued that Rorty's own conceptions of the public and the private are closely related (more of this below); but for the moment what is at issue is his contention that the line between these vocabularies can be shown to be sufficiently sharp to preclude any intrinsic connection between them. A pointed example both of this claim and of the difficulties it runs into occurs in the distinction Rorty finds between two different vocabularies of Heidegger. "On the general question of the relation between Heidegger's thought and his Nazism, I am not persuaded that there is much to be said except that one of the century's most original thinkers happened [!] to be a pretty nasty character . . . . But if one holds the view of the self as centerless . . . one will be prepared to find the relation between the intellectual and the moral virtues, and the relation between a writer's book and other parts of his life, contingent." (111)

This interpretation of Heidegger cannot, of course, be excluded a priori – but that fact should, it seems, cut both ways. Rorty's reader never learns *how* Rorty has determined that the two vocabularies mentioned *are* separate (he would have, incidentally, to override Heidegger's own insistence – reported in a conversation with Löwith – that they are not), and indeed in Rorty's terms there could be no criteria for making such a determination. Without this means, however, it remains no less plausible that Heidegger's politics were part of the same vocabulary as his metaphysics (and then, presumably, consistent with it) than that they reflect different sources. The danger that a new vocabulary might simply be announced whenever a writer or reader wants to protect one part or another of what has been said is obvious enough; it is not clear, however, what means Rorty leaves himself as a defense against just that charge.

The "contingency" of language – and of meaning and truth – is the basis of Rorty's account in *Contingency, irony, and solidarity* for his views of the self and community which are the main substantive concerns in the book. He writes, he informs the reader early on, as a "liberal ironist": "liberal" as believing that "cruelty is the worst thing we do;" "ironist" as a "person who faces up to the contingency of his or her own most central beliefs and desires." (xv) (Notwithstanding the book's title, the ironist practises "ironism" not "irony".) It is through this two-fold redescription – "ironist" reflecting the private self, "liberal" reflecting the public self – that Rorty elaborates his views of ethics and politics.

In his conception of the self, Rorty mainly reiterates its "self-lessness." Since there is neither a natural nor a transcendental self to be realized, the alternative of "self-creation" is all that remains. The terms of this process have been anticipated, among others, by Nietzsche and Freud. For Nietzsche, "to fail as a human being . . . is to accept somebody else's description of oneself, to execute a previously written program" (28) – and Rorty conceives this ideal as willing both what one is and what one was, proposing "to create one's own language." (27) Passages like the latter sound as if the individual "vocabulary" *is* chosen; indeed little seems to separate Rorty's view at this point from the Sartrian "absolute totality" of freedom. He even criticizes Nietzsche's conception of the "will to power" as presupposing a theory of human nature that infringes on the centerlessness of the self and its capacity for change. No more can be demanded – or judged – of a self than that it be original, committed to crossing the line that "divides the old from the new." (29)

Freud is a more surprising source than Nietzsche for Rorty to cite for the ideal of self-creation, since on most interpretations Freud is a foundationalist, tracing the variety of human expression to a basic instinctual source. Rorty's reading of Freud, however, emphasizes that variety of expression rather than its common source. It is, in effect, Freud's "nominalism," his reading of individual character, that attracts Rorty: " ... Terms like 'infantile' or 'sadistic' or 'obsessional' or 'paranoid,' unlike the names of vices and virtues which we inherit from the Freeks and the Christians, have very specific and very different resonances for each individual who uses them .... " (32) It might be objected here that a trait like "gluttony" might evoke resonances as individually personalized as any of Freud's terms. But even allowing for this possibility, Freud's method does complement Rorty's in a number of ways: by its primarily causal history of individuals and culture; by the neutrality with which it fends off evaluative distinctions among "vocabularies" or persons; and in Freud's refusal (according to Rorty) to deduce a public from his private ethic.

There is more to be said about Rorty's "reading" of historical texts and writers than can be discussed here, but certain of its general features are clear. His relation to the figures he cites are often a mingling of what he claims they said, what he claims they *should have* said, what he claims they said when a good part of what he admits they did say but objects to is dropped out, and what he himself says about all of these – the last of these gaining authority from the fact that there are, after all, only a variety of alternative and conpossible readings. Rorty's own reader might well wonder why he invests so heavily in sources from whom he invariably – and soon – parts company. One jarring result of this pattern is the dismemberment of authors: Nietzsche writes non-perspectivally and with a commitment to a theory of human nature – but this is quite apart from his claims on behalf of perspectivalism and of self-creation. Nabokov holds that literature has nothing to do with moral issues – but this has nothing to do with the evident relevance of his own literary works to moral issues. Etc.. To be sure, on Rorty's view of the centerless self, there is nothing surprising about such inconsistencies. Yet if there were nothing surprising about them, there would be no basis for understanding continuities or consistencies when *they* occurred. Why, for example, should the moral virtues (in his bifurcation of Heidegger) constitute one group rather than several? Indeed, why should we assume that an author's "centerless" self remains constant from one page or paragraph or sentence to the next? It would be no less likely that the author should change personas (i.e., vocabularies) with the page numbers of his book (Rorty 1, Rorty 2, Rorty 3 . . . .)

In keeping with the separation he asserts between the private and the public domains, Rorty's own public rediscription – the "liberal" half of the "liberal ironist" – starts from a different point than does his account of the ironist. He relates cruelty as "the worst thing we do" to the causing of pain, and pain in turn to a distinctively human exemplification, that of humiliation. (92) (This last step, in which Rorty distinguishes between humans and "brutes," takes him dangeroulsy close to a theory of human nature.) It is this basis that then projects the value of solidarity by which we "try to extend our sense of 'we' to people whom we have previously thought of as 'they.'" (192) If cruelty is fostered by a sense of others as alien, then the way to deter cruelty is to prevent or alter that sense. "We" treat others of "us" more or less as we treat ourselves – and the ideal of solidarity would thus expand this circle until it would presumably include all people. This ideal has moral force; indeed Rorty asserts that "we have a moral obligation to *feel* a sense of solidarity" (190, [emphasis added]), as though the feeling itself might be legislated.

A number of issues raised by this spare conception of politics are anticipated by Rorty. To the question of why *solidarity* is claimed to be the basis of obligation (and cruelty "the worst thing we do"), Rorty responds that "there is no *neutral*, noncircular way to defend the liberal's claim . . . any more than there is a neutral way to back up Nietzsche's assertion that this claim expresses a resentful, slavish attitude." (197) But the point, he suggests, is not to *justify* his contention; all that we – or anyone – can do is to describe it in terms of the causes which lead to the ideal as the liberal's own: "*We* have to start from where *we* are." (198) This response, too, seems to rely heavily on what history has decided for "us" – assuming once again a clear definition of who counts as "us" and who does not. If reasons do not underwrite the liberal "redescription," then the question of

"Why accept it?" has no other answer than that "we" liberals *do* accept it – and the justification for this is (apparently circularly) that the viewpoint represents the currently dominant vocabularly or redescription. "A liberal society," Rorty writes with emphasis, "is one which is content to call 'true' whatever the outcome of such encounters turns out to be." (52)

This assimilation of political justice to a "given" vocabulary is unsettling not only because it assumes that a judgment about what the current vocabularly is will not be problematic and that a vocabulary's status as given is sufficient reason for accepting it, but also because of other conditions that Rorty attaches to it. Notwithstanding his own distinction between the public and the private self, for example, the basis of the ideal of solidarity seems closely tied to his own ideal of individual self-creation. "J. S. Mill's suggestion that governments devote themselves to optimizing the balance between leaving people's private lives alone and preventing suffering seems to me pretty much the last word," (63) Rorty writes about the function of political structure. This comes very close to inferring the parameters of political organization from the justification for self-creation in the private realm – and although the order of argument here is reversed from that proposed by Plato or Aristotle for the relation between ethics and politics, this is a formal, not a substantive difference.

Also the second part of the role of government – "preventing suffering" – leaves itself open to the question of how that is to be accomplished; that is, how solidarity can be fostered and the narrow circle round the "we" expanded. Rorty's recommendation about this – what amounts to his political program – turns out not to be political at all, at least as that term is usually understood. If solidarity and the prevention of cruelty are furthered when we "*see* other human beings as 'one of us'" (xvi, [emphasis added]), then to accomplish this, Rorty concludes, might also be based on "seeing." He thus turns for the basis of political and moral cohesion to literary criticism in general and a number of literary forms in particular – "ethnography, the journalist's report, the comic book, the docudrama, and, especially, the novel." (xvi) So far as anything like a political or moral program is proposed by Rorty to replace the philosophical search for social foundations, we find it in the literary means which provide concrete redescriptions of the "kinds of suffering being endured by people to whom we had previously not attended" and of the "sorts of cruelty we ourselves are capable of." The view provided by such texts, Rorty contends, is "relevant to the avoidance of either social or individual cruelty" (141) – and his accounts of three writers in particular

(Proust, Nabokov, and Orwell) further indicate why the novel is a likely genre for Rorty's conception of moral education. The varieties of character and voice give the novel a nominalist cast; it is the individual who counts there, not general principles or a universal self. Furthermore, even so far as connectives occur in the novel, they are the connectives of narrative – the form of emplotment most resistant to theory and generalization.

This literary means makes no provision for political institutions, and although Rorty does not deny the need for such institutions, he says little more about them in this context than to acknowledge that "something like the institutions of bourgeois liberal society" (34) are needed. (He seems only to assume here that what these are is itself clearly defined and commonly agreed on.) On the question "What is to be done?" then, his emphasis is on the means provided by literature – and even there, it might be objected, with only a fragmentary view. For the moral instruction he ascribes to literature claims not only an expanded range of "seeing," but that this seeing will also induce changes in conduct. Literary perception, in other words, is assumed to affect moral practice. Rorty says almost nothing about the evidence which such claims presuppose, nor about the counter-arguments to them. Plato, for example, argues for the banishment of the poets on the basis of virtually the same premises from which Rorty draws *his* conclusion, that is, the particularity or nominalism of literature and the emotional enlargement to which it contributes. I would suggest, furthermore, that a ready, albeit rough test of what Rorty assumes to be the power of literary "seeing" is close at hand (ours and his) – available at any univesity in the same departmentalization of disciplines that Rorty hopes otherwise to subvert: Is there *any* evidence, it might be asked, that their reading of the texts that Rorty recommends has made university professors of literature more sensitive to cruelty, more "liberal," than their colleagues who have read less, or perhaps not at all?

There is an irony in Rorty's reliance on literature for moral instruction as this assumes a representational and thematic reading of novels – in contrast to Rorty's criticism of philosophy's past because of *its* representational form. And there is a deeper irony still in the fact that Rorty, intent on overturning a tradition of textual authority, himself calls on texts to answer the question of how moral and political differences are to be made. Rorty does not consider even as a possibility that sensitivity to cruelty might be enlarged by other activities than reading – by work in a hospital or a prison or on a farm, or perhaps even by wordless meditation. In fact, little is known about the process of moral education – this is surely the largest scandal of an increasingly professionalized system of education; but should not such other possibilities of learning at least be acknowledged before a decision is made for The Book? Dewey, to whom Rorty pays markedly less attention in *Contingency, irony, and solidarity* than in his earlier writings, adverts constantly to the priority of doing as a means for learning. He is arguably at least as surefooted a guide on this question as Proust or Nabokov, even if *reading* Dewey is less immediately engaging than reading them.

There are various reasons why Rorty's response to the question "What is to be done?" which is the constant if not always the explicit theme of *Contingency, irony, and solidarity* might lead so readily to what has been referred to in another context as "aesthetic pragmatism."[11] Literature is itself open, subject to change, nominalist in its plurality of texts, self-less. But a deeper issue here bears on pragmatism – and now liberal ironism – more generally. For better or worse – for better *and* worse – Rorty in *Contingency, irony, and solidarity* uncovers certain commitments of pragmatism that have not (at least not as clearly) been shown before. These features involve the relation of history (specifically, the connection between past and present) to truth – the latter conceived now as what contingently works or "pays" (a favored metaphor of Rorty's that turns into a verb the "cash value" favored by James). A decision on what works or pays is obviously not only retrospective, but directed to the present – and here the question of *why* what pays pays takes on an urgency which imposes the same question and terms on the past.

The question in the present of "What is to be done?" involves whatever can be known about moral agency, about the historically movable line between the public and the private domains, about the knowledge of "matters of fact" involved in decisions made about these in the present – all of these referring to a world and self still in the process of being made. But these questions addressed to the present have antecedents in the past. And one obvious means for responding to them in the present is by seeing not only what the answers to them have been in the past, but *why* those answers worked – what, in other words, can be surmised about the reasons for those results in the relations of world and self. The question of why what works works impinges unavoidable on the "world outside" that Rorty and the pragmatists prefer to avoid. The basis for their exclusion here is evident: the same question of "Why?" – in its Kantian version, "How is it possible that . . . . ?" – is accountable in philosophy's lurid past for the foundations it has sought, perhaps (but only perhaps) in vain. Rorty would prefer to emphasize the present, and in a sense this is understandable: see how the tapestry looks, we are told, feel it, *use* it. But this emphasis does not by itself entail that the question of why this or any texture of discourse has the use it does, either in the story Rorty tells or in those he means to displace, should not be asked. Indeed that question arguably has a connection to the use or look itself.

Even if one granted with Rorty that to assume finality for any particular answer to the question "Why?" ultimately results in circularity, this does not mean that the question of why what works or fits or "looks good" does so should not be asked at the beginning. In pragmatism's own terms, it could be argued that the most extreme versions of foundationalism – for Rorty, Platonism or Christianity – may themselves be read non-circularly and contingently; if literature turns out to be philosophy, then it is no less likely that metaphysics or theology can be read as literature. To move in this direction would be another way, it seems, of providing "novel" redescriptions. And unless one is willing to swallow whole the grandiose contention that the entire history of philosophy, incited by an errant but constant "metaphysical urge," has been only a corporate search for a philosopher's stone, one might suspect that even the search for foundations was fostered by an interest in what works, the same interest that Rorty himself defends. It could be argued, in fact, that this search carries that same interest from the past into the present only in order better to understand the difference between what does work and what does not. In this sense, there might indeed be a "reasonable" interest in the theory of human nature – not in the doubtful sense of an interest in squaring the circle, but because even if theories of human nature end in circularity, important junctures along the way would be missed unless one entered the process. And also because not all circles are vicious – and certainly not equally so – anyway.

There is at least some evidence that an answer to the question "Why?" – provided, for example, by a theory of human nature – may bring a sense of coherence, even of "looking good," to an array of particular things. To an extent, as I have argued, Rorty himself seems to assume the results of such a search, notwithstanding his claim that he is not interested in carrying it on. When he writes, then, in a response to Bernstein that "In the utopian postmetaphysical culture I envisage, nobody would see the point of *asking* whether or not 'there is a universal core of moral intuition in all times and all societies'.

...What difference would it make to *us* whether there were or not?"[12] he has the matter, I should argue, exactly right and exactly wrong: right, insofar as this is indeed entailed by what he has previously said, wrong insofar as the kind of question he cites might well be of interest to others, even if not to himself or his postmetaphysical fellows. The answers to it, moreover, might make a difference even for him in the present, as indeed it has seemed to for other thinkers in the past.

What Rorty – and pragmatism – say finally about this possibility of inquiry is that, like Melville's Bartleby, 'they would prefer not to.' No one can quarrel with this judgment, which is after all the choice of a vocation and one which has proved suggestive and valuable on its own terms for Rorty's readers over the years. But it seems contrary even to the spirit of pragmatism or liberal ironism – much like a "certain moral blindness" that James described – that what one person "would prefer not to" should be made into a general prohibition or, beyond that, into something that *can not* be done. When Bartleby, the conversation-stopping Scrivener, disrupted the world around him by responding "I would prefer not to," his mild answer was startling because it disclosed a choice where none had been recognized. "I would prefer not to," prosposed by Bartleby or Rorty is not the contradictory of "I would prefer to" expressed by someone else. The two are compossible – not because (as Rorty himself might have it) *everything* is compossible, but because they are expressions of desire rather than of fact. But the desires themselves have a basis in fact or at least in reflection. And one alternative to universalizing Rorty's "I would prefer not to" is to think about what it is that he prefers not to, with the possibility of finding there evidence of an account that goes underneath the prose of the world that Rorty himself favors. This is not incompatible with Rorty's "I would prefer not to;" indeed, it seems at least as consistent with his redescription of the role of contingency in the world as does the exclusionary, even repressive implication that he himself draws from it.

Notes to Chapter Six

1 *Philosophy and the Mirror of Nature (PMN)* (Princeton: Princeton University Press, 1979).

2 *Proceedings and Addresses of the American Philosophical Association,* LIII (1980), pp. 719–38; reprinted in *Consequences of Pragmatism* (Minneapolis: University of Minnesota Press, 1982).

3   That PMN was Rorty's first book – aside from his anthology, *The Linguistic Turn* (1967) – provides a footnote for the sociology of philosophy. Inflationary pressures on "professional" philosophy are such that it is improbable that anyone, however gifted, should now be similarly honored if only because – a book having been required for promotion or even tenure – it is increasingly unlikely that the circumstances *could* be the same.

4   "Pragmatism, Relativism, and Irrationalism," see note 2 above.

5   I should note that although not among the organizers of the "pluralist" group, I have since participated in a few of their discussions.

6   *Contingency, irony, and solidarity* (Cambridge: Cambridge University Press, 1989). Unless otherwise indicated, page references in parenthesis are to this work.

7   See Paul de Man, *Wartime Journalism, 1939–1943*, edited by Werner Hamacher, Neil Hertz, and Thomas Keenan (Lincoln: University of Nebraska Press, 1988).

8   Victor Farias, *Heidegger et le nazisme*, translated by Myriam Benarroch and Jean-Baptiste Grasset (Paris: Verdier, 1987).

9   Perhaps the decision was a more general one on the part of Cambridge University Press – but Rorty's "nominalism" in *Contingency, irony, and solidarity* extends to the book and chapter titles as well, with only the first word in each capitalized.

10   One of Rorty's polemical devices is to put the "redescription" of his own position by his opponents in unusually nasty and mean-spirited terms, although without claiming that these have actually been used. Rorty has indeed been attacked harshly and unfairly, but this tactic of making his critics "look bad" suggests that anyone who disagrees with him might be presumed to use the same terms of excoriation. So, for example, also in the chapter on Orwell, Rorty writes of the "metaphysical" interpretation of Orwell which by implication attacks readers like Rorty who dispute the status of "plain sense": "Only those who have allowed their own personality (and in particular their resentment, sadism, and hunger for power) to cloud their vision will fail to grasp the plain moral facts." (173)

11   Richard Bernstein, "One Step forward, Two Steps Backward," *Political Theory*, 15 (1987), p. 541.

12   Richard Rorty, "Thugs and Theorists," *Political Theory*, 15 (1987), p. 541.

7

Nostalgia for the Future, Waiting for the Past: Postmodernism in Philosophy

I do believe in beginnings, middles, and ends – but not necessarily in that order.

Godard

"Everything is now permitted," we tell ourselves, knowing as Dostoyevsky only imagined that God has in fact been found dead; confident, where Nietzsche could only speculate, that language itself no longer constrains us ("I fear we are not yet rid of God," Nietzsche would write apprehensively, "because we still believe in grammar.") We may inhabit the first period in history that has suspected everything that *can* be suspected – we as heirs of the nineteenth-century pioneers, those classical philosophers of suspicion, who were so convincing in their descriptions of life underground that other stories about life on the surface now seem to us as distant in their charm as the flights of Greek myth or the experiments of medieval alohemy.

It is not just skepticism that has come to hold us, certainly not the tendentious skepticism of Descartes who, like Job, in the end found all his worldly losses restored, not even of the Pyrrhonists or even of Gorgias, who would commit no more of himself to life or logic than the wiggle of a finger. The transformational grammars – of the psyche, of economics, of language itself – were yet to be construed, and only with those revisions do we begin to understand how difficult the labor of suspicion is: not a simple two-termed relation in which reality has to prove itself against appearance, but one in which the supposedly elementary distinction between appearance and reality is itself doubted. The institutions of the human world – art, political structures, science, social relations – are disclosed first as appearances moved by other forces: psychological, economic, literary – and then *these* examples of stratification: superstructure driven by base, sublimation by libido, historical representation by imagination – are in their turn suspected, no longer turned upside down as Marx had prescribed for Hegel but sideways, where there *could* be no privileged origins or conclusions. So the forces that Marx and Freud still, for all their revolutionary zeal, took as fundamental, foundational, and stable turn out also to be contingent features of experience; they, too, require explanation, with the concept of explanation itself also altered, no longer hoping for inclusive laws or models, but spinning new, individual narrative threads, flattening even causality into a virtual and non-causal present.

At the edge of postmodernism, then, no theory or word or even feeling is above suspicion, and whatever postmodernism does or says seems to take that fact, perhaps *only* that fact, as given.[1] This starting point turns out to be more demanding than that which challenges the oracle or the soothsayer: all *they* have to do is to predict a future woven from the same fabric as that used in the past – a continuity that offers both comfort and a means: with a modest reliance on Delphic ambiguity, most of us could do reasonably well as prophets. Postmodernism, however, not only has to predict but to constitute, since when nothing is given, when everything is possible (and more than that, *equally* possible), what is proposed cannot fall back on analogy or any other logical or literary figure, all of which presuppose versions of continuity; it is obliged to spin of whole cloth. How would Joyce (let alone anyone who was not Joyce) have *predicted Finnegan's Wake*? Well, in a sense, Joyce *did* make the prediction – when he wrote it. At that point, all the speculation that had preceded his writing about an impending revolution in consciousness, the possibility or impossibility of a contemporary epic, and so on, appeared suddenly in a different light. *Finnegan's Wake* itself – his prediction realized, the performance – was there, available to sight and touch, even in some loose way, since it must have been shaken up by the performance, to the mind.

We have then only an *apparent* choice in trying to anticipate the directions of postmodernism (whether in philosophical discourse or some other) in terms similar to those we would apply to *other* plans for the future. We might, on the one hand, speak *about* that future, extrapolating from the present (somehow overriding ther postmodernist claim of a sharp gap between past and present, the *dis*analogy); or we might, on the other hand, try ourselves to *do* the work of postmodernism, accepting as a premise that traditional philosophy, with its search for foundations and its representational theory of truth, is passé, over, done. But in both these accounts the work of postmodernism is defined only negatively, by what it *rejects* in the past and so by what it is *not*. This common and negative starting point, it seems, discloses an important feature of postmodernism, although perhaps not a feature that it recognizes in itself; it also points to the general thesis I shall be arguing here that one thread of discourse in the history of philosophy has been continually, repeatedly, postmodernist. How this is so turns out to be important for understanding both the history – and the present – of philosophy, on the one hand, and the phenomenon of postmodernism, on the other.

Let me rehearse a composite and so, bland but also standard account of the history of philosophy, as postmoderism – in such figures as Heidegger, Derrida, and Rorty – impatiently looks back at it. We mark off here the approximate distance between Plato and Hegel in a circle with a perimeter 2400 years long. At the center of this circle is a motivating distinction between, on the one hand, the apparent world – loose, disjointed, occasional; and, on the other hand, a second world that appearance both conceals and discloses, one which *includes* the apparent world and has enough left over to explain why the apparent world looks as it does without actually being it. The claim of displacement made by this second world, together with the related claim of truth as a form of representation, draws on a variety of ostensive powers: the role of a logos or god or causality that determines aspects of everything else; the idea of substance – an underlying stuff (or two or three) that is then somehow differentiated into a greater number of things; the doctrine of a soul or mind that is as invisible and active as the body it animates is palpable and inert. What appears in these numerous accounts at first as a genuine variety in the history of philosophical thought, however, discloses itself *formally* as no more than a series of variations on a single theme – that of hierarchical reverence: appearance subordinated to reality, plurality to the One. And just this suspicion – that it is a reverence for authority, the desire for a center (and then for its representation), that has motivated the history of philosophy – is the starting-point of the postmodernist diagnosis of that philosophical history. It is in the diagnosis of that origin, moreover – the moment of "rupture", in Derrida's term – that what had announced itself in the history of philosophy as the will for truth or wisdom is revealed as no more than a disguise for nostalgia, a form of wistfulness and finally of self-deception where the will, not the mind, has been accorded the last word. We ought, then, to interpret the traditional discourse of philosophy rather as expression than as idea, as manifestation, not assertion; there is no object or foundation driving the process, only *other* expressions and manifestations which philosophers in their weakness have reified after the fact, finding objects where there had been initially only tracks or traces.

Now it might well be argued that this revisionist history is based on fragmentary, and at points no evidence (suspicion, after all, is for some people a pleasure in itself). And it is, I think, a matter of fact that none of the several versions of philosophical deconstruction sponsoring the efforts of postmodernist philosophy has come close to explaining *why* the history of western thought should have gone astray as deeply and consistently as it allegedly has, resulting in a measure of falsification not much slighter than that of original sin (and like it, too, apparently, in being passed on as transgression to evey following generation.) But no matter – for this is history as the postmodernist imagines and so, we may suppose, lives it; and so there, again, at the alleged core of that history, the aspiration for authority, for structure, for beginnings, species, essences, categories, centers, natures, explanations, causes – all of these reflecting a malady that we now, postmodernly, are in a position to identify and then to overcome. At least we are able to reduce the symptom – but that is all, we are told, that there *is* to the malady since there is nothing that is *not* surface, even in illness – and we cure these, moreover, mainly by the recognition that they *are* symptoms (an invitingly docile malady, that). So speech, for Wittgenstein, is reconceived as a part, not a contrivance of the organism; the ghost in the machine, for Ryle, turns out to be only the cogs and levers that anybody not put off by the fear of blood will find for himself if he has the courage to look inside; for Sartre, human nature is precisely the absence of any such nature; for Derrida discourse is about discourse and even then, more about its absence than its presence – in any event, not about subjects and certainly not about objects. The motivating image here is also of a circle, but undifferentiated now, designedly anti-hierarchical and thus verging on the possibility that everything is itself only by being everything else as well, that distinctions are intrinsically suspect, unnatural. Given this starting point, even to ask simply "What now?" is already to beg the question, since it revives from the past an ideological commitment to the "what" – things – and to a "now": the present as implying a precedent, something it is not. And although these may be evoked by the headiest of nostalgias (our own), they too must be suspected.

There are, it seems to me, two possibilities open to postmodernist thinking beyond this point, the one consistent but self-defeating; the other, inconsistent, revisionary even of the starting pont in its conception of history, but nourishing a hope of survival. We can think of the difference between these as a difference between two theories of time. On the first (consistent) one of these accounts, the linear conception of time dominant in western history is alleged to be part of the problem. Lines imply beginnings and ends; they also imply continuity, inferring from the reality of a past the probability of a future. If, then, as this first version of postmodernism maintains, we are not entitled to such claims, then time must be *dis*continuous, unmotivated – and we are talking here of separation not only between periods of time (years or generations) but between moments or instants, where even personal identity becomes an arbitrary and mystifying fiction, where proper names or the meanings of common terms cannot count on reidentification either. Not only institutional or corporate continuity is denied here but also continuity as it has been alleged for individual persons or objects; the very conception of an identity is suspect.

It can, I think, be reasonably objected to this (consistent) version of inconsistency that little in the appearances of culture – in ethics or law, in science, in the arts – is in accord with it. In the phenomenon of "style" (of individuals or groups), one recognizes the dependence of expression on the assumption of continuity or, still more rudimentary, of repetition. If these are required for style – perhaps, in Freud's suggestion, for the mind itself – the sacrifice of cultural or human anatomy might seem too high a price to pay for a new theory no matter how enticing it otherwise is. To be sure, the phenomenon of style itself – its domestication of novelty, its reliance on categories that pass themselves off as nature – has been accused of an all too easy nostalgia, but this objection itself has a price: to live only with the supposed neutrality of "stylessness" would be to threaten nature and not only art (even without assuming a notion of "natural" style). We would find ourselves here in a domain of pure contingency where the purpose of all writing or thinking is mainly to defeat expectations, to deny reference, and thus to reiterate continually the absence of continuity. The prospect, it needs to be said, is not entirely unfamiliar. Dadaism, surrealism, the so-called "experimental" novel, have been partial attempts to move in this direction, and without judging them in other ways, we recognize one feature common to them all: much of their power comes precisely from the expectations they work to defeat. Like the jiu-jitsu wrestler, they get strength for their throw from their opponent's rush; without that, they have no more power than he has by himself. They flourish, then, by contrast, by reaction – and although this may be a way *into* the future, it hardly promises survival there; it is also, of course, itself a form of continuity insofar as it presupposes the past. Moreover, the philosophical or theoretical past that postmodernism (on this first view) simply writes off has, even in postmodernism's own terms, had unmistakably compelling consequences – in poetry, in science, in social institutions.

By contrast, the new present announced by postmodernism has as yet been mainly declamatory (Yeats and T.S. Eliot were reactionaries politically and arguably poetically as well – but postmodernist theory applied in practice has not come close to producing rival poetic imaginations.) Hegel suggested that philosophy's Owl of Minerva would fly only at dusk, and perhaps, as postmodernism now intimates, he was mistaken; perhaps criticism, theory, philosophy, can *anticipate* rather than follow objects of experience such as literary texts or paintings. But even then they would not need to be identical to the latter; thus the strain is evident when postmodernist critics and theorists of art, for example, represent their own work as displacing the art from which they ostensively had set out. (There is an analogy here to a more traditional failure in which the artist views his work as the equivalent of theory.)

Still, there is no assurance that the second, contrasting version of postmodernism, as it disputes the alleged rupture in the history of western thinking, promises any improvement. Such an alternative, it might be argued, would forfeit not only a potent criticism of the past but also the new beginning in the present that might be extracted from that criticism. But it is precisely this sense of a beginning, it seems to me, that can best be sustained by the alternative outlined above. Here, in the interest of postmodernist survival, I appeal to a military analogy – but irenically, designed to beat the swords of deconstruction into the ploughshares of pragmatism. The analogy is in the distinction between a conception of *strategy*, on the one hand, in which it is ends or goals or principles that are asserted, and the idea of *tactics*, on the other hand, where it is the means, even beginnings, that are sought and those only in order to serve the context in which they appear. Characteristically, postmodernism has opposed itself not only to *particular* strategies in one or another critical system, but to the possibility of strategies altogether. What happens to strategists, on this account – here the analogy to military history is pointed – is ossification, reification. Generals, we know, are constantly preparing to fight the war just past (this is true even when they have been victorious, but especially if they have been defeated – as in criticism they always are). And the strategic ends are still more implacable: only the incidental names of the enemy change over time, and even then, in cultural warfare, not by much. Looking out on the debris of the battlefield, we might thus willingly say with the postmodernist, "Enough and no more; after this only tactics – the response to a moment, and always in a context, *always* in the spirit of contingency, that is, with the present always in part absent. A celebration, in effect, of mortality itself."

And here we note the beginning of a small deceit as it grows, like most deceits, from a small truth. That rupture in the history of western philosophy, the diagnosis and then rejection of logocentrism: might we not suspect that this claim is itself open to suspicion? Do we not have, in the distinction between strategy and tactics, a weapon to be turned against the *reading* of history as well as against history itself? My thesis here comes in two parts: first, that the traditional discourse of metaphysics, supposedly ruptured once and for all at its first moment, was itself – notwithstanding its high talk of God, substance, soul, logos – a sequence of tactical variations that only *came to be seen* (by advocates and critics alike) as committed to strategic ends. Its own intention reflected a design that was contextual not transcendent, historical not atemporal, practical, not theoretical. And, secondly, that the postmodernist attack on philosophy's history is itself a tactic much in the tradition of other tactics in that history – not, as it professes, a strategy, not even a meta-tactic, to end all strategies.

These are large claims to make good on: the ascription of such a tactical impulse to the full history of philosophy is not easily substantiated, and I do not mean to suggest that the impulse is everywhere apparent (certainly not in the same measure) in that history. What I am recommending in fact is only the prudence of an even hand: that where logocentrism or reification are alleged, we look for the occasion of those charges in the dramatizing eyes of the beholder, among the reader-historians of logos, as well as in the supposedly guilty texts themselves. There is considerable evidence that *this* mote too may be in the eye of the reader, not of the author; ideology, after all, does not play favorites.

I can hardly defend this general claim for all the texts and philosophers that have been accused of deviant practices (the history of philosophy written by postmodernists has closer textual affiliations to the Marquis de Sade and Kraft-Ebbing than to more recognizably philosophical sources). But since the Greeks were on most versions of postmodernist history originally responsible for the fall into logo-centrism, let me refer to them and in particular to Plato who is in so many ways a "paradeigma" of the doctrine of presence. It is easy enough, in reconstructing Plato's dialogues, to regard the questions he raises in them also as establishing their answers: "What is justice?" "What is piety?" "What is knowledge?" "What is courage?" – we hear, finding in this catalogue of questions the merely assumed existence of the "things" in question which are thus given life immaculately, without having labored, virtually a priori. Around them the representational world of the philosopher then turns; nothing more, it is inferred, need be added by Plato except for a brief and always *ad hoc* specification in the definition itself. There, in the questions he asks (and then, unsurprisingly, in his answers to them), we have Plato's theory of Forms: immobile, abstract, other-worldly – patterns to be known and then imitated by the rational self, at once explanations and directives for action.

The one thing missing from this common portrait, however, is Plato himself, specifically the act – the motives, the reasons, the practice – of his writing and philosophizing. *Is* the genre of the philosophical dialogue a means of objectification and representation, or even of assertion? Do Plato's dialogues provide definitions or rules – for justice or temperance or courage or piety or whatever – which demand allegiance, or at least imitation, from the reader? *Is* the Good quite other than the individual items that experience sails past in its tours? One need not agree to the flat 'No' by which I should answer these questions myself to concede its plausibility – and this in itself suffices as a wedge to loosen the rigid distinction that the ideologists of the historiography of philosophy have in general taken for granted. It hardly makes a crypto-Marxist of Plato to acknowledge that his eye for the work of the shoemaker, the sailor, the horse-trainer was the same eye with which he looked for and then at the Forms. What many readers of Plato have done on the assumption that psychology duplicates ontology, is to read backwards from the Forms to experience – rather than the other way round, which is the way that Plato himself almost certainly proceeded and in any event assumed that his reader would.

This historical revision does not deny that, once conceived, the Forms might or did take on a life of their own – but it is at least a cautionary warning that Plato (and then the Forms) may have found their hands forced by the evidence, that they may have been driven rather than driver. In any event, it underscores the importance of avoiding interpretive placebos (like nostalgia) to explain Plato's allegiance to the Forms as long as other less reductive explanations (including Plato's own) are available. Perhaps the theory of the Forms is not strictly *required* to account for the possibility of Platonic experience – but Kant's transcendental formulation is surely relevant to understanding how Plato or his readers could possibly take the Forms seriously. To be consistently or even occasionally suspicious may well argue that we should not take philosophers at their own words, but this hardly entails that we should not take their words at all.

One advantage of the account I have begun here is that it suggests an *explanation* of what it is that the deconstructionists have objected to in the history of philosophy itself – something to which Heidegger, Derrida and Rorty have, it seems to me, given little more than a few firm moments of intuition and a metaphysics of history then cobbled together out of them. There is no conspiracy theory of history required here, no need for the invidious contention lurking in the work of these figures that we – or at least, *they* – are more astute, more circumspect, more enlightenedly suspicious than past figures, singly or together, in the history of western thought. It turns out for one thing – what the readers of ancient philosophers, like the reader of the ancient poets, can hardly be surprised at – that the occasions of philosophical experience from which those writers set out resemble our own. Abuses that occur, moreover – fetishism, for example – may be endemic to the process of thinking itself rather than peculiar to the history of a single-minded ideology. So, for example, the fallacy, in Whitehead's phrase, of "misplaced concreteness," where the price exacted by abstraction for the power it provides to memory (itself, as Nietzsche argued, a human creation) is forgetfulness of its origins. This theoretical version of religious idolatry appears when symbols, signs, constructs, representations become things-in-themselves, when their history is repressed. And there is, of course, an irony in the association of this particular fallacy with the deconstructionist view of the history of western thought: that the latter view, meant to destroy the idols of the past, is true only or largely as it is false, when it itself totalizes or fetishizes history

One could go further here, incorporating even the rupture announced by postmodernism into the very history it claims to have ruptured. For if we ask now not why the past was misread, but, more substantively, why the claim should now be made that the history of philosophy is over, finished, that it has, in Heidegger's words "come to term", we see *that* declaration too, in full hyperbole, as continuous with the past of philosophy. Not only is it not the first time that philosophers have seen themselves as starting anew, shrugging free of the past which they pronounce as over, finished – but this is what philosophers have repeatedly asserted. Aristotle, Descartes, Locke, Kant had little "philia" left for their predecessors; they were not more inclined than the more recent and explicit advocates of postmodernism have been to place themselves in a continuous line of indebtedness. The voice speaking in the preface of a literary work is as close as we ever come to the person of the author; and the history of prefaces to philosophical writing – Descartes in the *Discourse*, Locke in the *Essay*, Kant in the *first Critique* – is in fact a history of revolt, less nicely, of murder, where the sons pit themselves against the fathers, promising a future that is now to begin with the present authors themselves. That such writing condemns the past does not necessarily mean for its authors that there is no future for philosophy (as Heidegger and Rorty propose) – but for the former as for the latter, it is the rejection of the past that determines a radically different prospect.

The impulse behind this rejection is more than psychological; it is, we might say, philosophical, an appeal to reflection where the assertion of distance is a prerequisite for the act of discourse itself. The life of philosophy is in these terms paradoxical – since we know that the claims of distance, of detachment have repeatedly been superseded, upended by history itself as it works to close the gap. (Nature may abhor vacuums in principle, but for history they are unintelligible in practice.) Thus philosophy succeeds only when it fails, when it evokes the past by rejecting it in favor of the present, when it wins access to the moment by imagining the whole. The moral that emerges here may seem Calvinist in its anticipation of defeat, but it has the large advantage of addressing the history of philosophy as a history. To win the partial glimpse which is in the end what philosophy settles for is along the way to presuppose a rejection of one whole and to seek after, to desire another. An *original* impulse for fragmentation or partiality promises at worst fetishism, at best a glimpse of pleasure – but little, in either direction, of a habitable world, let alone of the reflections of philosophy. Lionel Trilling suggests that the concept of modernism soon came, in one of its main proponents, Matthew Arnold, is to lose its standing as a chronological category: "By [his] definition, *Periclean Athens* is a modern age, Elizabethan England is not." Can we not then think of postmodernism in the same way – not simply as a present possibility, now, at *this* moment, but a possibility attached to the present whenever the present occurs?

The historical occurrence of this prospect is not difficult to find. Descartes' eventual claim of certainty for what he knew came neither as a straightforward rejection of his philosophical past nor merely as a step added to it: in the very skepticism that he disputed, as it turned on itself, he found a ground for its denial and then for personal, eventually for systematic certainty. That alteration, we understand, was more than an appeal to rhetorical irony; it was a re-direction of speculation back to its own means, conveying the force of a "postmodernist" break with its past, something on the order of a "paradigm shift" in philosophical discourse and method. Similarly, Kant, responding to Hume's critique of causality, turned the mechanism of cognition inside out, assigning to the subject or knower the power that Hume had conclusively found wanting in the object – a strong example of the way in which the means of discourse, as the poststructuralists (themselves heavily indebted to the Kantian tradition) have insisted, can be turned back on itself, deconstructed. There is, then – although the general claim requires further elaboration – a *history* of "postmodernist" moments within the history of philosophy. It might be argued that the notion of *the* history of philosophy itself is tied to another one of those moments, in the Romantic assertion of philosophical hegemony over time – specifically in the Hegelian account of philosophical time. Also in that account, we note a ready source for the postmodernist fascination with the death of philosophy: as Hegel himself heralded the deaths of art and religion, he might well appreciate the cunning of history which would then go on to write an obituary for the author of those death-notices.

But what then, looking from *this* present, of the postmodernist future in philosophy? For even if the much-qualified version of postmodernism presented here were granted for the sake of argument, there is nothing predictive about it; and we also have the constant obligation of responding to those thinkers who, standing at the brink, have cordially pronounced the death of metaphysics – not the beginning of a new version, but simply the end. There is Wittgenstein for whom, mimicking his compatriot Karl Kraus' words about psychoanalysis, philosophy was the disease it had been supposed to cure; there is Heidegger who found that Nietzsche had once-and-for-all settled the traditional philosophical accounts; there is Derrida for whom discourse is now disclosed as entirely its own object and in which then, philosophy, no more than the other addictive sciences of representation, has a future. Could philosophy survive such confident obituaries?

One path here might be towards quietism – in the prescription of a character of Unamuno's, simply "to catalogue the world and return it to God all in order." There has indeed been something of this conservative affirmation of things as-they-are in the mood of those thinkers themselves, and it is important to keep in mind how this comes about. Consciousness itself, Nietzsche had proposed, was to be suspected as a malady – and with *that* suspicion, it is understandable that tactics no less than strategy should be viewed with a wary eye, hinting that there was no particular goal either to reach or to avoid, no distinctions to stand on, no references to hold to. Pleasure and the will might at first seem likely replacements for truth and understanding, since the latter could inevitably harden into abstraction – categories, foundations, ends-in-themselves. But then we find that the former may also become objectified, also doctrinaire, also punitive. And if the will can ensue in foundations and principles, then would not what starts there as tactic also lose its sense of origins?

I have suggested here that this impulse for displacing its past may be native to philosophy – repeatedly to privilege the present over what has been judged in the past. But looking at the recent present also as a past, we also may see something omitted there, something that philosophers in the tradition were more candid about, even if they could not, any more than the philosophers of suspicion, respond to it conclusively: the possibility that philosophy begins not in suspicion but in the quite different phenomenon of wonder. The difference between those two is much like the distinction emphasised by Kierkegaard between fear and anxiety, between the problem and the mystery that Gabriel Marcel distinguished – with each of the former terms reacting to a specific object, in contrast to the latter terms whose reference was diffused, a general feature of experience. I do not propose here to define the concept of wonder except in its least technical sense which still suffices to disclose it as at once a postmodernist and constant feature of philosophy. For wonder, unlike suspicion, is attached exclusively to the present, a function of the here-and-now. As a motive of philosophy, then, wonder compels philosophy to begin in the present, that is, always to start anew – thus, to reject the past even with the full knowledge that this rejection is a function of the present as present, not the rejection of some particular past. So we understand the mild irony of the ninth-century Arab writer Ibn Qutayba, when he reminds his readers that "God has so ordered it that every ancient was modern in his own time." To which might now be added " . . . and that some ancients were also postmodern in their own time."

This may seem to offer a peculiarly disembodied view of the history of philosophy (past and future), with its fate left entirely in the hands of individual philosophers (as individuals) who whether they wish it or not, will always be breaking free of their philosophical pasts and even of the world itself. In these terms, postmodernism would be not an option but a necessity – a supposed consequence that, for the postmodernist, would be as much an outrage as an irony. There is, indeed, a social history of philosophy yet to be written, one which reflects on that history as history and not just as word and which, in doing this, describes the contexts of meaning for philosophical discourse that the discourse has not said for itself. I suggest, as a link between this unwritten history and the more formal analysis I have been giving, that philosophy has itself been openly ambivalent about its social status. Nietzsche objected that the idea of a married philosopher was a joke, and we might predict from this the harsh words that he would also supply about "institutional" philosophy on a scale larger than that of the family. Philosophy seems itself to have realized well before this challenge that the phrase "institutional philosophy" was arguably an oxymoron – that even if philosophical discourse might evolve *in* institutions, it could never be honestly *of* them. One way of understanding the recent proclamations of the end of philosophy, in fact, is as a reaction to the institutionalization of philosophy that occurs mainly in the nineteenth century, associated there with the more general phenomena of bureaucracy and professionalization of which philosophers now, permitting themselves a guarded optimism, might hope to be the tail end.

I do not mean here to draw an image of the philosopher as an outsider or an alienated consciousness (insofar as this holds at all, it applies to only a small number of figures in the history of philosophy) – but rather to suggest that there is a difference worth building on further between institutional philosophy and a conception of philosophy as "polyphonic" in which the voice of any one philosopher is recognizable as an overlay of many other individual voices. The latter, it seems to me, has in fact been a recurrent feature of philosophical discourse that has come increasingly – and recently – to be discounted in the conception of a "heroic" history of philosophy. As the arts in the Renaissance discovered and then celebrated the artist as individual, so philosophy, tardily, would then in the eighteenth and nineteenth centuries learn to forget the metonymic function that proper names serve in the history of ideas – ostensively referring to an individual but standing in fact for a practice. We have recently heard much about the "death of the author" (proposed by authors who seem willing to observe that phenomenon for everyone but themselves); but it seems likely in fact that philosophy in its most compelling moments has long known about that death, indeed that it has even willed it. This is but one more way in which proclamations of the "end of philosophy" have continually shaped its history.

None of this is to claim that the non-institutional philosopher, unlike his counterpart, will manage to escape the constraints of ideology – that because he is unfettered in this way, he can hope somehow to jump out of his skin. There are always certain matters that will not be spoken of; repression in its many guises will see to some of this, and when repression fails, finitude itself may suffice. Thus, philosophical wonder itself will also turn out to be partial, embodying particular interests and idioms, and so always with an object not fully of the philosopher's own choosing. But there is a difference between speaking *for* a context and speaking *out-of-context* – and it is the latter, as a violation of the taboos of the understanding, that philosophy seems to me to accomplish when it succeeds. That we can in retrospect find ways of neutralizing these violations is less unsettling than is the effort of those who would, even if only in principle, escape all retrospection. The denial of ideology occurs at the point where ideology is most active and most determinant. And like positivism and existentialism which have thought to privilege themselves in this way, postmodernism in the fundamentalist version criticized here has victimized itself by the same denial.

Thus, irresolute and absent-minded an answer as it may seem, a plausible response to the question posed for philosophy, "What now?" is, "Go and do it." For as wonder is spontaneous and cannot be coerced, neither can its objects or shape be anticipated. There is at work here a theory of time which escapes both the lockstep of historical determinism that postmodernism finds in the pre-post-modernist history of philosophy and the radical discontinuity or randomness that the latter would substitute for the former. Is it so improbable that the present can be new without being quite other than the past? Or that it can be indebted to the past without merely repeating it? This conception of philosophy's history would offer a means of thinking in the present without being quite of it; it would also, along the way, validate one side of postmodernism's view of the history of philosophy without the menace of its other consequences – founded again and again, in the present without the claim of a miraculous creation (again and again) *ex nihilo*.[2]

This all may seem to promise a future for philosophy that is either hopelessly amorphous or, still worse, that bears an uncanny resemblance to the past – that is, a "new" present in which nothing has changed. But consistent with these alternatives is another one – and this is the "possibility of everything," the postmodernist theme with which the discussion here began and which turns out now to be an illusion (a creative illusion, its own "Noble Lie") by which philosophy has constantly lived in the past, watching what it envisions as tactics continually turn into strategies. What this means is that also in its own design, philosophy, waiting always on the new present, will be tactical, setting out from the immediacy of particular moments of experience. We may indeed look forward then to the philosophical "conversations" that Rorty anticipates, although these may not be as novel or unfamiliar as Rorty's readers have been led to expect. They will – if we are fortunate – be like (perhaps even *be*) Plato's dialogues, Montaigne's *Essays*, Descartes' *Meditations,* Hegel's phenomenologies, Kierkegaard's points-of-view for his work as an author. Like them, but of course also not like them – by as much, at any rate, as those works themselves were, are, like and not like each other. Does not this leave matters exactly as they had been? What would be *post*modernist about this? But the occasions will be different, the angle of vision will vary, the intersections of history will be occurring for the first time – and with these differences, also the constantly new questions of address, of tactics. What this amounts to, then, is the appropriation into the present of a past that can be advanced, subverted – or, with the tactics of postmodernism, turned on its side: certainly not for the first time, probably not for the last, but nonetheless. Thus, everything *is* possible – including philosophy when it flatly asserts that not everything is possible. In this way, Aristotle argued for the law of non-contradiction as itself not requiring or even as capable of demonstration. The proof of *its* ground, even of its possibility, was for him the actuality of everything else around it – and there too we may find if not a foundation, at least the origins of a discourse that, in the testimony of the past, turns out to be philosophical. To demand more than this is to will oneself either a captive of the past or a fugitive in the future; on these terms, the next step is only to come back once more to the present work of philosophy, at once familiar and novel. Nostalgia, when it is spontaneous, is for the future; anticipation, when it is not merely wistful, is of the past. This is why philosophers would in their history say at first – and then again and again – "Let us begin." Let us, then, begin. Again.

Notes to Chapter Seven

1   I do not attempt to assess here the numerous (sometimes conflicting) definitions that have been given of postmodernism; originally quite

modest in its applications to architecture and to poetry, the term stands now as a general (if vague) term of cultural reference. (See for the historical background to the term, Jerome Mazzaro, "The Genesis of Post-modernism," in *Postmodern American Poetry* (Urbana: University of Illinois Press, 1980), pp. 1–31; also, Marjorie Perloff, *The Poetics of Indeterminacy* (Princeton: Princeton University Press, 1981), pp. 28–44, and Richard Palmer, "Towards a Postmodern Hermeneutics of Performance," in *Performance in Postmodern Culture* (Milwaukee: Center for Twentieth-Century Studies, 1977).) For a more speculative historical reconstruction, see J-F. Lyotard, *The Postmodern Condition: A Report on Knowledge*, translated by G. Benington and B. Massumi (Minneapolis: University of Minnesota Press, 1984). Its latest transformation has been an ingenious turn into the "post-contemporary" (see Stanley Fish, *Doing What Comes Naturally* (Durham: Duke University Press, 1989) although this, too, it may be predicted, is not the last word.)

2 Although coming from a different starting-point, this formulation converges on Habermas' objection to postmodernism as a form of *anti-modernism*, with its aestheticism a cloak for conservative or reactionary ideology. (So, the postmodernists " ... remove into the sphere of the far-away and the archaic the spontaneous powers of imagination, self-experience and emotion." J. Habermas, "Modernity – An Incomplete Project," in H. Foster, ed., *The Anti-aesthetic: Essays on Postmodern Culture* (Port Townsend: Washington Bay Press, 1983), p. 14. See also in the same volume, F. Jameson, "Postmodernism and Consumer Society," pp. 114–18; Jameson, associating postmodernism with the genre of the "pastiche," argues still more sharply for the incapacitating social consequences of postmodernism.

Part II:

Literary Form and Non-literary Fact

8

Hamlet's Grandmother(s)

Q: Did Hamlet have a grandmother?

A: Yes, of course. Two of them, in fact.

Q: What's the evidence? Shakespeare doesn't mention them.

A: Imagine the alternative.

We have Claudius' word for it that Hamlet had once had a grand-
father and even a great-grandfather ("Your father lost a father, and
that father lost, lost his"); and although Claudius is not quite a
disinterested chronicler, we might decide to believe him here if only
because the forebears of Hamlet whom he recalls were also his own
(and nothing much rides on his mention of them anyway). But what
then of the likelihood of Hamlet's grandmother, neither one of the
usual two referred to, let alone named in the drama where so much
that is known about Hamlet (and to him) is revealed? Is it only that the
present or the near past are more important in the lives of dramatic
characters (as seen by them or by us) than their earlier history? Surely
this disproportion constantly shapes literary practice – and what is to
that extent true of dramatic or fictional characters is true-to-life as
well. Shakespeare's failure to introduce or even to mention Hamlet's
grandmother(s) is in the end no more unsettling than his failure, so far
as we know, to mention his own (and surely *he* had them) – or our
own failure (in context or out) to speak about ours. Even the fact that
Shakespeare had easy access to all the information one could possibly
require about Hamlet's grandmother (undoubtedly more than he had

about his own) hardly makes him more culpable for not having reported any of it.

And yet, of course, not to be mentioned is not necessarily, for any of these, not to exist; their omission raises the question in fact of what relation there is between literary mention and existence (literary or not), and we find in this connection a pattern of causality in dramatic or fictional emplotment that closely resembles causal patterns in the emplotment (i.e., the actions and events) of everyday life. Whenever someone (or -thing) is referred to in a text, we expect to find reasons – in the form of literary consequences – which explain why that reference appears when and as it does. Such reasons draw on a variety of possibilities, ranging from the single expression of emotion or idea to a collective representation of emotions and ideas-realized (i.e., action), and sometimes as well to the shapelessness of free association that depends for its literary effect on the denial of any such causality (*that*, then, becomes the cause). Literary structure, whether at the level of trope, genre, figure or even of grammar, turns constantly, in fact, on causal sequences of mover and moved (ultimately, for each structure, of Prime Mover and moved); even the complex systems of *physical* cause and effect, a close reading of each shows, fall well short of the networks of causality at work in literary events.

One source of this causality in literature no less than in nature, moreover, is in causes which have not been mentioned even though they *could* be; it is in certain respects crucial to their causal role that they should *not* be mentioned although they are no less active causally than are other factors or causes that are mentioned. Chekhov wrote that if a gun is seen hanging on the wall in Act I of a play it must go off before the play ends – but there are also effects in the last act (or even in the first) for which no such explicit precedent is given and yet for which no less firm a basis is understood.

This, in fact, is the point of speaking here about Hamlet's grandmother when Shakespeare himself, so far as we know, never did. For as the brief exchange cited as an epigraph to this chapter suggests, the answer to the question of whether Hamlet *had* a grandmother is obvious and "yes, of course he did." The reason for claiming that response as obvious is itself evident (only too evident) in the combination of non-literary and literary consequences that follow if, alternatively, the answer to the same question were held to be "No, he doesn't (or didn't) have a grandmother – not even one, let alone two," on the grounds that all we know about Hamlet is what Shakespeare himself tells us in the play. For this denial – here is the obvious point – will not do, since then we have to imagine the Hamlet we encounter in *Hamlet* as a young man with the standard attributes of persons and males and youth, who walks and talks and thinks and act (sometimes), who has a mother whom we also meet and had had a father whose ghost he encounters before our eyes (as much before ours as before his) – and yet had no grandmother. Is it possible? What could we make of whatever else Hamlet allegedly does or is if, after duly weighing the evidence, we also decided that he had no grandmother? Surely it would put many if not all of our other findings about Hamlet in a different light – starting at the beginning, fittingly enough, with his father's ghost who would undoubtedly be quite different even as a ghost if Athena-like, the father himself had sprung full-grown into the world (Hamlet's grandmother would have been *his* mother – both now, alas, non-existent). And then we must ask ourselves about the other, even biological consequences that would unavoidably accompany this breach in the continuity of generations (and also, to be consistent, in the act of generation). Etc., etc..

The literary consequences that come at us from these many sides would not change much even if we limited the denial that Hamlet had a grandmother to a more oblique agnosticism, holding more modestly that "We can't be *certain* if Hamlet had a grandmother or not." For this too suggests that Hamlet (in contrast, one supposes, to Shakespeare himself) *might* not have had one (or no less oddly, two); and such possibilities are only slightly less unsettling to our understanding of Hamlet (and *Hamlet*) than the flat denial must be.

What difference does any of this make one way or the other, it might be objected. Is not Pandora's Box waiting to be opened with even a discreet nod to Hamlet's grandmother? For we know well that grandmothers also have grandmothers, and their grandmothers have theirs – and we should soon find ourselves committed here to a genealogical survey of the links between Hamlet and Eve, as well as to a near-limitless anthology of other persons, events, and qualities which pass unmentioned by Shakespeare but have significant roles in Hamlet's history, not only during his appearance in the play but before the play even begins (and perhaps, in consideration of his immortal soul, after it is over as well). Hamlet himself, for example, mentions certain details of his physiognomy ("Who breaks my pate across?/Plucks off my beard and blows it in my face?/Tweaks me by the nose?/Gives me the lie i' the throat,/As deep as to the lungs?") but not at all others (eyebrows, teeth). Yet presumably he also possessed the latter (or at least *had* had them) – since again, not to have would argue that much else must also be different about Hamlet (and *Hamlet*); the same conclusion holds for the color of his hair (that is, that it had a color) and that he was so many feet and so many inches tall (that he had a height). And of course, by inviting this construal of Hamlet's person, Pandora's Box may be expected to contain many other occupants as well, each with many of the same properties, also unmentioned by *their* authors, that Hamlet then turns out to have: Mr Pickwick and Medea and Young Werther, and also Peter Rabbit and Aesop's fox who decided that the grapes were sour after all (and then, too, by the same reasoning, the vines that bore those young but so untender grapes.)

Why should we believe – why *do* we believe – that literary characters are surrounded by such an aura, not quite visible but quite real, of properties translated literally; that is, carried over from the non-literary – nonfictional – world? Because, again, of the requirements of literary causality that allow us, *compel* us, to see what happens literarily in the sequential ways that we do, depending not only on the author but on an unspoken world he shares with his readers. It is so much a commonplace that people walk on their feet, not on their hands that it would be extraordinary for an author to bother to mention it (we would require a subsequent literary reason to explain the reference) – but the fact itself is no less causally and literarily efficacious for being unmentioned. People inside and outside of texts almost always walk in this way, as they also do many other things that do not warrant mention. If that (admittedly vague) group of ostensively non-literary properties were *not* understood in the literary characters and actions we read about, much else must also be different about the literary world they constitute: even surrealism would fail as a form of representation because, quite simply, there would be no norms of realism to deviate from – and surrealism has at least to be able to presuppose these.

We infer then that the imaginary musings or whimsies of the literary world, fictional as we are meant to think them, take many of their cues from a bedrock of fact in a nonfictional world shared by the author with both the characters he creates and the imagination out of which he creates them – and also with his readers who themselves move in the continuing traffic between the two worlds. There seems in effect to be a large unwritten text surrounding the written and more overt one, one which does not strictly *cause* the latter to take the form it does but which makes that form possible, thus causing it to be *what* it is, if not quite *to be*. The possibility of individual literary facts depends on the reality of non-literary facts that the author has not written about and may even be quite unaware of. The reader presupposes this unwritten text in order to establish a sequence for his reading, as the author has presupposed it in his writing; it is a contractual presence, fuller and broader because it is tacit than it could be if all its details had to be made explicit. And there is a need for this unwritten text in both writer and reader, if only because we can hardly imagine – indeed we would not know where to begin – what could on either side be imagined without it.

It might be objected, even sympathetically, that this nonfictional underpinning to fictional worlds makes no literary difference, whether to the shape of literary characters and events that populate those worlds or to the reader's understanding that starts outside them – if anything, that it detracts from these both. For one thing, the additions supplied by this source would be so numerous and extensive that if we try to distribute them equitably in the fictional world, little space will be left in that world for those of its inhabitants to whom the author himself had set out to call attention. And surely it is relevant that the author, entitled as he is to the last word – we would not venture to say that Shakespeare had got it wrong, Lear *really* had four daughters, or it was really Rosenstern and Gildenkrantz – has chosen *not* to mention them (at least in the sense that he has, by contrast, chosen to name the characters and events that he has.) And lastly, the newly literary but unwritten facts that would show up in this way are so uniform, so generally applicable – many would be approximately the same for every character and event in the long history of literature: the law of gravity, the anatomy of the gallbladder, the will to power – that they seem at once to neutralize each other and to be neutralized collectively. Why should any of them, let alone all together, matter when it is the individuality and difference of literary causes – events, characters – that reward the reader's attention by making what happens in the text to happen, moving the reader by way of its own movements. It is this process of action and reaction, of non-literary give and literary take, moreover, that stands at the crux of the author's purpose and distinguishes whatever claim he has as author.

We might well agree that item by item, these matters of commonplace fact do not often appear openly as literary causes. Indeed the unusual instances when they do appear in that role attest to the general rule: Alice thrives in the literary association of Carroll's Wonderland because people outside that Wonderland (as well as most inside it) do not grow or shrink instantaneously; the literary reason why Gregor Samsa wakes up as an insect one morning is that this violates the reader's non-literary expectations (and quite reasonably, Gregor's too); Sherlock Holmes solves a mystery by reflecting on the dog that didn't bark because (in ordinary circumstances) the dog would have barked (as everybody inside or outside the text must know: Holmes, the dog, the reader). Thus, too, another facet of the general denial is significant: that the non-literary terms to which it refers are not only co-present with but affect – give content to – the standards which underwrite the interpretation and then the assessment of literary structures; those standards, too, start out in the world of commonplace belief.

It may still be objected that the assembly of non-literary facts, even as *admitted* to the literary work, remains only neutral background, a periphery largely unnoticed for the good reason that like the nonliterary facts of the author's own life – his genetic make-up or the history of his schooling – they only make possible what is literarily unforeseeable and indeed not yet actual in them. They are, then, passive, almost by-standers at the literary spectacle, colorless or invisible. But invisibility can occur because of the constancy of what is seen no less than because something has gone out of existence or did not exist in the first place (who would claim to see, day-in, day-out, the doors we shut behind us?) Moreover, even as the literary violation of the non-literary facts happens only occasionally and piecemeal (so again – Alice in Wonderland), not *en masse,* familiar expectations and rules are always and omni-present, not *only* in the literary work, but there also. (It is the explicit purpose of science-fiction as a genre to violate familiar expectations – and even so it succeeds in this purpose only partially; it pays for the blatancy of these efforts, moreover, by its standing as a minor form.)

The neutral background to the literary work set up by non-literary facts, then, does not mean that such facts are *literarily* neutral or passive. At the very least, they have the status of a "material cause" – perhaps best understood in this role in terms of the literary medium (akin, for example, to the marble of a sculpture – although for sculptures, too, beyond the sculptor's marble or bronze, there would be an unwritten – and unsculptured – text, e.g., the book of anatomy). Like the artistic medium, the unwritten text of commonplace fact would then be a necessary condition (although surely not a sufficient one – but what *would* be that?) and perhaps regarded as having a lesser (and unrelated) role literarily than the "final" or "formal" causes which point more distinctively to the individuality of literary characters and events and, finally , of texts. (So, too, persons, characteristically associated with limbs and genes and blood pressure, yet always seem more than these, even in combination.) To draw a more invidious line of demarcation than this would be to assume that the status of the unwritten text of commonplace facts is non-literary only *because* such facts go unmentioned in the literary text – and again, this, on the one hand, begs the question of what distinguishes literary from non-literary fact; on the other hand, runs counter to the literary evidence itself. Does the mere *mention* of his beard by Hamlet make it more of a literary presence, more *real*, than is his grandmother whom he does not mention or have mentioned at all? Surely, whether referred to or not, less rides on the existence of the one than on the existence of the other – and with this understanding, we may well begin to wonder if there is any way at all (or reason to, either) to distinguish literary from non-literary matters of fact.

Perhaps a more fruitful means of coming at the issue that allegedly divides these two is to start before they *are* two, asking, for example, why the world of commonplace belief provides so constant, even a necessary background to the world of literary fact. One answer to this question is given in the question itself – that the background is unavoidable: the most powerful and resourceful imagination still could not spin out of whole cloth. But this again presents the unwritten text of commonplace only as a constraint or limitation – one that would be, if it could, exceeded or perhaps dispensed with. But a second answer is that the necessity acknowledged in this way has its own virtue, a literary virtue at that: that literary worlds may themselves be embodiments of the same facts that comprise the unwritten and non-literary texts surrounding them. Aristotle prefers the probable possibility of literary representation to its possible probability – and the measurement by which for him the probable and the possible were to be distinguished is not only analogous but virtually identical to the standard required of us as well; it is a world largely shared. Chekhov, again, is the master we might listen to here, reporting to us a text that other authors had assumed but left unwritten: "Let the things that happen on stage be just as complex and yet just as simple as they are in life. For instance, people are having a meal, just having a meal, but at the same time their happiness is being created, or their lives are being smashed up." There are, we recognize, even simpler events than "having a meal" – many of them off-stage altogether – that are nonetheless fully literary.

To be sure, mimetic theories of literary discourse have had their up's and down's (recently, their down's), and we might agree that one reason for the persistence of such theories in the history of criticism is itself mimetic – the conservative power of tradition in which critics and readers imitate *their* predecessors. It is difficult, moreover, to quarrel with the objections to mimesis drawn from experience – that the figures of poetry and drama, the fictive gathering of character and action in the novel often seem so unexpected, so evocative and unpredictable as to exhaust mimetic explanations long before they reach literary comprehension. But there is nonetheless a ready although prosaic counterstatement to this thesis: that novelty and originality gain their force from what it is that they are novel or original *about* (or in respect to, or in). Literary light at its brightest shines always on a familiar world, known from the past and the present or even from the imagined future. Literary facts need not be entirely non-literary or other in order to be literarily distinct (or other); they acquire their force precisely in relation to what has preceded them – sometimes by contrast, but more constantly and dramatically by accrual, by refraction, by displacement and by embodiment, all of these presupposing something given and known. To be sure, a question remains of how *real* literary facts are; but that question is now not nearly so invidious as it once set out to be: the same question remains to be answered also for non-literary facts. And it is possible, even *likely*, that for neither of those questions is there a general answer at all.

We do not hear, when the play is the thing, of Hamlet' grand-mother. But we do hear of his mother, his father, his uncle, his enemies, and of course about the Prince himself; we learn what they do to each other and to themselves and to still others. We find the consequences of these actions, moreover, not only in the dramatic fiction, but also in ourselves, the listeners and readers, and we take these consequences with us beyond the written text, beyond the unwritten text on which the written text depends – where? There is, to be sure, a way out available to us from any particular literary world, if only by closing the book we have been reading or by walking away from the theatre we have been sitting in – but there is hardly a way out of the world on which the various literary worlds impinge. There are, admittedly, many times when we have good reasons for wishing such a way out – for calculating escape, or more high-mindedly, transcendence. But the price exacted by transcendence often leaves us more needy and further in debt than we had been before; "escapist" literature, the higher critics tell us, is a low form of literature (we know this well enough, when it is the excess of life in the immediate present that turns us in that direction). Is it not, in any event, the very sanity of literary facts that they first provide assurance that we cannot succeed in such attempts – and then extend a lingering gift, in the form of reasons why we should not want to or why we do well to want something else even more? The hunger for literary fact, unsurprisingly, is also a hunger for ourselves non-literarily; we should hardly be surprised then that what we measure or test literary facts by, the means we have for comprehending even literary *possibilities* – what we want them to be and what we take pleasure in when they are – have much in common with non-literary ones, and most generally, with the hope of existence. It is not a matter here of duplication or repetition, but of realization, of the urge toward more (and more of) life. And imagination and play can no more easily be separated from that life than physiology can in all of its non-literary commonplace. "There is nothing outside the text," Derrida admonishes us – and Lear, long before, knew better, although he himself was confined – lived and died – inside the text. "Nothing can be made out of nothing," he says, and then Shakespeare compels two other characters in the play to repeat the same line as if to suggest that the audience outside the play is more likely to bear it away with them if they hear it independently from several witnesses.

Q: So the world of literary facts turns out to be like the world we live in. Isn't one of the damned things enough?
A: No. Imagine the alternative.

9

Autobiography as a Matter of Literary Fact

> ... It is, after all, always the first person that is speaking.
>
> Thoreau

> I am like no one in the whole world. I may be no better, but at least I am different.
>
> Rousseau, Confessions

Reflexive questions are invariably a nuisance and often an embarrassment. But an age of subtlety and suspicion that nourishes doubts about the face value of everything that has a face can hardly hope to avoid the same doubts itself (reflexivity, after all, starts at home), and a concise meta-history of modern thought might well be written of questions turned back on the thinkers of suspicion who earlier, only a brilliant moment before, had so startled their readers that no further questions of any sort, reflexive or straight on, seemed possible. Is the analysis of class ideology not itself ideological? Can the transvaluation of all values also be transvalued? Are the claims for relativity – in so many places: ethics, culture, taste, space – themselves relative? Is the principle of verifiability verifiable? I mean here to add still another question to this list and then, in considering its implications, to say something about its – shaky, I shall claim – foundations. For although the corporate list of reflexive questions probably tells us more even by its extent than the questions disclose singly, they impinge on theoretical discourse and method most immediately as individuals. Even if we choose finally to view them (or doubt them) collectively, moreover, it is by themselves that they lead to self-knowledge, recalling the historical routes by which presuppositions made in the past have landed us – singly *and* collectively – in the present.

The question I propose to set out from reflects the modern estrangement between the domains of rhetoric and poetics that had traditionally lived more harmoniously, shaping language for related if not quite identical ends. What is proposed here, in fact, is a new conciliation between those two spheres – and the possibility of doing this through the marginal literary form of autobiography. But in order to follow the line of this argument, the reflexive question for which so much is promised must first be introduced. Like many reflexive questions, this one, too, is irritatingly simple: "The distinction between fiction and nonfiction," it goes: "Is *that* distinction fiction or nonfiction?"

Unmaking the Distinction

Motivated as they are by history as much as by logic, reflexive questions can hardly be as innocent as they seem; to doubt the division between fiction and nonfiction is thus to address both its current applications and the assumptions made in the past that have led up to the present. Thus, too, we quickly recognize that although the two sides of the distinction are commonly held to span the universe of discourse (so, the two charts displayed weekly in *The New York Times Book Review*), the distinction does not serve quite adequately on either of those sides. Does the fact-free inventiveness associated with fiction apply also to poetry or drama? The events which the latter cite or announce have not, of course, "happened," but neither, on the other hand, have they quite *not* happened: the connotations of fictionality are not so much wrong in this connection as beside the point. One could admit (who would doubt it?) that the recurrent "I" in Emily Dickinson's poems does not exist in the same sense that Emily Dickinson herself did without denying that it has a firmer historical purchase than does its apparent "contemporaries," Hester Prynne or Moby Dick. And again: does the supposed facticity of nonfiction apply equally and in the same senses at once to the plots of a geophysical survey and to the steps in a baking recipe, to the biography of a late military hero and to the brief formulae of a telephone directory? Unless differences in purpose and method (to say nothing of form itself) are simply ornamental, indifferent to claims of meaning, theories of reference or representation that impose a single index of literary understanding on texts so diverse will almost certainly pay the price of vacuity.

Historically, furthermore, the fiction/nonfiction distinction offers even less reassurance than do the vagaries of its applications; the very brevity of this history should itself be a warning. The Greek theoreticians of discourse, whether from the side of rhetoric or from that of philosophy (and science), avoided the distinction altogether, and seen against the background of their premises, this was not only understandable, but inevitable. If, as they constantly assumed, discourse is characteristically mimetic or representational, only the most marginal appearances of language could escape assessment in terms of correspondence and to that extent, of truthfulness (or falsity). So Aristotle would distinguish history from poetry, but not because one had and the other lacked truth or nonfictionality; they *share* this quality, with the truths claimed for the one only less general and conclusive than those realized in the other. Aristotle approximates the strong distinction between fiction and nonfiction only when he cites the (for him) peripheral examples of nonmimetic music or painting that should, he notes in the *Politics*, be viewed and termed "recreational" and that remain, accordingly, morally or cognitively insignificant. The distinction passes largely unnoticed through the Renaissance, effectively denied in the Platonic (and more generally, the rationalist) tradition with its characteristic hostility to the "falseness" of fiction and also by the critics of that tradition for whom the capacity to instruct is as native to literary discourse as its capacity to delight.

The positive history of the fiction/nonfiction distinction depends theoretically on the development of formalism initiated in Kant's critique of aesthetic judgment and then elaborated in the post-Kantian response to that critique. This history is too complex to be detailed here, but certain social factors affecting it are usefully noted. These include material causes such as the development of newspapers and jouranlistic writing in the eighteenth century and *their* relation to social urbanization and to the "simultaneous" texts made possible by the printing press. If the factuality of "news" is to be privileged referentially and thus to be distinguished as a form of discourse, it achieves this status only by being contrasted to other writing for which reference and interpretation mingle – and it is with this disjunction, in the declaration of a social or cultural equivalent to the independent "facts" of nature, that the break between fictional and nonfictional discourse finds itself in modern theories of discourse.[1]

These compressed historical comments on the background to the fiction/nonfiction distinction turn finally on epistemological concepts of truth and reference, and more specifically, in *their* history, on the new role of fact that evolved mainly in science, but in other institutional settings as well in the seventeenth and eighteenth centuries. The course of that development identifies the concept of fact and its attendant fiction/nonfiction distinction as historical contingencies – a qualification which itself reinforces a recurrent skepticism in the history of philosophy against the privileging of empirical data ("facts") as a ground for epistemic assurance. The conception in modern science of the facts of nature as disinterestedly available and verifiable is openly at odds with an older Platonic model according to which the general principles or laws are primary (ontologically or at least epistemologically) and the testimony of empirical appearance, in contrast, subordinate and "theory-laden." It takes nothing away from the suspicion cast by a Nietzsche or a Marx on certain common varieties of "fact" to recognize that related charges of tendentiousness – the grounding of facts on ideals or first principles rather than the other way round – had been recognized before them as well.

The questioning of the logical status of the fiction/nonfiction distinction – in the issue of whether the distinction applies to itself – is thus reinforced by the distinction's problematic historical background that is itself supplemented by other prima facie evidence and practice. Name what one will among the most evident fictions – Homer's or Kafka's or Cervantes' – the pressure for contact with a reality brought to the reading from beyond the text, for reaching in or through the reading to something more than text (at least to more than *that* text), has continually affected their authors and readers, and then, too, their critics. Gestures such as Coleridge's appeal to the "willing suspension of disbelief" or Keats' recommendation of "negative capability" serve only to defer the task of reconciling claims of the literary world with those of the reader's pre- or extra-literary dispositions. Plato's quarrel with the poets in the *Republic* has sometimes been construed as an attack on the *abuse* of poetry, that is, against the way in which the discourse of poetry had been mistaken by Plato's contemporaries for historical truth; but even when his objections are understood in this way, finding in poetry no intrinsic falsification, it is the criterion of truth (at any rate, *his* criterion of truth) which is appealed to[2]. The conception of literature as set in a social reality to which it constantly answers has had an uninterrupted, if not uncontested, history ever since.

From its side, nonfiction has been slower and less consistent in acknowledging its loss of independence, but there, too, the evidence has been increasingly compelling of a presence in critical, historical, philosophical, and scientific discourse of the full range of imaginative devices: tropes and figures of speech, genres, authorial point-of-view, implied reader, stylistic "choice" – virtually all the means for enlarging the space between discourse and whatever exists outside it, a space more familiarly associated with fictional discourse[3]. To be sure, the ideal has also persisted, in the theoretical concept of a meta-language, of a universal and artificial discourse, referentially transparent and mimetic vis-à-vis the reality represented by it. But the consistent failure of the sciences ("literary" as well as "philosophical" sciences) that hold this ideal to realize it in practice suggests an ideological impulse at their source; it stands in effect as a secular counterpart to religious fundamentalism with its insistence on the text as transparent and thus as interpreting itself.

It may seem that this line of argument must conclude by denying the distinction between fiction and nonfiction altogether, eliding fact with nonfact and construing discourse as a form of play or improvisation constrained at most by self-defined criteria. Exactly this position has been taken by the poststructuralist writers,[4] but it is not one that will be defended here. Even a flat rejection of the fiction/nonfiction distinction does not imply or even, I should argue, support that conclusion. To question that distinction is neither to assert the homogeneity of discourse in respect to truth nor to conceive truth or fact as *only* modes of discourse. Viewed more modestly, the objection entails no more than a revision in the order of argument which had taken the distinction between fiction and nonfiction as foundational and only then constructed an anatomy of discourse. The sequence of argument could with fewer presuppositions and more fruitful conclusions move in quite the opposite direction: from a functional conception of discourse to an account, only *then*, of truth or reference as one among its variable – and various features.

The latter revision leaves open the possibility that the fiction/nonfiction distinction may simply reappear at a later point in the same form it had earlier assumed. But even if this should occur, the revision would provide for literary discourse a more accurate view of its own history and identity, with substantive implications for an understanding of literary and even non-literary matters-of-fact. I shall be attempting here to show how one form of discourse – the writing of autobiography – establishes the connection between literary and non-literary matters-of-fact as fundamental, thus leaving the fiction/nonfiction distinction to be asserted (if it is at all) only as a further and contingent development.

Admittedly, autobiography as a genre stands on the margins between fictional and nonfictional writing; and it may seem unlikely that an account of the role of literary fact in fiction and nonfiction should emerge from a form of discourse that combines the problems of definition which those ostensibly conflicting modes face by themselves. But it is precisely the marginality of autobiography, its place on the verge of both fiction and nonfiction, that discloses aspects of the matter of literary fact which otherwise go unnoticed. One way of proceeding here is to address the question of whether autobiography itself is a form of fiction or nonfiction. The reasons for and against each of these characterizations will provide a basis for defining certain systematic issues about literary matters-of-fact; those issues turn out, in the concluding part of this chapter, to suggest a revision of the fiction/nonfiction distinction and to propose, beyond that, the elements of a general account of literary discourse.

Privileged Access and Autobiographical Discourse

It is a commonplace among students of autobiography that the genre itself is largely a modern development, unavailable to the Greeks or in the Biblical writings, and flourishing mainly with the texts of Romanticism in the nineteenth century (the term itself is associated with Southey's usage of 1802.)[5] This reckoning is at best an approximation, since there can be no good reason for excluding Augustine's *Confessions* (sometimes cited as the first "true" autobiography) from any such history; as Plato's VIIth Letter and Socrates' reflections on his philosophical education in the *Phaedo* join the confessional mode of his *Apology*, the impulse for autobiography is recognizable in the fifth century BC as well. Admittedly, we encounter in these and other possible examples the familiar difficulty of specifying the necessary or even "typical" characteristics of literary genres (perhaps more so here, since autobiography is less clearly than many other candidates a genre at all). But if the conception of literary form as a "natural kind" goes beyond the evidence, the flat denial of generic comparisons that Croce asserted and that, more recently, Derrida takes for granted, stops well short of what the evidence does suggest. In the case of autobiography, in fact, the cluster of forms which approximate that genre but are yet distinguishable from it make a suggestive pattern around a center; one thinks here of such variations on autobiography as the memoir, the diary, the travel journal, the personal essay, and, of course, the *bio*graphy.

The characteristic design of autobiography to which these contrasting forms attest becomes most explicit in Romantic and postromantic writing, reflecting the indebtedness of that writing to the Idealist view of the constitutive role of the mind. In autobiography, the latter role ensues in a narrative history – a constitution – of the self as conceived by that self. The autobiographer looks back from the moment of writing to the past which, as the author recounts it, has led up to that moment. The narrative characteristically follows a unified line of development in which the author's self is the constant subject; the end of that development – what it is directed towards – appears as a motif which the writer "finds" in the events he describes and which, read backwards by the reader (who is *also* required to keep the present and the past simultaneously in mind) provides an explanation of the way in which the writer's self in the past has "intended" his present. A paradigm example of this causality is the constant presence in Augustine's *Confessions*, even when he is describing his childhood, of his conversion at the age of 33 that he represents as the end or *telos* of the whole of his life up to that time.

It would be unusual, to be sure, if *every* event mentioned in an autobiography were made to revolve around a single motif (Augustine is exceptional in the degree to which this connection is made, and even for him there are lapses). But such motifs distinguish themselves nonetheless as "causes" in autobiography (both of texts and of lives), whether they are cited explicitly or appear only in the unified point-of-view from which the individual, often disparate events recounted are elaborated. so, for example, the larger part of Mill's autobiography involves a description of the political positions he arrived at as an adult and continued to hold at the time of his writing – but they, too, are viewed by Mill as related to the unusual childhood and education described in the first part of the autobiography, and then to the two decisive events which followed that – the crisis of his break with his father and his relationship with Harriet Taylor.

The application of "history" or "narrative" to the process of autobiographical discourse is hardly a neutral use of those terms; the issue is joined in them between the characteristic structure of auto-biography and the question of the status of literary facts. Except as the autobiographer's account approaches the present (*his* present), the act of writing is distanced from the past he writes about. Although he may rely on documents or other evidence that bear on the past (here too, of course, the author depends on "present" evidence), he rarely troubles to do this. Even when he does, the autobiographer still relies mainly on his own discrimination and judgment of past events – and this dependence on memory, even if the events recounted were less emotionally charged than those that shape a life as seen from within, would in itself open autobiographical statements to epistemic doubt.

It can be objected that events cited from memory will be suspect in *all* first-person historical discourse, whether that discourse has the writer as its main subject or not – thus, that we find nothing distinctive here about autobiography. But such doubts only reinforce those provoked by a more basic feature of autobiographical discourse; namely, the central role of the autobiographer's *present judgment* of the events in his past and of the pattern that he "finds" there. For it is not simply individual historical moments that autobiographical writing enumerates; a detached recounting of such moments might suffice for biography or even for the memoir, but could not serve by itself for autobiography. Autobiographical authors vary in the emphasis or explicitness with which they identify patterns in the events they recount, but autobiography must do this in *some* measure if only because the autobiographer presupposes a disjunction between the past he describes and the present – the single present – from which he writes. (Starobinski argues that a radical sense of this distinction is required even as *motive* for the writing of autobiography.[6]) The author of autobiography who characteristically speaks in a narrative voice brings together in that point-of-view events which are otherwise disparate, conveying to them the unity of at least that point-of-view. In the role both of speaker and subject of his discourse, moreover, he presents the subject under the guise of a description which is more accurately seen as a determination or decision; he asserts the definition or meaning of the events of his past as *present* even though that meaning and the events on which it is based are in the past. The writer thus causally establishes a present view of himself, indicating or implying what he affirms or denies in it with his formulation. The autobiographer in this sense not only describes the events of a personal past – for that purpose, a *biographer* would do as well or possible better; rather, he locates those events in a present which he alone *could* confirm and which, circularly, influences the details of the description itself. It is what the writer now makes of the past that distinguishes the modality of autobiographical discourse; the claim is hardly too strong that this "performance" constitutes what is distinctive in autobiography.

One way of understanding this characteristic modality of autobiographical discourse is in terms of "first-person" or "privileged" knowledge[7] – knowledge (or, more generally, representation) in respect to which the speaker or writer has special access and thus special authority, not as it happens (as if, for example, he were the one surviving witness to an accident), but, intrinsically, on the basis of its *kind*. The assertion that "Today is Sunday," is open to correction by persons other than the speaker; in contrast, the statement that "Today *feels* like Sunday" would ordinarily be the end of the discussion so far as doubts about the truth or falsity of the statement itself might go. Admittedly, the person who makes the statement might be pretending or lying: it does not really feel like Sunday to him, but he wants to give the impression that it does, etc., etc.. And there may also be external checks by which a listener might dispute the speaker's truthfulness ("If it feels like Sunday to you, why do you look as grim as you do on Mondays?") But except in extreme circumstances, such possibilities finally give way to the statement itself and the speaker's privileged access to its claims. On the question of what he perceives or how he perceives it, the speaker or writer is judge, and this premise is ordinarily assumed in the response to the reports of such perceptions. Such statements are thus said to be incorrigible; they are immune to any external test and are unverifiable except by the speaker (arguably, as Wittgenstein insists in his objections to the concept of a private language, not by him either). Thus, whatever engages the reader about such statements, it cannot be due to any external assurance of their correspondence to facts or events. The reader's confidence in the "description" of such facts or events can only depend on the authority of the writer or speaker.

There are, admittedly, instances of such statements for which the question of authority is unlikely to arise at all. We ordinarily accept without question the occasional statements in which a speaker reports, for example, on personal likes or dislikes. Such reports may occur in contexts where the reader or listener has confidence in the speaker's statements because of prior acquaintance with him – but even where there is no such specific ground, the expression of likes or dislikes leaves little room for dispute. As the description of feelings or perceptions becomes increasingly complex, referring them to public events or objects, the reader may think to distinguish those references from what *must* be conceded because of the speaker's or writer's privileged position – but even here, the authority of autobiographical discourse persists. Here, too, the autobiographical author retains his privilege, since the pattern by means of which he identifies the events of his past constitutes, by a decision that only he is in a position to make, the present self which "reports" both the pattern and the particular events in relation to it. It has been argued, for example, that Mill's claim in the *Autobiography* of the influence of Harriet Taylor on him is exaggerated – but Mill's contention retains its autobiographical (and privileged) authority even against this reasonable doubt; if this is not exactly how he *saw* it, this is what in writing he commits himself to – and the reader has no means from within the writing itself for judging that there is a disparity between these. All that is required so far as concerns the "truth" of autobiographical statements is that the author should indeed have made it. We may detect exaggeration (or mistakes or even lies) in such claims either from evidence internal to the autobiography or from external information provided by letters, contemporary accounts, etc.; but even after drawing on these sources, the reader then returns to the present character of autobiographer as he asserts himself in the text. The external references may enrich, elaborate or even controvert the understanding of that assertion – but they remain always subordinate to it.

It is thus the autobiographer's representation of events or states of mind, not their independent historical standing, that preoccupies his reader, subsuming even such rudimentary questions as what the representation is "of." This emphasis in the reader's response to autobiography distinguishes that response from the reading of standard "nonfictional" discourse with its implied or explicit claim of an "objective" authority independent of figures or *personae* who appear in the text. The feature of authorial privilege, moreover, is by no means an accidental or merely syntactical feature of autobiography. As has been suggested, for certain classical autobiographies (again, as in the *Confessions* of Augustine or in the *Confessions* of Rousseau), it is precisely the representation of himself as reported by the author – sometimes the untrustworthy or obviously mistaken representation – that compels the reader's attention. And even more notable than this is what might be seen as a characteristic purpose of autobiography more generally to justify – i.e., to establish the truth of – the status of the autobiographer at the time of his writing. (Gusdorf speaks in this connection of autobiography as a *"theodicy* of the individual being.") The feature of authorial privilege itself thus contributes to a more basic purpose.

A rough measure of the relative significance of such statements for any given autobiography can be made by determining how much of the autobiographical narrative would have to be omitted – that is, could not have been known to the writer or asserted authoritatively by him – if the autobiographical "indicators" had been set in biographical locution, where the text was written by someone other than the autobiographical subject. Admittedly, conventional third-person historical narrative which is not autobiographical may include first-person locutions, as a biographer or historian acknowledges a role in selecting and interpreting the events recounted; he may, in these locutions, use such characteristically autobiographical (and privileged) markers as "It seems to me that . . ." or "I find here such-and-such a pattern." But prefixes of this sort in historical narrative typically appear in a context of corroborative evidence, and this would justify the reader's refusal to take these prefixes as the *subject* of the discourse. For autobiography, in contrast, the relative significance in historical narrative between assertion and context is reversed: here it is the context, the point-of-view in the narrative present, that is primary and incorrigible even when individual items cited within that framework (for example, Rousseau's sometimes mistaken references to the dates of his journeys: *those* do not depend on his feelings about them or even on his memory of them) can be independently verified or disconfirmed. The author's present perception of what has happened and the way in which he locates himself in the present vis-à-vis that past are foregrounded for the reader. Where this is not the case (for example, where the reader looks to an autobiography for corroboration of facts that might otherwise be obtained from civil records or other third-person reports), autobiography simply merges with biography and history more generally.

To be sure, the world of non-literary matter-of-fact beyond the autobiographical text impinges on the reader's (and before that, on the writer's) judgment in a number of ways. It is hardly accidental, for example, that the authors of the most notable autobiographies would otherwise be known independently of (and almost invariably, prior to) those works, sometimes for other writings, sometimes for accomplishments that do not involve writing at all. Such "para-history" is not, strictly speaking, part of the individual autobiography, but it serves as a tacit preface, often establishing the occasion for both the writing and the reading. An autobiographical author whose *only* claim on a reader was the autobiography itself *might* sustain that claim (so, for example, Leiris' autobiography which at the time it began to appear (in 1939) – and, arguably, later as well – *was* his main accomplishment); but the scarcity of such instances suggests that the author's history outside the autobiographical text persists as an "aura" for autobiographical discourse.

For certain autobiographies, moreover, the possibility of reformulating them in third-person discourse – in effect, as *biography* – without causing significant omissions in the autobiographies as written could be almost fully realized (*The Education of Henry Adams* and *The Autobiography of Alice B. Toklas* are autobiographies written in the third person – for the latter, even in the "fourth" person – but are emphatically *not* examples of this.) But the noticeable difference between such autobiographies as they recount individual events detached from the writer's present and what has been pointed to here as the more characteristic structure of autobiographical discourse underscores what is generically distinctive in the latter. In works of the former kind (for example, in Emma Goldman's *Living My Life*), the writer as privileged subject is virtually omitted from the text; interest roused by the autobiographer's hand in such writing turns out to be of little more consequence than does the external and anecdotal interest evoked by Rembrandt's house in Amsterdam or Marx's grave in Highgate Cemetery: in both these instances, it is the associations aroused for the reader from outside rather than the autobiographer's privilege that matters.

A more significant role of matter-of-fact in autobiography is defined by the large body of commonplace information assumed first by the writer and then on the part of the reader; that such assumptions are relevant for *all* discourse means only that it is not peculiar to autobiography, not that it is any the less important there. As I have suggested in Chapter 7, the commonplace assumption that people do not shrink or grow instantaneously, for example, is not usually a literary issue (except, of course, in Alice's Wonderland where its denial is a causal element in the text). But that biological rule is inevitably presupposed in the structure of literary plots, and an indefinite number of similar non-literary matters-of-fact are presupposed in all writing and reading. In this sense, a larger, unwritten and "nonfictional" text accompanies every written one (fictional or not); the Russian Formalists' reference to "defamiliarization" as a defining feature of literary discourse discloses the potentially literary importance of the unwritten commonplace text as a foundation for the written one.

Again, however, such broad associations of text and the common matter-of-fact world apply generally; for autobiography, they remain secondary to the claim of privilege asserted by the authorial "I." The emphasis of the autobiographical narrative is not on the world assumed or on public events from the author's past but on the autobiographer's assimilation of them both at the moment of writing (however long that moment is). This act of assimilation, moreover, is at once incontestable in historical terms and central to the autobiographical representation; it is, again, the writer's definition of himself that is the subject of the autobiographical discourse. Even when the narrative emphasizes events of the past as isolated from each other and distinct from the present, it is the single voice or point-of-view as it makes these assertions that engages the reader – since it is this that

is the ground for those other assertions. A reader may judge the autobiographer's view of his past (and so, of his present and himself)
to be partial, foolish, deceptive – or acute and honest. But whatever
its character, the reader's response first presupposes acceptance of the
author's statements as constitutive, immune at the level of assertion
either to doubt or corroboration. To measure the statements of autobiography as if they were historical statements of biography would
be to conflate the two forms; the difference of autobiography entails
acknowledgement of the distinctiveness of its discourse. In doing this,
the writer anticipates and the reader endorses a bracketing of the
question of historical accuracy or "nonfictionality." The justification
for this bracketing is based on the autobiographical indicators or
"operators" that ascribe privileged access to the statements of autobiography; those indicators force the question of historical or literal
truth in autobiography to a secondary role.

  One implication of the foregoing comments is that in autobiography, the conventional lines between fiction and nonfiction seem to
disappear, at least as breached from the side of nonfiction: to read
autobiography as history (or biography) would be to repress both the
logical and the representational distinctiveness of autobiography (so
Frye refers, in an aside, to autobiography as "this very important
form of prose fiction.")[8] The pressure from the other side – that is, in
the referentiality of fictional discourse – will be elaborated below,
but for the moment it is the threat to the distinction itself that is
singificant. The most concrete evidence of this effect appears in the
small difference it would make if what had been read first as an
historically authoritative autobiography was then revealed a "only" a
first-person fictional narrative – or conversely, in the case where a
supposedly fictional first-person (or for that matter, third-person)
narrative turned out to be a "literal" recounting of the narrator's life.
The expectations of a reader – what Frye refers to as the "radical of
interpretation" – are unquestionably significant in shaping literary
effects; for autobiography, the consequences of the shifts in expectation mentioned are so minimal as to make that fact itself symptomatic.

  For a reader who only later discovers the contrived features of
Walden – the compression of the two years that Thoreau lived at
Walden into the single year of the narrative; the information from
outside the text that Thoreau would occasionally escape the austerity
of life in the woods for some of his mother's pies; even the number of
versions (eight) of the manuscript of *Walden* which suggest an artful
shaping of the material – it is doubtful that the interjection of such

factors in the apparently historical *appearance* of that work will significantly disrupt that appearance. The same point applies more strongly to Rousseau's *Confessions* where the reader learns from the text itself that the line between fiction and nonfiction is constantly being subverted – and accepts this also as a premise of his reading, because it is then a feature of Rousseau himself.

The explanation for such indifference to autobiographical "facts-of-the-matter," for putting to one side in the reading of autobiography the issue of historicity, is provided by the notion of privileged access, as it also accounts for the converse of the argument. When we learn, for example, that David Copperfield (in parts of the early chapters of the novel) *is* Dickens, that knowledge hardly make more difference to the reader than would evidence about the *dis*similarity between the respective lives of the author and the principal character of the work (which indeed holds for the later parts of the novel). Flaubert's dramatic identification of himself with Emma Bovary is surely intriguing – but, again, however we understand this, it hardly affects our reading of the novel which she/he dominates. Information of this kind and inferences based on it, even if they reveal the historical inaccuracy of certain statements in the autobiography, either become simply *another* story or make a place for themselves in the story as it has been read: nothing in the status or interest of the autobiographical statements themselves is changed by them.

Although the claim of privileged access in autobiographical discourse is the single most important indicator there of the problematic status of literary facts, it is not the only one; other of its features also locate autobiography in the margins between fiction and nonfiction. Thus, for example, the standard questions about literary beginnings and ends – what causality controls them, what "happens" before the beginning of the narrative or after its conclusion – which arise in relation to narrative fictional discourse, retain much the same character in relation to autobiographical writing. The "natural" solution to such questions as addressed to autobiography – that an autobiography should begin at the writer's birth and conclude at the time in his life when the author writes – is far from universal in practice. Augustine concludes the *Confessions* chronologically with his conversion to Christianity, 15 years before he wrote; and Sartre's *The Words*, written when he was 59, follows the events of his life up to the age of 10. (*The Words* was supposed to be the first volume of a sequence; but if Sartre allowed the one volume to stand by itself for the 15 years he lived after its publication, that is at least as much reason for taking its ending to be "conclusive" as for crediting his statements outside the text which deny that.) And when Goethe in the opening line of his autobiography follows what might seem to be the archetypal autobiographical convention ("I was born at Frankfurt-on-Main on the 28th of August 1749, on the stroke of twelve") the artificiality of that beginning is itself unmistakable. Even more rudimentally, of course, any expectation that an autobiography will provide the full account of a life is, for obvious reasons, unwarranted. Neither the beginning of the narrative nor its end is available to the autobiographical author: he has no more access to the beginning than any biographer (perhaps less); to the end, he has none at all.

Both in practice and in theory, then, the chronological limits of the autobiographical text also turn out to be functions of the privileged view of the writer. Even if the autobiographical narrative extends fully to the time when it is written, that extent too must be understood as a decision by the autobiographer – who chooses that moment as the terminus and who, as he would in any case, selects and shapes the events which bring him up to that point. (It is possible to imagine a number of autobiographies by a single author, each successive one incorporating the writing of the earlier texts as part of the author's new "present.") Thus the conclusion of an autobiography, whether set in the writer's present or in his past, has a figurative and not simply an historical function; it is an element of the representation which, as one decision among others, shapes the motif or theme that the writer "discovers" in his life. So Rousseau, viewing himself as an outcast, looks backwards in the *Confessions* from his "present" condition to the virtues in his past actions – the combination of feeling and sincerity that will, he believes, vindicate him to his readers (and possibly to his enemies); so also we note Sartre's determination at the end of *The Words* of his lifelong "project" as a writer, the project that engaged him as the subsequent author of that account of his childhood and that retrospectively shapes the events of that childhood which he recounts.

A similar conclusion applies to the beginnings of autobiographical texts. Here again, contrary to the "natural" starting point (whether at birth or in the author's coming to consciousness), autobiographies sometimes start out with references to ancestral generations (so Sartre begins the account of his life three generations back), or with events in his life prior to adult consciousness (Augustine includes a remarkable reference to his *prenatal* desires), or with events that occur relatively late in the author's life. There is, in other words, no necessary moment of origin for autobiography, and this openness points again to the distinctive modality of autobiographical discourse: as the autobiographical subject is determined by the subject as writer, so the decision of where the beginning of that representation "is" is part of the determination. The autobiographical frame – the narrative's beginning and end – thus turns out to be a function of the narrative structure itself; like the justification for the frames of "fictional" narrative, its justification, too, reflects the intentions of the text – how the author conceives it as a whole and what he then chooses to disclose in its parts.

Another characteristic feature of fictional discourse which recurs as a compelling presence in autobiography is the unavoidable division within what is typically, in other literary genres, a unified authorial point of view. For the "author" of an autobiography, as has been suggested, occupies two places in it, one as its subject and one as its writer; and although the point-of-view defined by the latter is in one sense chronologically later and in any event more comprehensive than that of the former (and almost invariably more consistent, since it is the point-of-view of a single moment), the relation between the two is not that of straightforward historical subordination in which the past appears only as an inert object. Rather, it is the *juxtaposition* of those points-of-view that constitutes the subject of the autobiography – how the writer *now* joins impressions, views, opinions held separately or in diverse patterns in the past and still more pertinently, how that past itself shapes the present view of it. The autobiographical author-present holds a privileged position in respect to events in the life of the author-past; but the content of autobiography emerges from the joining of those two temporal positions, not in maintaining (usually not even attempting to) their separation.

Here, too, then, the autobiographical narrative voice – which belongs to the implied author, not necessarily to the "actual" author – is also a *persona* within the text, active on and in the discourse, presumably with the full range of literary tropes among which to choose: romance, comedy, irony, tragedy. That the "plot" of auto-biography is characteristically motivated by an idea or conceptual pattern might suggest a special relation between autobiography and irony, but the tropes of autobiography seem in fact to vary. Rous-seau's *Confessions* approximates the standard, morally static pattern of comedy, even of farce; Augustine's *Confessions* progresses towards the unification and renewal characteristic of romance; Socrates in the *Phaedo* provides an anticipation of tragedy. Is it perhaps that the lives disclosed in autobiography – or indeed all lives – follow the defini-tions of tropes? The autobiographical voice often proceeds with no pretense of objectivity or neutrality; even if it adopts that stance, the question would persist of how that stance was itself to be understood literarily. The unified authorial voice or point-of-view thus becomes a *persona dramatis* – distinct from the historical author to whom the reader may have access quite apart from the autobiographical text and the "facts" of whose life remain for the reader of autobiography always subordinate to the assertion of the autobiographical text (to this extent, the "Intentional Fallacy" applies here as well). Rousseau is but one, if the best-known example, of an autobiographer who insists on the truthfulness of his account while repeatedly providing evidence to the contrary in that very account. The narrator's insistence in fictional discourse on the historical veracity of the narration (as in Defoe's *Journal of the Plague Year* or in Hawthorne's *The Scarlet Letter*) is a common fictional device; this should itself be a warning about such references in the context of autobiography.

Autobiography and Aesthetic Inference
(Or: Saving the Literary Facts)

The distancing of autobiographical discourse from the domain of historical fact, as the autobiographer has the "last word" irrespective of whether that word is historically true or false and only because it *is* the last word, may seem to imply the conflation of fiction and nonfiction in autobiographical discourse. But the implications of autobiographical discourse are more complex than would be captured in a reduction of nonfiction to fiction from the other direction – in the formalist denial, for example, that facts have any literary future at all. For even with the displacement in autobiographical discourse of historical fact by authorial privilege, truth and referentiality persist as features of that discourse and as factors in the reader's response to it. It makes a significant difference that Augustine's account of the pleasure he took as a boy in stealing pears was in the stealing rather than in the pears – and this is the case, even if, as I have argued, the reader of the autobiography finds himself bracketing the question of whether, historically, that was indeed the young Augustine's motive. It is his *account* of his motive that matters – as a fact to be assimilated with the text and also beyond it, if only as *possible* – impinging then on the background we recognize as the extra-literary understanding of the reader. (We might compare Augustine here with Rousseau who apparently reflects backwards quite differently on *his* childhood motives: "I would have stolen fruit or sweets or any kind of eatable, but I never took delight in being naughty or destructive . . . . ")

Augustine's description, displaced historically, still bears directly on the reader's comprehension, directed inside or outside the text, of the motivation for wrong-doing or sin – Augustine's or anyone else's, including the reader's own. It thus involves the reader in a way that would be unintelligible if Augustine's description were measured by Sir Philip Sidney's often-cited apology, that "the poet nothing affirms, and therefore never lyeth" which epitomizes a characteristic and traditionally influential formulation of the fiction/nonfiction distinction. According to the latter claim, Augustine's account must be read hermetically, as referential (at most) to Augustine himself – and although this captures one side of the autobiographer's "authorial privilege," it suggests that this privilege is exclusively emotive, with *nothing* more to be said about the author's claim than what the author himself says, much as if everything he said might be contained in the simple prefix "I feel . . . . " It is this preemptory conclusion that needs now to be further discussed – disputed, in fact, on grounds which are, like the others cited, internal to the text itself. Even if Augustine's "present" view of his past is privileged in terms of its truth status, the representation of that view remains to be judged by the reader *as* a representation – and the issue of truth, of the way in which the representation supervenes on the reader's world, is arguably, at least until it is for some reason excluded, one part of any such judgment.

A second example puts the same point more explicitly. When Rousseau writes in the *Confessions* that "No passions were ever at once so pure and so strong as mine," autobiographical privilege conflicts with the reader's sense that Rousseau could not possibly have known enough – *no one* could after all – to justify his claim. But the very extravagance of the statement then affects the reader's conception of Rousseau's autobiographical self – much in the way that the equally extravagant statement by Oedipus in *his* fall ("No living man has loved as I have loved") extends the reader's conception of that self. For both of these statements, it is a literary issue for the reader, beyond the question of their internal coherence, of how the textual representations engage the reader's experience outside the individual statements or words that constitute them, that is, in the reader's world itself. Whether we speak here about the literary enlargement or consummation of extra-literary experience, of literary representation as "true to" or "true of" or "true in the same sense as" the reader's dispositions, the cognitive issues of truth (and so also of falsity) impinges. There is no need to demonstrate that this issue pertains to autobiographical discourse differently or more basically than it does in other forms of discourse; its relevance is attested *there* in any event by the characteristic structure ascribed above to autobiography and by the inadequacy of alternate accounts of autobiography which deny its role or attempt to explain it away.

I am proposing, then, that the privileged access which establishes autobiographical discourse as incorrigible, with the combination of power and limitation that this provides, nonetheless leaves open the possibility – indeed the inevitability – of assessing the discourse in terms of the status of truth which emerges from what might be called "aesthetic inference." The reader infers from the combination of individual autobiographical statements (and before that from the individual words) the representation of a whole which then, circularly, affects the meaning and reference of the parts. To assess the individual statements of Augustine or Rousseau as descriptive or historical statements ignores their standing as autobiographical – but to read them only as *that* would ignore their standing also as discourse; the latter requires judgment of the representation which the individual statements in their sequence constitute and which then affect their meanings individually. As it would be a "category-mistake" to judge questions or exclamations as true or false, so it would also skew their meaning to deny, in judging autobiographical statements, the context of general representation in which they appear; and that context adds the possibility of a different measure of truth to the incorrigibility with which they begin.

The claim for autobiographical privilege, then, governs only one aspect of the truth-status of literary statements. The author who cannot be mistaken in what he thinks – and then writes – *of* himself, still, in the outcome of his thinking and writing, displays that self; in that display, the issue of literary matters-of-fact reappears, joining the literary representation to the reader's experience and dispositions outside the text. Autobiographies differ more sharply as texts than as records of the events that make them up: lives that are the agents of important events may yield dull autobiographies, and startling autobiographies might be written about unexceptional lives. But if the analysis of autobiographical discourse is distinguishable in this way from the historical lives which occasion that discourse, such analysis also compels a subsequent return to other, inferred literary "facts of the matter." Neither the motives for reading autobiography nor the discoveries initiated by that reading are restricted to finding out only "what happens" in the text. To follow those processes to their conclusion, that is, to determine how the reader is engaged by them, is to see the reader addressing the autobiographical *persona* beyond the literal limits of the autobiographical text itself.

It is at this point that the implications of autobiographical discourse for a broader account of literary fact become evident, since a strong parallel emerges here between the modality of autobiographical discourse and the modality of "fictional" discourse. I can in this context only suggest how that analogy might be further developed, and indeed it is important to keep in mind the evident *dis*analogy which any claim for this parallel must overcome. On the one hand, the autobiographer's "I" is a constant presence in his text, both as speaker and as subject. Authorial privilege depends on this conjunction: the autobiographer's statements, finally, are "about" himself in a way that writing by any other author could not be (except in the attenuated sense in which every statement whatever involves its speaker). Responding to this feature of autobiography, the reader's interest also sets out from what the autobiographer says about himself rather than from what the historical "facts of the matter" disclose (whether inside or outside the text). But fiction presupposes no such intrinsic relation between author and representation, no autobiographical "operators" as preface to the individual statements, no apparent joining of the author's memory to an affirmation of the present. Where, then, the parallel?

It is useful to note here two accounts of literary matters-of-fact that are disputed by the analysis based on authorial privilege in autobiographical discourse. The first of these appears in a tradition that extends from Plato to Russell, according to which the elements of literary discourse (for Russell, the propositions) that bear the weight of verification turn out to be largely, if not entirely, false. If there never was a Mr Pickwick as there was an historical Dickens, and if (as in Russell's theory of definite descriptions) the use of a proper name asserts the sometime historical existence of whoever or whatever is named, then the statement that "Mr. Pickwick went to Bath" (and indeed virtually all other statements in *Pickwick Papers*: *all* of them, if they are viewed, as a single long conjunction) is false.[9] The same conclusion would hold for virtually all the fragments and wholes of fictional discourse (including drama and poetry); in the "Ode to a Skylark," the statement, "Hail to thee, blithe spirit, Bird thou never wert" turns out to be not only false but false because *self-contradictory* – to the extent that one might find falsehood itself to be a distinguishing mark of literary discourse. (It might be argued, given the premises stated, that for no other common source of false statements – political pronouncements, newspapers, advertisements, – is falsehood *intrinsic* on this scale.)

It is impossible to review here the arguments that have arisen in respect to this conception of literary fact; in this sense, what I propose is an alternate view rather than a refutation. But it is at least clear that on the prima facie evidence to which such theories answer, the assessment of literary matters-of-fact by the criteria of a literal understanding of historical discourse (thus, largely as false) is quite inadequate. It may be, as writers on literary truth have sometimes claimed, that the disclosures of literature, abstracted from their contexts in order to be judged independently as true or false, turn out to be banal or trivial even when true. (Abstracted in this way, of course, most "non-literary" truths would seem no less banal; the conclusion that over-reaching oneself may lead to sorry results is not more or less a cliché as a summary of Aristotle's *Ethics* than it is of Sophocles' *Oedipus*.) But insofar as this view allows *some* place for literary facts, it avoids the consequences that follow if literary statements are, as a class, judged to be false. For although the cultural and intellectual importance traditionally ascribed to literature is logically compatible with a view of literary discourse as false (in Plato's extreme thesis, the attraction of art reflects precisely the *appeal* of falsehood), any such conjunction would obviously be strained; on the view of literary discourse as false by its nature, western cultural history, with its strong and persistent ties to literary expression, appears as a form either of mass error or corporate self-deception, having mistakenly associated literature with a positive moral or theoretical content. The latter assessment cannot be ruled out as possible, but it is prima facie implausible and would in any event require evidence that has not been forthcoming. Alternatively, attempts such as Goodman's to sustain the positivist view and yet to provide *some* basis for claims of the significance of literature – in his case, by claiming that fiction although literally false, may nonetheless be "metaphorically" true – seem only to defer the question of how the terms of such a sharp distinction can be joined.[10] It is significant that without exception, none of the recent discussions of the logic of fictional discourse in which literary matters-of-fact turn out to be false consider the social or historical role of literature as a possible source of evidence. The assumption apparently underlying these accounts is that the conditions or consequences of literature could add nothing to the understanding of the literary text. This in turn presupposes – contrary to the facts – that the text and its implications are themselves non-empirical and non-historical.

A similar objection applies to the second of the two views that traditionally have contested the one that is defended here. Referred to above in the quotation from Sydney, this view conceives of literary discourse as non-cognitive, not even intended to make or deny truth-claims. On this account, the ostensive assertions in literature are "pseudo-statements" – utterances which look like statements but which are not genuine (that is, subject to judgment as true or false). Literary works are to be judged for their emotive or (related to this) their formal qualities, not as representational or referential; to find them or their implications true or false misconstrues their function, much in the way that labeling an exclamation true or false also "misfires."[11]

Underlying the dissociation which this theory asserts between the literary imagination and the world of fact is a non-cognitive theory of emotions which holds emotions to be non-referential, and thus also, detached from their "objects." The most immediate consequence of this view of literary matters-of-fact is its failure – much like the first alternative noted above – to account for the historical role of literature. For again, without at all denying the emotive force of literature, it would be arbitrary to define the historical influence of literature – and the history of literary criticism and theory – as having been *exclusively* emotive (even if one assumed the theoretical viability of a sharp emotive-cognitive distinction). To be sure, the prima facie evidence against the view of literature as non-cognitive may be disputed – but it cannot simply be ignored or explained away, as formulations of the position have characteristically attempted. The historical contexts in which this view has been prominent are worth noting: Sydney, responding to the Puritan attacks on art's alleged falsification; Richards, looking for a response to the devaluation of literature implicit in the Logical Positivist account of verification and meaning. The pressing issue at both those junctures was how to defend the art of literature against a restrictive view of truth – and although in those contexts the failure of the defense to contest that view of truth rather than to revise the conception of literature is understandable, the effect is to throw the baby out with the bath water: literature is defended against charges of falsification by being divorced from knowledge altogether.

Although developed only in outline, the methodological premise of the position argued here against these other views is explicit; namely, that a theory of literary discourse must account, among other "matters," for the role of literary matters-of-fact – and that in this account, the close connection between literary and non-literary matters-of-fact is unavoidable. A summary of the modality of autobiographical discourse in the history of its own reading thus brings together three principal features. First, autobiographical discourse displaces the response of the reader from the individual assertions of the literary text to their common preface, to the "operator" which directs his response. Secondly, it privileges the discourse in such a way that its statements are (initially) incorrigible – thus accounting for the "aesthetic proximity" that invariably accompanies even the strongest versions of the concept of "aesthetic distance."[12] The "I" which is emphasized as the subject of autobiographical discourse will in *some* way – although not, as we have seen, by historical disinterestedness – be appropriated and joined by the reader's "I." Thirdly, it suggests that the status of matters-of-fact in autobiographical discourse reappears as an issue when the representation of the text is seen not by way of its individual assertions but as they are brought together – when, through inference, the reader constitutes a whole out of the individual "assertions," finding the justification – the necessity – for doing this in directives of the text itself. The conclusions of this inference, as they constitute the view from the autobiographical self of the disparate parts of a personal history, thus challenge the reader's self as well. The challenge here is not that the reader's self should become the autobiographical self, but that the process of constituting a self – non-literary, we have seen as well as literary – is joined between them.

The proposed analogy between autobiography and fictional discourse is hardly self-evident in these respects, and indeed the proposal itself may seem no less doctrinaire than the denials of literary matter-of-fact to which it is opposed: are all fictional statements now, like those of autobiography, to be privileged or "true" as a class? But the conditions of the analogy are not unlimited. In autobiographical discourse, the reader credits the writer's word initially because it is the writer's self – as writer – which certifies it; in fictional discourse, similarly, the reader credits the writer's word because of the analogous domain constituted there by the authorial voice or point-of-view. Like the autobiographical rendering of characters, figures, dates, actions, the authorial voice in fictional discourse is also, in its first appearance, infallible. The reader may ask *why* Lear decided to divide his kingdom among his daughters – but there can be no doubt that this was what Lear decided; the reader could hardly object that Shakespeare "got it wrong," that Lear had two daughters, not three, etc.. At this level, the authorial voice is also incorrigible, and this status is unchanged even if the reader might argue, at a different level, that a given text would have been more compelling or even more consistent if the author had arranged the literary facts differently.

In fictional discourse as in autobiography, moreover, an "operator" which serves as preface to statements in the text is implicit in the text itself. The preface tacitly attached by the autobiographical author is also a constant presence in the reading of the autobiography – author and reader in common reflecting, then, on the events recounted. This preface or operator is a condition set by the text – and the process of inference that follows from it is unavoidable; an explicit claim within the text for its autobiographical character may be a misrepresentation (conversely, it is possible that autobiographical discourse might be prefaced by the denial of that status). Similarly, the fictional text, by a variety of literary conventions – figurative language, judgments by the implied author about the thoughts or feelings of characters, etc. – distances itself from alternate forms of discourse, thus providing directives for the reader. Admittedly, it is not clear what non-circular term would serve as an "illocutionary" prefix to fictional discourse, and the attempts that have been made to do this only underscore this difficulty. (So, for example, Searle's proposal that the writer of fiction "pretends" to make assertions seems only to beg this illocutionary question.[13] Other alternatives range from ones that are specific but problematic (like "imagine") to others that are general but vague ("describe" or "narrate").) The question of this characterization thus remains open, but that does not alter the status of fictional statements as embodying a form of action in which the author's word is, initially at least, also "authoritative."

Again, for fictional discourse as for autobiography, the statements grounded in authorial privilege do not preclude questions about the truth-status of literary "matters-of-fact"; these questions require only a shift of the context in which the latter are assessed. For although fictional utterances would not now be treated as discrete or independent – or as independently verifiable by the criteria applied to ordinary "matters-of-fact" – they shape a representation which, viewed as a whole, impinges on matters-of-fact, illuminating them or misconceiving them, deepening them or revising them. For fictional as well as for autobiographical discourse, readers who analyze individual statements in the text as directly and literally referential do this at the cost of denying the functional context by which the meaning of the whole and thus also of its parts is determined. Such statements *do* impinge on the reader's world outside the text, but they can be judged as doing this *literarily* when they are viewed through the representation they constitute and by the inferences involving reference and truth drawn from that representation. They *can* be judged otherwise, of course, – for example, as the individual "statements" of literary discourse might be judged by the criteria of historical or scientific truth; but to take these as the norm to be applied is no more likely to produce conclusions pertinent to their literary status (whether as fictional or nonfictional) than would the chemical analysis of the paper they are written on. Again, the immediate question for Augustine's reader is not whether Augustine – historically – took pleasure in stealing the pears but how to conceive a self struggling with desire which retrospectively sees the lure of that pleasure as something to be overcome – a much more complex matter-of-fact, but one nonetheless. So, too, the reader of *King Lear* who does not doubt that Lear divides his kingdom must still judge the person – in the reader's own experience – who would make that decision and who would further act and suffer as Lear does.

The logic of this form of inference requires examination in its own right, but that task is separable from the contention that the process itself is unavoidable; we have only to consider what the act of reading would be without it. By "aesthetic inference" the individual parts of a text – questions, exclamations, statements, even omissions – are brought together in a way that makes inferences to a conclusion, to the shape of a whole, at once possible and necessary: possible because actual, and necessary because the alternative is to read only in fragments (of sentences, even of words). This process, for fiction as well as for the exemplary case of autobiography, starts out from an authorial "I" which, in its initial assertion of privilege, engages the reader's "I" by a literary version of cathexis. Enlarging on this starting point, it establishes a frame of reference more general than the initial one but still individuated: the reader must confirm for himself the inferences that emerge. Thus, the literary "speech-act" is carried on jointly, by the reader and the writer together. The initial displacement of the issue of matters-of-fact turns out then to be a postponement: the reader returns to it under the compulsion of the text.

Autobiographical discourse thus indicates more directly and explicitly than do other, superficially less marginal forms of literary discourse how the incorrigibility of an authorial "I" can yet found a role for literary matters-of-fact that is not incorrigible at all. The authorial "I" and the privilege it conveys in autobiographical writing turn out not to settle the status of autobiographical matters-of-fact since those, in a variety of ways, reappear subsequently. The force of autobiographical writing is a function of truth – but not characteristically of "literal" truth, since for autobiographical discourse, the distinctive role of privileged access disposes of that stage early and once, if not for all. In what is conventionally distinguished as fictional discourse, too, there is authorial privileged access – and here, too, the question of truth and of the status of matters-of-fact subsequently recurs, as the conclusions of aesthetic inference revive the issue of reference which, if raised earlier, would easily be (and have been) misconstrued as having no specifically literary character.

One way of bringing together the several lines that converge in the thesis argued here is in relation to the question commonly posed for reading of what a particular text is "about." The obvious answer to that question when posed for an autobiographical text is that it is "about" the autobiographer – the self both written and writing. But this, no less obviously, is only the beginning of a response: the *persona* disclosed in Augustine's *Confessions* engages the reader not only beyond the isolated historical references to Augustine himself, but also beyond the figure constituted as those individual references are together assumed to be true because of autobiography's privileged access. So, too, the claim that *King Lear* is about King Lear is true but trivial, and even the more complex claim that *King Lear* is about a king who in old age disinherits one daughter and entrusts his fortunes to his two others only to find both judgments misplaced – which is also true – is only slightly less trivial. On the other hand, the process of aesthetic inference is presupposed even in these statements. In neither the *Confessions* nor in *King Lear* does a statement appear that they are "about" anything at all; this first step, then, is itself a matter of inference. For the reader to reach even the minimal conclusions cited, moreover, is to be driven further by the same logic of inference: in *King Lear*, to a conception of the destructive power of human vanity and self-deception that is more fundamental to its causal structure – non-literally *and* literally – than the claim that the play is "about" King Lear.

Thus, the way in which the standard question about the status of literary matters-of-fact is put, assuming a direct representation by the ostensive "statements" of literary discourse of a world of external facts, is misplaced – in fiction no less than in autobiography. "Did Mr Pickwick *really* go to Bath?" the question asks, and the tendentious "really" (sometimes explicit, sometimes only assumed) reflects the arbitrary obtrusion of a literalist or historical criterion. The answer to that question is obviously "No" – but even more certainly the question itself is misconceived. To ask "*In what sense* did Mr Pickwick go to Bath," on the other hand, acknowledges what is surely indisputable, that Mr Pickwick did, in *some* sense indeed go to Bath. With this formulation, we also recognize that the conventions of historical description do not – should not – serve as the basis for assessing or even understanding fictional statements – not even for determining the status in fiction of what in another context would be a straightforward historical matter-of-fact. (Wolterstoff's proposal to view fictional characters as "character-kinds" rather than as individuals goes some way toward addressing this issue, but insofar as it is restricted to persons (or other nouns), takes account of actions or assertions only indirectly or not at all.[14])

The question remains, of course, of the sense in which Mr Pickwick *did* go to Bath – and, from the side of autobiography, of the sense in which Rousseau *did* feel more intensely than anyone who had ever lived. Only to have shown that the fiction/nonfiction distinction is inadequate for answering this question is not itself an answer to the question. But it does provide a framework within which an answer may be found. Before we begin to judge the status of literary – e.g., autobiographical, fictional – matters-of-fact (and also, we infer, non-literary ones as well), it is necessary to determine what the discourse in which they appear is *doing*, what action is engaged in or undertaken by it. One way of accomplishing this is by seeing how far and in what way the literary text diverges from the privileged status it claims initially *because* of the form of its discourse. An implication attributed to speech-act theory (and often cited as an objection to it) has been that all speech-acts, inasmuch as they share a performative aspect (in the terms cited here, as they share an "authoritative" preface) are to that extent equal in "force." But this apparently indiscriminate claim, far from blocking referential distinctions among types or genres of discourse, provides a means for deriving just those distinctions. In asserting a role for the agent of discourse (in its exemplary form, the autobiographical "I"), this account calls atttention to the elements of agency – history, purpose, function – which permit distinctions among forms of discourse as *they* provide a more general means for distinguishing among types of action or performance. Thus, someplace between the logical claim of privileged access and the prima facie claims of reference or truth in autobiographical and fictional – *and* historical – writing, a means may be found for distinguishing them by their "performance" and by the means of reference characteristically associated with the discourse that they set in motion.

If we return, then, to the question initially raised in this discussion, of whether the distinction between fiction and nonfiction is itself fiction or nonfiction, the answer arrived at now turns out to be – perversely – "yes." That is, it is both of them at once, with the ostensive distinction between the two now a function, not a foundation of the common worlds of literary and non-literary discourse. In other words, the role of discourse, not the characters of fiction or nonfiction, becomes the primary consideration – and discourse itself only as one among the varieties of human action or doing. The difference between fiction and nonfiction thus appears as one of a number of distinctions tied to the functions – themselves various: moral, political, psychological, *and* epistemological – of literature.

Seen in these terms, the fiction/nonfiction distinction, as it has been traditionally accepted as fundamental to the epistemology and philosophy of literature, as well as in literary criticism and theory, does not settle – if anything, it obstructs – the question of the truth-status of literary discourse; indeed it seems to have little to do with literature at its ground level at all. Its most immediate practical consequence has usually been to impose "nonfictional" criteria on the "fictional" world – which is itself, we might conclude, a fictional device. At the very least, this tactic begs the question which it professes to answer concerning the relation between literary and non-literary matters-of-fact, revealing this arbitrariness in its conflation of the character of Mr Pickwick with the arbitrary designs of gold mountains and unicorns and the present King of France – references which are overtly non-literary, although designedly fictional, in their origins and purposes.

Much more needs to be said, admittedly, about distinctions among the functions of discourse: how, if the standard fiction/nonfiction distinction is rejected, the differences it had obscured would now be characterized – for example, what the differences are in respect to reference or truth among the types of figuration or among the varieties of authorial point-of-view. On the terms proposed here, literary discourse is a form of action, – with literary matters-of-fact now aspects of that action. The theoretical analysis of discourse in which rhetoric occupies a central position has long emphasized the role of discourse as a form of "doing," and the account given here suggests a means of reasserting that emphasis in the domains of fiction and nonfiction which, from each of those directions, has come to be dissociated from the rhetorical center. Autobiographical discourse provides a clue at once to the possibility of this connection and to its importance. The relation suggested here between literary act and literary fact may seem also to suggest a more general thesis, intimated in the epigraph by Thoreau, about the status of all discourse as autobiographical; but although there is an important sense in which this thesis is true,[15] it is not required for the conclusions drawn here. For if we consider only writing which is ostensively autobiographical and thus only one among other forms of discourse, we find there a role for literary matters-of-fact that undermines the suspicion which autobiographical discourse itself initiates – that there are no such things, that the phrase itself is an oxymoron: if literary, not a matter-of-fact; if a matter-of-fact, not literary. A similar role for non-literary reference also appears, it seems, in fictional discourse, and the reflexive question raised at the beginning of this chapter thus concludes in an irony: that the fiction/nonfiction distinction leads eventually, still in its own terms, to the reinstatement of literary, that is, "fictional" matters-of-fact – which the distinction had been initially intended to repress.

Notes to Chapter Nine

1   See Ian Watt, *The Rise of the Novel* (Berkeley: University of California Press, 1957); Raymond Williams, *Culture and Society, 1780–1950* (New York: Harper and Row, 1966); Lennard J. Davis, *Factual Fictions: The Origin of the English Novel* (New York: Columbia University Press, 1983).

2   E.g., Iris Murdoch, *The Fire and the Sun* (Oxford: Clarendon Press, 1977).

3   See, e.g., Hayden White, *Metahistory* (Baltimore: Johns Hopkins University Press, 1973), and *The Content of the Form* (Baltimore: Johns Hopkins University Press, 1987); Richard H. Brown, *A Poetic for Sociology* (New York: Cambridge University Press, 1977); Berel Lang, ed., *Philosophical Style* (Chicago: Nelson-Hall, 1980).

4   See, among other exmples, Jacques Derrida, *Of Grammatology*, translated by Gayatri Spivak (Baltimore: Johns Hopkins University Press, 1976), and *The Postcard: From Socrates to Freud and Beyond*, translated by Alan Bass (Chicago: University of Chicago Press, 1987); Roland Barthes, *Image-Music-Text*, translated by Stephen Heath (New York: Hill and Wang, 1977); Richard Rorty, *Contingency, irony, and solidarity* (New York: Cambridge University Press, 1988).

5   On the historical development of autobiography, see, Georg Misch, *A History of Autobiography in Antiquity*, translated by E.W. Dickes (Cambridge: Harvard University Press, 1951) and William C. Spengemann, *The Forms of Autobiography* (New Haven: Yale University Press, 1980); see also Robert F. Sayre's more speculative history, "Autobiography and Images of Utopia," *Salmagundi*, 19 (1972), pp. 18–39. For a general account of the issue of truth in autobiography, see

Roy Pascal, *Design and Truth in Autobiography* (Cambridge, Massachusetts: Harvard University Press, 1960), and on the question of autobiography as a genre, see Paul Jay, *Being in the Text* (Ithaca: Cornell University Press, 1984), pp. 14–21.

6   Jean Starobinski, "The Style of Autobiography," in James Olney, ed., *Autobiography: Essays Theoretical and Critical* (Princeton: Princeton University Press, 1980), p. 178: "If such a [radical] change had not affected the life of the narrator, he could merely depict himself once and for all, and new developments would be treated as external (historical) events."

7   For a summary of the issues concerning "privileged access," see William Alston, "Varieties of Privileged Access," *American Philosophical Quarterly*, 8 (1971), pp. 223–31.

8   Northrop Frye, *Anatomy of Criticism* (Princeton: Princeton University Press, 1957), p. 307. Cf. also Patricia Spacks, "The Soul's Imaginings," *PMLA*, 91 (1976) p. 425, and Paul John Eakin, *Fictions in Autobiography* (Princeton: Princeton University Press, 1985), pp. 3–26. For a more radical view of the distance between fact and autobiography, see Paul de Man, "Autobiography as De-facement," *Modern Language Notes*, 94 (1979), pp. 919–30. Barnet J. Mandel argues the opposing case for autobiographical historicity in "Full of Life Now," in James Olney, *Autobiography: Essays Theoretical and Critical*, see note to above.

9   See Bertrand Russell, "On Denoting," *Mind* (1905), pp. 204–19, 336–54, 509–24; and for a summary of discussions about Russell's position, cf. Israel Scheffler, "Questions of Fiction," *Poetics*, (1982), pp. 279–84. One account would translate "Mr Pickwick went to Bath" as "There is a novel by Charles Dickens which either contains the statement, 'Mr Pickwick went to Bath' or contains other statements which entail it." (See Richard Rorty, "Is There a Problem about Fictional Discourse?" in Rorty, *Consequences of Pragmatism* (Minneapolis: University of Minnesota Press, 1982), pp. 111–12. On this reading, "fictional" statements would be true if (and then because) accurately reported from their original texts – but this only defers the assessment of the statements themselves.

10   Nelson Goodman, *Of Mind and Other Matters* (Cambridge: Harvard University Press, 1984), p. 124.

11   A notable source for this view as applied to literature is I.A. Richards, in *Science and Poetry* (New York: W.W. Norton and Co., 1926) and *Principles of Literary Criticism* (New York: Harcourt, Brace, and Co., 1938).

12   A fuller account of the concept of aesthetic proximity appears in Berel Lang, *Art and Inquiry* (Detroit: Wayne State University Press, 1975), ch. 4.

13   John Searle, *Expression and Meaning* (New York: Cambridge University Press, 1979), pp. 58–75, and *Intentionality* (New York: Cambridge University Press, 1983), p. 18 ff.. J.L. Austin's "Performative Utter-

ances," in *Philosophical Papers* (Oxford: Clarendon Press, 1961) and *How To Do Things with Words* (Cambridge, Massachusetts: Harvard University Press, 1962) are important sources for the issues raised here (and for Searle's account).

14   Nicholas Wolterstoff, "Characters and Their Names," *Poetics*, 8 (1979), pp. 101–27. See also Kendall L. Walton, "Fiction, Fiction-making and Styles of Fictionality," *Philosophy and Literature*, 7 (1983), pp. 78–88, and Thomas G. Pavel, *Fictional Worlds* (Cambridge, Massachusetts: Harvard University Press, 1986).

15   Rudolf Gasché argues persuasively that such a claim can be supported not simply on the obvious historical ground that discourse implies an author but from the internal character of discourse itself. See "Autobiography and the Problem of the Subject," *Salmagundi*, (1978), p. 574 ff..

10

The Animal-in-the-Text:
Fables and Literary Origins

*When someone has behaved like an animal, he says "I am only
human." But when he is treated like an animal, he says, "I, too, am a
human being."*

                                                                    Karl Kraus

*The anatomy of people holds a key for understanding the anatomy of
apes.*

                                                                    Karl Marx

One thing that fables have in common and that non-fables lack in
common are the animals that populate the former and are absent
from the latter. To the extent that fables *have* plots, animals are
usually in the thick of them, causing what happens to happen and
almost always, moreover, making it happen to themselves. It may
seem then that to ask why fables revolve around animals is to ask why
fables exist at all, and the answer to *that* question turns out also to
point at the animal kingdom, the animal-in-the-text serving as Prime
Mover for fabled texts as a genre. Indeed, once we reach this point,
we can hardly avoid going one step further, asking exactly what is
literary about the fable which is, after all, known first for its didacticism and morals and which we recognize now to have mainly brute
rather than artistic or spiritual origins. The answer to this more
general question, I shall be suggesting, leads to the unlikely moral of
this chapter itself, namely, that fables provide a notable key to the
anatomy of literature as literature. Just so the large stakes of literary
theory mount from the brief transparencies of the fable.

I do not mean with this promissory note for a conception of "literariness" to imply that the fable is the historical source from which other literary forms evolved – as it were, an ancestral Ur-test or literary missing link. (Although there *is* some truth, that is, some history, in this claim: the first traces of the fable – *not* its early stages, since it seems to have sprung to life full-grown – reach back at least to Ur and the first texts of Sumer, that is, almost to the first texts of any kind whatever, demonstrable "Ur" texts).[1] But I shall be suggesting that in understanding how fables work, more exactly, how the animals in them make them work, we learn something about literary texts in general, including texts that on the surface seem to have little to do with the animal world and its colorful *dramatis personae*. Name whatever literary character you choose – Isabel Archer or the Young Werther or Emma Bovary or Josef K: we may yet find their forebears in fables, familiar to us there by animal names, animal aspirations, and animal fates. This, at least, is the improbability promised in a view of the fable which assigns primacy of place to animals first within the genre and then outside it, as its literary artisans – a view which then also ascribes a morphological primacy to the genre itself.

The gross anatomy of the fable might go something like this: what is required in the fable is a body of narrative that is characteristically brief, ranging from a single sentence to a number of paragraphs, but not longer in any event than what can be encompassed by a single sweep of the eye or mind. (So, for example, at the beginning of this scale, the one-sentence fable of Aesop: "When the hares addressed a public meeting and claimed that all should have fair shares, the lions answered: 'A good speech, hairy-feet, but it lacks claws and teeth such as we have.'") Part of the text, moreover, consists of a "moral." that is, an edifying conclusion, sometimes unstated, sometimes explicit. The lead character of the narrative is an animal (or a single group of like ones) who acts on the basis of desire and who is thwarted in that desire because another character (also an animal) opposes and defeats it, also by desire.[2] Desire is thus vanquished by desire. In that defeat, the first agent is left with something less than what he started with although with the benefit of a lesson. Attempting to be more than he is, the lead animal who in the end would settle for his beginning, finds that it is too late. A conclusion or moral thus emerges which threads desire with irony: attempting more, we – animals and humans together – open ourselves to having less.

This is evidently a complex structure (predictably, not every fable fits the pattern); and it is, I propose, the animal-in-the-text who provides the succession of clues that establish unity in the complexity.

Why, we ask, coming face to face with the various menageries: Aesop's hares, lions, and foxes; La Fontaine's gnats and donkeys; Thurber's bears and moths – why all the animals? And the answer to this question, circular but cumulative, demonstrates at least that the presence of those animals is not accidental. They could *not* just as well have been people – and this is true despite the fact that people are present in some fables and that they are quite central to the morals of all fables.

Let us consider again the dramatization of the fable: desire, counter-desire, defeat, moral conclusion – all of them impelled by the animal-in-the-text who acts to produce them quickly and briefly (even if this is the only time that he acts in this way: to reach the end of the *fable* of "The Tortoise and the Hare," the tortoise moves as swiftly as his rival). Brevity may seem only a literary means (an incidental one at that), not an end; but so concise is the narrative of the fable that the distinction between means and end itself merges. The feature of compression tells us something significant, in fact, about the concluding moral-in-the-text which closely follows the animal there; we do well, then – in asking why the fable is what it is – to begin by considering the constant feature of brevity, first in its relation to the animal-in-the-text and then, once again, as that relation produces the single whole of fable and moral.

Almost necessarily, any writer who aims for conciseness in narration attempts to enter the narrative world *in medias res,* without providing or presupposing an explanatory past. Ideally, in other words, the *personae dramatis* would live only in the present of the narrative itself – or in that present no differently than they had in the past and in any event with no causal relation between past and present to muddy the waters of the present (with or without a past, it is *always* in the present that literary action occurs). It is possible, admittedly, to write about human characters in this way – but the effect then (as in Kafka) will be surrealistic, coveying a sense of arbitrariness and dislocation which then itself becomes an element of the literary intention. To represent as natural a self for whom past history is of no present consequence requires an unusual kind of self – one that typically would not be a human self at all (in the genre of the parable, all human selves are alike – which is not, after all, quite human). Such a self *does* appear, however, in the kingdom of animals (at least in the human view of animals) where history, past or future, hardly matters. This abridgement of time implies an abridgement of consciousness that the fabulist can then rely on for naturalizing what otherwise would be an unnaturally brief narrative.

To be sure, there is a biological history, in both the individual and the group, for animals as well as for humans – but with the former, in contrast to the latter, no consciousness reminisces about that history or looks expectantly towards its future; there are none of the regrets or hopes or regressions and denials that complicate human stories in *their* present. For much the same reasons, furthermore, the absence of individual variation *among* the animal members of a kind is also useful: the kind is all one. Even if there were a history to be told, then, telling it for a single animal of a kind would be to tell it for all. And there is no need to tell the history even once, because, again, there is none to tell; they live all and only in the present. To have a narrative revolve around characters who are credible as characters and yet for whom nothing in the past bears on the present – not the image of parents or childhood impression or the emergence of self or the nostalgia of failure, not even the present swerves of conscience or expectation: this surely is an effective way to make a long story short – which is, after all, what fables do.

The same feature of conciseness, in fact, is relevant to the plot of the fable no less than to its characters, as it shapes the conflict of desire around which the plot moves. For again, human desire, insofar as it is more than simply biological and involuntary – and no story of human desire is limited only to that since there is here no story at all – also attaches to itself the various indirections that reflection may think up (often including the concealment of desire itself). All of this, the desire of the animal-in-the-text simply avoids, since with animals, we believe, everything they want is unambiguously in the open (as well as in the present), as clearly visible to an observer as it is to the animals themselves. It may seem unfair to lions to measure them always by the standards of courage, and even more unfair to represent snakes only as treacherous, or wolves as constantly vicious and foxes sly. But what is at issue here is not justice for animals but literary practice, and the assumptions about animals in this practice are clear: birds of a feather are for *literary* purposes identical – an identity which puts the single stamp of biology also on character. To name an animal by species is also to identify a constancy of will, character, ethos – and so also to build the plot of the text which the animal will be in (or, more exactly now, which will be in the animal).

Thus, when an animal acts in a fable, his actions hold no surprises for the reader; indeed the reader would be surprised only if the animal acted in a way that was surprising (if, for example, the fox were candid and ascetic, the crow, quietly modest, and so on). Even for animals that are not so completely stereotyped, the principle of this same effect persists. The deer may in one fable be vain, in another, shy; but these two portraits coexist only so long as they do not, from either side, contradict a common stereotype: a wolf would never, even metaphorically, *be* a sheep (even if he happened to wear sheep's clothing). As animal, the animal justifies a writer's representation of single and uncomplicated characteristics or motivations which move consistently to predictable ends; it is just this narrowness of focus that provides the writer with both a literary subject and a literary means. Even when the animal seems to be of two minds, this soon turns out to be an only apparent confusion; it is a resolvable – and soon resolved – aberration, a near-lapse into the human condition quickly remedied as the animal remembers, and reminds the reader, of his (the animal's) single-mindedness. That is, his single-"mindedness".

The claim that it is the desires in animals that motivate fables is underscored and elaborated by the counter-desire by which the first is opposed, and which, through the conflict it produces, establishes whatever there is in the fable of the literary element of plot. In this complication, desire, will and character (the literary progression here is swift and inevitable) run up against the desire that has already been established and is no less pointed and assertive: the forces are quite nearly equal as well as opposite. There is action in the fable, then, however direct and simple – and also the complication of action calling for resolution which we recognize as plot. But the action and plot evoke neither past history nor future nuance: desire is active only in the present. Thus again: what more natural source for so limited a range of impulse and attention than the motivation of animals? Or by contrast: what more doubtful source for such limits than people? The fox wants the grapes (until they turn out to be sour) as the crow wants to show off his voice (until he discovers that it will be at the cost of his cheese): at those first moments, these are the *only* things that they respectively want. Desire and counter-desire are thus each unambiguous, explicit, and – without at all impeding the moral progress of the fable – brief.

And yet, fables apparently have morals in the senses both of ethics and of conclusions – which animals customarily do not have and which, we assume, they do not think about having or lacking. Why should animals claim a central role in fables if it is conclusions of *that* sort at which the fable's narrative aims? Would not the fabulist find a more convincing object for his ironies if he wrote about human rather than about animal beings?

Well, of course, the fabulist *is* writing about human beings, and he also compels his readers to think of them, whether they recognize this hand of compulsion or not. The animal-in-the-text is the means, moreover, by which humans are discovered in the text – and this animal origin is neither accidental nor independent of the view proposed of these humans. But the process by which this occurs is an important part of the story – indeed it arguably *is* the story.

If we consider for a moment how the moral of a fable emerges from the plot, the most striking features and certainly the most familiar one in that process is that the moral does not "emerge" at all. For some fables, the moral is not even stated independently; there is in them *only* the progression of plot and character. So: "A vixen sneered at a lioness because she never bore more than one cub. 'Only one,' she replied, 'but a lion.'" What, after all, is the moral of this story? The writer does not tell us – and the authorial premise evidently assumed by Aesop himself (who was never, we might guess, at a loss for a moral) is that to read the fable just is, in that act, also to identify the moral. Not because the moral cannot be stated apart from the narrative and not because the moral is ineffable, but because it *has* been said: that is, in the fable itself. No independent conclusion or inference would make either narrative or moral clearer or more compelling than they are as disclosed together in the fable itself. To insist on the distinction between moral and fable might well, in fact, only confuse the reader: he must wonder then what he had missed in reading the fable – since it had not seemed to leave anything over or to require a mediating voice at all.[3]

Much the same argument applies even to fables where the author does draw the moral and writes it down for the reader. Sometimes in these fables – as if to demonstrate its independence – the moral appears first, not last. So La Fontaine writes in one preface, that "we all occasionally have need to call on the services of the weak and the small" – and only then describes how the lowly rat saves the mighty lion. And indeed the moral appended to a fable might just as well be placed first as last, because it tells the reader no more (and no other) than the text does itself. It is, in a way, a gift from the author – but a gift with strings attached, or more exactly, with the strings part of the gift itself. Even where fable and moral are separated on the page, the distinction between them is without a difference, and this becomes evident through the implausible possibility that a reader might accept the one but *not* the other. So, for example:

A wolf was carrying to his lair a sheep which he had lifted from a flock, when a lion met him and took it from him. The wolf stood at a safe distance and cried: "You have no right to take away my property."

"You came by it rightfully, of course" replied the lion. "No doubt it was a present from a friend."

Moral: This story is a satire on thieves and greedy robbers who fall foul of one another when they are out of luck.

What, we ask, would it mean to read the "plot" of this fable but then to reject the moral, on the grounds that the moral is not entailed by the fable? The point here is that the moral of a fable is not an interpretation, at least if we believe that for interpretation there must always be a plausible alternative to the one given. (No *one* interpretation, the rules of reading go, without a likely other.) And it is not only the fact that the moral is integral to the fable (as the title given to a text, for example, might well not be) that ensures this. There is no room left for doubt or speculation in the plot of the fable, partly because it is brief but also, more importantly, because of the structure itself: what the fable is *about* is so much of a piece with what it *is* that to view those two aspects as distinct would be a conceptual conceit, needlessly multiplying entities. A reader of the fable who failed to read the moral appended to it (before or after) would hardly notice the difference – so long as he had read the fable itself. In this sense, it does not matter whether the moral is drawn explicitly or not, or whether it is drawn by the author or left to the reader to draw; the moral just *is* the fable. The only differences between fables in which the author draws the moral and those in which the reader is left on his own are in the author's eye; so far as the fable is concerned, the author might just as well have added only an exclamation mark. (And so far as the *moral* is concerned, he might just as well have omitted the fable.[4]

To call attention to this interweaving of fable and moral, however, may seem to add little to the primacy claimed here earlier for the role of the animal-in-the-text. To make the connection between moral and animal, we have to go a step further, even beyond the conclusion we might have reached on other grounds as well, that it is the lack of animal consciousness, certainly of animal self-consciousness, that accounts for the absence of critical space evident in the reading of fables. There is no more room for the reader of fables to doubt or to speculate outside the text, to distinguish the literary act from a moral conclusion implied by it or to reflect on alternate possibilities for either – to *interpret* – than there is for the animal characters themselves to reflect within the fable on who or what they are. The animal-in-the-text is more aptly defined by desire than a person-in-the-text could be: insofar as that desire (and counter-desire) also, at the same time, define the action of the fable, a large source of interpretive incentive (and often of critical disagreement) is foreclosed. In other words, the fact that animals do not *have* ideas leaves the reader freer to treat the animals themselves *as* ideas – and this is indeed what happens when the fable, impelled by the animals at its center, unfolds its moral as part of its action.[5]

Still, although the animal-in-the-text fosters the proximity of act and idea as well as that of act and desire, neither of these relationships (even taken together) accounts for two other prominent features of the fable's moral or conclusion. The first of these is that an "ought" occurs in the conclusion of the fable that seems to have no precedent in the "is" of the narrative: the animal-in-the-text does not think of morals at all. And secondly, the "ought" of the conclusion turns out to apply not to animals (not even in a sense), but to human readers: the moral of the fable – and so the fable – is *their* moral (and not only, one supposes, because it is so likely that any reader of a fable will *be* human).

The first of these features calls attention to a point which will be obvious as soon as it is mentioned: that the morals of fables are not "moral" – that is, ethical – at all. To be sure, an "ought" does emerge from the conflict of desires that constitutes the fable's plot, but it is an ought of prudence, not of ethical obligation. The fact that it is desire alone, even in its complications, that evokes the fable's conclusion makes it probable – or even, ensures – that the moral of the fable will not be "moral" in that word's more usual sense. Fables describe how the animal-in-the-text does act, often and characteristically if not necessarily – never how it *ought* to act (whatever that could mean for animals, and it could not mean much). When the animal-in-the-text is thwarted by the desire that conflicts witth his own, the motive on either side is animal nature as it is, not as it ought to be: the lion is naturally more powerful than the mouse, in the same sense that a mouse (any mouse) may be of assistance to a lion. As desire and self-interest are the motives for action in the fable, so too they are the clues to its resolution: if the crow's craving for praise makes him forget for the moment his taste for cheese, he may wind up, because of his single-"mindedness," with neither.

There is surely a counsel of prudence in such "morals", and no doubt a morsel of straightforward truth in them as well (although usually no more straightforward than its contradictory, which prudence might also teach; Aesop's Crow, for example, had probably been brought up on the adage that insists "Nothing ventured, nothing gained"). But there is little that is *moral* about any of these, in the sense that they attach an ethical stigma to wrongdoing or approbation to right-doing. It is not in itself immoral to want more than you have, nor is it immoral to lose what you already have as the result of an attempt to get more – but it is dumb, and also, from the point of view of bystander or reader, ludicrous. (Only recall here the standard definition of humor as a version of detumescence: what was hoped for and supposed to exist turns into nothing.) There is no *ethical* "ought" in the fable, and to this extent we see again the role of the animal-in-the-text: the amorality of desire and any of the other motives of nature's *persona* (if there *are* other motives – there can't be many) is all that is asserted in the conclusion to the fable. And this is as it should be, or more correctly, as it *must* be, since there is only desire in the fable's premises, acting first to define the character of the animal-in-the-text and then to impel the fable's conclusions.

Yet it may seem, in respect to this, like any requirement of consistency between premises and conclusion, that the fable itself suffers from desire in conflict, that it would like to have its cake and eat it too: professing the conditions of logic, the fable itself violates them. For unlike their premises, the conclusions drawn from fables are not about animals but about human beings, the ways they act (or do not) and the cost to them of acting in that way (fables almost always ending in defeat for *someone*). But here the animal-in-the-text also reveals how this apparent inconsistency is in point of fact consistent: it is precisely in the animal, in the straightforwardness of its desires, in the brevity of its past and its lack of anticipation for a future, that we also see something of what it is to be human, however less brief and less uncomplicated the human character is. Admittedly, the animals of fables are not also human; but humans, unmistakably, are also animals – and the narrowed view by which animals show themselves in the fable then provides a view of humans as well. The clue here is in language: when the fox or the lion or the donkey speak, the reader knows (and is meant to know) that they are not only foxes or lions or donkeys. The moral is for the reader to draw immediately and conclusively, since there is only one that can be drawn: if the fable is not about foxes or lions, whom *could* it be about? The animals – like the facts – speak here for themselves (even if what they say is in an alien tongue). Foxes, unlike people, have tails and fur – but like people, are sly; lions, unlike people, have claws and manes – but like people, they assert their power. The one set of qualities is no less visible than the other – and the evidence of both is on display in the animal-in-the-text. We follow this convergence of sameness and

difference, moreover, without causal speculation and without genealogy, and this is another reason for the brevity of the fable: if the idea
is the action, the two will be visible in one sweep of the reader's eye.

According to the rules governing the syllogism, if we refer in a set of
premises only to a particular fox, we are not entitled to speak in the
conclusion drawn from those premises about the family of foxes, let
alone about the members of another family, for example, that of
humans: you cannot have in your conclusion what you do not have
in your premises (this is a moral that *logic* insists on). But the
apparent narrowness of the premises of a fable, I have been suggesting, conceals a breadth which makes it possible, even on logical
grounds, to draw from them a conclusion about human beings –
about all (or at least any) of them. For as it is also part of that premise
that all foxes are of a kind (and all crows of another), then the subject
of the fable's premise is not Fox A or Crow B, but a collective: *The*
Fox or *The* Crow. And if what motivates The Fox or The Crow is a
form of desire which in its same narrow form also motivates the
human animal, then the animal-in-the-text of the fable could only be
a creature who somehow manages to bring together in himself the
individual desires that singly animate The Fox, The Crow, The Bear –
and this is, of course, not necessarily but in fact, the human animal.
This does not mean that humans may not also be *more* than animal
(although the fabulist willingly leaves what more that is to other
writers) – it means only, for the fabulist, that to be human is *at least*
to be animal. Thus, as man is a wolf to man, man is also a fox to man,
a crow to man, a lion to man, a mouse to man: what is metaphor in
the hands of philosophers writing the story of human nature by
figurative allusion to animals, is more forthrightly, in the hands of the
fabulist, literal assertion.

How, one asks, could this claim for consistency in the fable between animal origins and human conclusions be proven? Some of
the difficulty here is that of providing evidence for *any* literary
theory (whether of history or anatomy.) Yet, beyond this, there *are*
specific reasons that can be appealed to, some already mentioned and
one other in particular which is itself something like a fable with
animals at its center. Consider for a moment that the role ascribed to
the animal-in-the-text – the life it provides for the fable, the evocation
of likeness and affinity in the eye of the reader – is much like that of
the animal-in-the-zoo and *its* evocations. The pleasure in looking at
the varieties of figure or motion or habit of the animals in zoos (or,
for that matter, out of them) is not simply an interest in oddity or
variety (although also these); it is an interest in the variations on a

human theme that a text might do well to imitate or elaborate – but only on the assumption that the subjects of the fable (like the occupants of the zoos) are not only its animal characters. "When an ape looks into a mirror, it is no angel that looks back at him," Lichtenberg wrote sharply but too easily; the harder question is what an angel might see in an ape that keeps the angel looking at *him*. There is, in any event, a rare opportunity here, so far as concerns literary theories, for verification: readers attracted to fables and their morals will also be attracted to zoos and *their* morals. And also obversely: the reader who finds no affinity in fables (who might be inclined, for example, to settle for the moral by itself) will also be impatient with zoos. There is, the claim would go, a common ground in those two sources; we should be able, then, to look and see.

Earlier, I made a suggestion in the form of a promissory note that not only does literary analysis – the standard discussions of genre, character, plot – disclose the special role in the fable of the animal-in-the-text, but that fables, in turn, would have something to say about literature *tout court*, the animal in the one text leaving its tracks on other texts as well. Think here in terms of an analogy – first, then, of a balloon before it is inflated. On the sides of the balloon appear what look like the outlines of animals and other figures and objects; perhaps we make out the form of a fox looking upward, wistfully, it might seem, at a cluster of grapes dangling beyond his reach. We begin to inflate the balloon: the figures expand, and as they grow, the lines which had given the figures their contours begin to separate into what, although they are still illegible, look like the lines of a text. The balloon expands further, and the lines separate; we begin to see divisions among paragraphs, the spaces between individual words, and then, very finely but growing slowly, the words themselves. These eventually compose themselves, when the balloon is further inflated, into the text of the fable of "The Fox and the Grapes". Thus we find ourselves in the midst of "iconic discourse," where the characters of the narrative become the characters as letters – and so then the words – of the text. For the viewer, it does not matter which of these came "first", and indeed there is no way of ascertaining that order from the balloon itself: one of its sizes or shapes is not prior or more "natural" than the others. In reading the one of them, at any rate, the reader, wittingly or not, is also reading the other. There is no reason, moreover – since *we* are responsible for the balloon – for stopping here, for not inflating it futher. Then the words and lines of the fable themselves begin to separate – and we find other texts emerging from them, from single lines or even from single words. The moral of the fable, for example, may become another full narrative, much longer in fact than the fable of "The Fox and the Grapes" but still iconic, still with the theme of desire first frustrated and then turned on itself (perhaps now under the name of *Notes from the Underground*). And so on.[6]

To be sure, it might be objected that this analogy is tendentious, that there is no justification for privileging the fable or for claiming *its* figures or literary parts as emblematic of the larger ones of the novel or the drama. And yet reasons there surely are, however peripheral they seem. Even the *argument from history* – that fables were in at the literary beginning – brings some weight to the role thus proposed for the fable; nor is the related *argument from size* quite irrelevant (if we admit that as a rule beginnings tend to be small). Beyond these, however, it is mainly the structure of the fable that supports the claim of the analogy, as features prominent in that structure are elaborated in other and larger literary forms. Consider then again, as functions of the animal-in-the-text, three also literary functions: the presence of a moral principle or idea, the interweaving of idea and the narrative, and the move to generalization. These characteristic, perhaps even defining, features of the fable and of the animal-in-its-text are also, we discover, prominent in the fable's literary afterlife.

(a)   No narrative form is more concise than the fable. The chronicle and the list are undoubtedly literary forms, and they are at least as brief and rudimentary as the fable – but there is no agency or character in them, and their plots (if they have any) do not thicken. On could hardly imagine the possibility of narrative discourse on the basis of those forms alone (except perhaps by making a fictional list on which narration was itself an item). The fable, on the other hand, although no less concise, includes the elements of narration. And if the turning-point here at which isolated facts turn into narrative tale has the animal-in-the-text as its means, then the many other, lengthier narrative texts – the short story, the novel, the epic – appear as collateral offspring (even though many times removed) of the fable. In them character, and characters, become human; the first and narrow shadow of desire moves to enlarge its field, evoking consciousness and memory and then too conscience. The smallest unit of a chronicle, for example, may consist of nothing more than the name of a battle and a date: the author's point-of-view is only minimally present in this conjunction (the formula "A.D." attached to a date, for example, shows the chronicler as writing in a "Christian" time but means nothing *inside* the chronicle, for the event recorded). To be sure, chronicles or lists normally include more than one such unit, and patterns of representation and action emerge as those accrue; but the single items of the chronicle or the list do not by themselves *require* that accrual. And although it might be claimed, teleologically, that even the single items in a list or chronicle presuppose the author's prior conception of a longer whole, the fable requires no such covert literary or metaphysical faith. For *it*, plot, character, and idea are present at the first moment; only their permutations and elaborations are left to be worked out in the varieties of fable and in its grander literary successors.

(b) Is the fable fiction or nonficction? Yes, I should say – affirming the question and by way of the fable challenging the supposed disjunction (is it itself, after all, fiction or nonfiction?). Animals do not ordinarily speak (at least not English or French or Greek): thus when we encounter them speaking those languages, we recognize that we are in the midst of a fiction (imagine what future the fable would have if animals *did* begin to speak English or French or Greek). But the animals in fables also tell (and suffer) some hard truths, that is, nonfictions. And these two sides do not conflict in the fable; in fact they are not even separate from each other.[7] By speaking, the animal-in-the-text implies as well as shows that there is a story to be told here. But the conclusion or moral of the story is the animal unspoken: the moral, like the joke, is *on* him, not *by* him. Thus, although in settling literary accounts, we customarily start out from the assumption of a separation between fiction and nonfiction and only then find ourselves wondering how it is possible for fiction to tell the truth, or for truth-filling to appear in a literary guise, we learn now that we *should* have begun elsewhere – with the question of how the two sides of the distinction between fiction and nonfiction came apart in the first place. In the fable, at least, they do not – and insofar as they later may be separated, the distinction then is, at least in its origins here, without a difference. If the distinction had only the fable to rely on, in fact, it would never have been imagined; that radical act of discrimination is subsequent, present only by intimidation in the fable itself. The "fact" that animals do not speak outside of fables foreshadows the many other facts in larger fictions that also have not "happened;" the fable is only more candid than other literary forms in admitting the dependence of invention on what is already known and known to be true, that is, to be fact.

(c) There remains then the issue – in three parts: literary, logical, moral – between the particular and the universal. On the one hand, the texts of literature are not themselves, at a literal level, inductive. We learn this as we find that the proper names that appear at the beginning of literary texts (Josef K., Emma Bovary, Isabel Archer) and which are also the subjects of their conclusions: the bearers of those names may change, may diminish or die, but literarily, they remain the same persons they initially were. On the other hand, the reader reading the names thinks at the same time, in the same act, also of himself and of others, even of mankind or human nature: the proper names serve as indicators of much else, even though, as individual names, they provide no warrant for this expansion. And in support of this, the fable's progress, too, demonstrates that there is no logical misadventure in the literary appeal to human nature: the animals-in-the-text *are* collectively human although they are also animal and individual; their names and words and actions establish a narrative space and then a reflective aura that none of them, by itself, could create. This is not two different ways of seeing the same creature, but one way – as looking through binoculars still produces one view.

When we read in a text about individual persons, the issue will always be in doubt whether it is not specifically on those persons alone that we should linger in the conclusions to which the text draws us. With the fable's animal-in-the-text, such scruples are soon put aside: it is the generic One which each displays – *The* Fox or *The* Lion or *The* Crow – and finally and quickly, then, the generic One not of an animal species but of the "creature" who writes and reads them. (This excludes gods and angels, but only because narratives about supernatural beings immediately become human ones; as humans cannot escape time, the gods cannot be caught by it.)

This process of inference is motivated by the moral of the fable which is, I have suggested, exactly equivalent to the fable itself and in the end not much of a moral (that is, not very moral) at all. Certain other literary forms that have been referred to – the list or catalogue, the chronicle – describe things only as they are; more elaborate literary forms on the other side of the fable incite moral visions of what ought (or ought not) to be: so Hamlet's conscience, if we took it seriously, might make heroes of us all. How does the fable establish the transition here, passing over the supposed distinction between facts and values as if it had no stopping power? It is, again, the role of the animal (non-human and human) that mediates here, displacing desire and want by need and idea, moving from what is to what might be – both of these conditions for the realization of what ought to be or at least for the realization that there *is* an "ought-to-be." Thus it is the animal-in-the-text who proposes to make the reader human and the moral moral, who shows that the first conditions for the process of narration can be met. Thus, too, it is the animal-in-the-text who provides assurance that there will be life – literary *and* non-literary – after the fable.

I have not intended with these suggestions to represent the fable either as a purer or "higher" form of literature than others or as their historical ancestor, but as providing an anatomical clue to literariness. The principal features of the fable, in one or another elaboration, also appear in every literary or at least in every narrative form; the elements of character, plot, and idea or moral appear in the fable as though in a seed which has the literary future inscribed in it. Thus, the animal of the fable who disappears in subsequent literary forms – more precisely, who evolves in those forms into other creatures: human characters, literary ideas, moral principles – rightfully, justly, is given the central role in the primordial literary scene which would later be thoroughly repressed. No one connected with the "higher literature" – authors, readers, the characters within it – has an interest in being reminded of their animal origins; a suspicious critic might well accuse them all of a common ideological conspiracy.

There is, furthermore, a sense in which the animal-in-the-text may be responsible for the very act of reading without which there would be no literary effects (or causes) at all. Whatever else the animals in fables do, there is one thing that they do not do, and this is to read the fables in which they appear. The morals of their own fables are thus entirely lost on them, and there is no reason to believe that the morals of other fables are any more accessible (what *would* Thurber's moth learn from La Fontaine's gnat?). Speech for them, in any event, is not only prior to reading but independent of it (but then, of course, not reading anything, they could not have read Derrida either). The moral of the fable is thus for someone else to draw, someone outside the text, even of a different nature – and that turns out to be, in fact if not by necessity, the human reader. For one thing, the fable presupposes the reader in the sense that without him there would be no one to draw its moral, to move from the desire which initiates it to the desirable inferred through it (or from repulsion to the reprehensible); the fable, in short, would not be a fable. And then there must also have occurred that one extraordinary moment when the reader himself first came into existence. We do not know the details of that moment – when it occurred or even how long it was – but we are able nonetheless to imagine it. Accidents, of course, do happen, and they might also have happened here, but there is also one *necessary* event in that history. This occurs when the reader of the fable draws the moral of the fable, that is, in the account given here, when he *reads* it. If the reader did not exist at that point, the fable would have had to invent him (no reader, no moral; no moral, no fable) – and perhaps, in its origins, as it sprang into existence full-grown, the fable did just this. That too would have been made possible, with all the other promises of the fable, by the animal-in-the-text.

Notes to Chapter Ten

1   On this early history of the fable, see Robert S. Falkowitz, "Discrimination and Condensation of Sacred Categories: The Fable in Early Mesopotamian Literature," in Oliver Reverdin and Bernard Grange, eds, *La Fable* in *Entretiens sur l'Antiquite Classique* (vol. XXX), Geneva, 1983, pp. 1–24. Falkowitz claims that a principal use of the Sumerian fables – beyond, or more likely because of, their edifying role – was for the teaching of Sumerian as a *language*.

2   There are, to be sure, fables that do not involve animals (see, e.g., Helen Waddell, *Beasts and Saints* (New York: H. Holt, 1934)) and animal "stories" that are not fables (so, for example, Richard Adams' "animal-novel," *Watership Down* (New York: Macmillan, 1972). But it is difficult to avoid the conclusion that the fable and its animal-means are peculiarly suited to each other: consider, for example, the improbability of animal "parables" – a genre which in its formal structure is otherwise closely related to the fable. (For the purposes of this account, organic life that is not human but also not animal – e.g., trees – are considered also as "animals-in-the-text." (Cf., e.g., La Fontaine's fable, "The Oak and the Reed."))

3   For a contradictory view, of the moral as indeterminate or "open," see H.J. Blackham, *The Fable as Literature* (London: Athlone, 1985), p. xiii. Even this view agrees, however, that the fable is characteristically linked to a moral; *that*, in any event, is not open. The evidence against Blackham's more specific thesis seems to me conceptual as well as empirical, and obvious on both counts – although this claim itself, I recognize, invites a moral.

4   This does not mean, of course, that the fable as a genre cannot be misunderstood or misread. So, for example, developmental studies suggest an approximate point (ages 9 or 10 in American children) at which fables are read as representational wholes. (See, e.g., Paul E. Jose, Marcy Dorfman, and Lisa Sliwa, "Development of the Appreciation of Fables" (unpublished paper) and Ellen Winner, Anne K. Rosensteil, and Howard Gardner, "The Development of Metaphoric Understanding," *Develop-*

mental Psychology, 12 (1976), pp. 289–97.

5　That fables characteristically "have" morals is acknowledged in virtually all accounts of the fable (see, for example, such otherwise different perspectives as John Locke, "Some Thoughts Concerning Education," *Collected Works*, Vol. VIII (London, 1824), p. 147, and Hans Robert Jauss, *Untersuchungen zur Mittelalterlichen Tierdichtung* (Tubingen: Max Niemeyer Verlag, 1959), pp. 16–17, 201–18). What the status of the moral is vis-à-vis the fable and as itself "literary" is much more in dispute.

6　For an account of other "formalist" analyses of the fable, see Helene Innendorffer, "Der Beitrag der Formalisten zur Gattungsgeschichtlichen Untersuchung der Fabel," *Poetica: Zeitschrift fur Sprach- und Literaturwissenschaft*, IX (1977), pp. 116–22.

7　Aristotle, in his discussion of the fable as a form of oratorical argument, refers on this issue to the fable's characteristic use of "invented facts" (*Rhetoric*, 1393a).

11

The Politics of Interpretation: Spinoza's Modernist Turn

Although the label of modernism is well known for its elasticity, the usage may still seem stretched by the claims I shall be making here for that remarkable seventeenth-century modernist, Spinoza. But the connection can, I believe, be demonstrated, at least with respect to the concept of interpretation which, whether at the level of theory or as it is applied to the "texts" of culture and experience, is an identifying mark of modernism in almost all the diverse accounts given of thatistorical turn. Interpretation acquires not only a logical form but a constant origin and purpose in the work of Spinoza, specifically in the radical *Tractatus Theologico-Politicus*[1] which Spinoza brought out anonymously although still bravely in 1670. I use the term "bravely" because Spinoza bases what we can now read as a general theory of interpretation on the dangerous text of the Bible (Hobbes, who had thought at least some of the same thoughts, admitted to Aubrey, that "he durst not speak so boldly"). Spinoza's initial anonymity, moreover, did not, and could hardly have been expected to, protect him for very long from defenders of the faiths who claimed jurisdiction over authors even when they were *not* writing about the Bible.[2] The *Tractatus* is radical because it asserts for the theory of interpretation a character which even now, 300 years and much enlightenment later, has won only grudging acknowledgement – the view, that is, that interpretation presupposes or implies a political framework, in effect, that interpretation is *itself* a politics.

Admittedly, neither in the *Tractatus* nor elsewhere does Spinoza propose a role for interpretation as intensive as that later claimed for it in the aftermath of Kant's Copernican Revolution. One consequence of that Revolution was to encourage the further conclusion that *all* knowledge is intertwined with the act of interpretation. This expansion, beginning almost immediately after Kant's writings appeared and lasting into the twentieth century, expressed itself in ways that Kant himself did not foresee and would undoubtedly have rejected. So, for example, the Hegelian insistence that interpreters are themselves inside their interpretation – its subject as well as its agent – implied an historicism that Kant's own ahistorical categories of the understanding had avoided. Almost a century-and-a-half later the contention by Heidegger that even the far reaches of ontology are at once ground and exemplar of the hermeneutic circle of interpretation dramatized what Kant had asserted, more restrictively, at the level of epistemology. Notwithstanding their differences in scope, there is no escape in these accounts (Kant's included) from the dominance of interpretation – and the recent discovery that the replication of physical life itself is also a function of interpretation serves them as a fitting epitaph: the authority of nature is now added to the authority of reason. (Is it so unlikely that the conception of the genetic code was itself induced by the post-Kantian imagination?)

Measured by these increasingly reflexive versions of interpretation, Spinoza was a rationalist in the strongest sense of that term, insisting on the "natural light of reason" as the foundation for all knowledge and thus also for the process and conclusions of interpretation. For him, neither the basis nor the goal of interpretation *themselves* involve interpretation – nor does Spinoza hold that knowledge or, for that matter, meaning is dependent on this process. Where reason has spoken or written, in fact, there will be no occasion for interpretation, since what is rational is also, by definition, clear and intelligible, and thus requires – or for that matter, allows – no mediation. In this sense, the very need fo interpretation is symptomatic of a defect; aside from writing which for prudential reasons has disguised its meanings, any text that requires interpretation is not what it might have or should have been. Indeed it is not what it *will* be once the process of interpretation is completed.

On the other hand, even granting the distance between this restricted and therapeutic view of interpretation and its modernist counterpart, Spinoza's conception of the *logic* of interpretation – its theory and presuppositions – subtly anticipates many of the issues and a number of the problems in much later elaborations of the theory of interpretation; these anticipations are important even where those later accounts (for example, in the current "reader-response" theorists or the "hermeneuticists") diverge sharply from Spinoza's own conception of what interpretation is and does. Certain philosophers are important for the difference they make historically to the developing thought of their successors, within philosophy or outside it; others endure as contemporaries, to be read for the continuing power of their own work, irrespective of disciples or of a posterity in schools. Spinoza's *Ethics* has often been viewed as a work of both these types; the *Tractatus*, with its immediate object the Bible and the practice of what we now patronizingly look back on as the literal-mindedness of "higher criticism," might seem exclusively an example of the former, and certainly it was *at least* that. For a society which had moved gingerly around a number of soundings of the same themes, Spinoza's confident learning and theoretical acuity made a startling and probably irreversible difference, and the echoes of his Biblical critique are very much present both in the Enlightenment and in the Romantic reaction to it in the nineteenth century.[3] I mean to suggest beyond this, however, that like the *Ethics*, the *Tractatus* also warrants reading as a contemporary text, now or whenever the question arises of what interpretation is and also, in fact, when the question does not arise – as a challenge to that omission.

This representation of the *Tractatus* as a modernist work presupposes that the role of the Bible in Spinoza's theory of interpretation should be understood as exemplary; his references to "Scripture," on *this* interpretation, stand instead for "scripture," and his richly detailed citations from the Bible have then to be construed as the particular means to a general theory. Spinoza himself nowhere explicitly states or recommends this displacement, but it is, I believe, implicit in the argument of the *Tractatus*; not only does the account of interpretation which Spinoza gives apply to other texts as it happens, but insofar as it holds for the Bible, it holds for other texts strictly and *a fortiori*. The Bible, in other words, is paradigmatic; the theory exemplified in his reading of *it* might apply to other texts even if it did not apply to the Bible – but if it does hold for the latter, with the unusual demands met there, it even more certainly holds when those exceptional conditions are absent.

Spinoza's conception of the Bible as a decisive test of his theory of interpretation comes into view as an implication of his continuing criticism in the *Tractatus* of the two theories of interpretation that were the principal alternatives to his own. The first alternative locates the key to Biblical interpretation in a source external to the Biblical text itself – mainly in the institutions and doctrine of religious authority. Spinoza's objection here, concisely put, is that interpretation requires reading before submission, not the other way round. The

second alternative which he rejects is the view of the Bible as trans-
parently clear for individual reading, in effect, as self-interpreting.
Consistently followed, this view leads to the literalist superstitions
which, in Spinoza's view, dominate the common, unreflective reading
of Scripture. (In the "Preface" to the *Tractatus* (p. 11), Spinoza asks
readers guilty of this tendency also to forego reading *his* book – a
warning evidently directed not only to them but to other readers as
well.)

Spinoza thus accepts the obligation of demonstrating the inadequacy of these alternatives – and also of demonstrating both that his own
account of interpretation avoids those difficulties and that there is no
alternative other than his own to the positions that he has shown to
be flawed. Unlike the first alternative, his theory argues that interpretation must set out from the object to be interpreted, not from an
external source; against the second alternative, he argues that the
process of interpretation, far from being immediate, requires a system
of inference and evidence which only then leads the interpreter to
meaning. Spinoza's objections to the alternative theories, and his
defense of his own, will be further discussed below; more important
for the moment is the question of what it is that is at stake in these
theories of interpretation. Here at least, he and his antagonists are in
agreement – since also for them the Bible serves as a test case. In each
of the alternative theories, too, if *any* text warrants interpretation
along the lines respectively prescribed, it is the Bible – and conversely,
if the Bible is open to such interpretation, any less problematic text
must be measured by the same standard. In no other text is it so clear
– on the first view – that an external authority, like the Church, is
both required and available; or (in the other view) that the text,
because of its own great power, would reveal itself immediately and
easily to the individual reader. (So, for example, Luther's statement
that "Scripture is through itself most certain, most easily accessible,
comprehensible, interpreting ittself, proving, judging all the words of
all men."[4]) Thus, insofar as objections undercut these two accounts
of Biblical interpretation; and since an alternative is available which
avoids those objections, then the alternative – Spinoza's – gains force
both as prescriptive for Biblical interpretation and as the basis of a
general theory. (The argument here has the form of a disjunctive
syllogism: (a v b) v c; ~ (a v b), therefore, c.) What the logical structure of the general theory is and how it turns, in Spinoza's view, into a
politics of interpretation are the larger questions to be addressed in
the discussion which follows here. Admittedly, these conclusions
move far afield from what starts out in the *Tractatus* as only one more

reading of a much-read text. But it is hardly surprising that Spinoza, instructing his reader on how to read the Bible, should also give the reader directions on how to read *him* – or that this in turn might grow into an analysis of reading itself.

To be sure, the theoretical claims of the *Tractatus* depend initially on Spinoza's exposition of *Biblical* meaning, and that exposition is extraordinary in its imaginative and detailed scrutiny both of the text and of its echoes in later sources. But if Spinoza's Biblical interpretation claims a place even in the rich tradition of Biblical commentary, his *conception* of interpretation is ground-breaking in a more basic sense still. With his thesis that "the whole knowledge of the Bible must be sought solely from itself," (p. 101), Spinoza formulates – discovers – a methodological thesis that had been absent from earlier accounts of interpretation, Biblical or not. It is not only that he here declares independence for the act of interpretation, but that with this declaration he also asserts a connection between practical interpretation and the theory of interpretation: interpretation is always embedded in a theory which must be argued in its own terms. Both the text and the medium by means of which it is comprehended are now contingent, within history. This is not the contradiction it might seem to be: the independence of interpretation is implied by a theory (namely, Spinoza's) – but the claim of an intrinsic connection between interpretation and its theory is itself part of the theory.

In introducing the latter condition, Spinoza by implication questions whether the two principal accounts of Biblical meaning which he criticizes are, strictly speaking, theories of interpretation at all. For where a text is transparent or self-interpreting, the reader can read, as it were, with his eyes closed: the text does the work for him. And where an external authority imposes an interpretation, the reader need only recognize that authority: he does not have to know (he is usually discouraged from knowing) much about its method, and the words of the authority carry so much weight that the reader might do better to read them than the text itself. The two alternatives, then, are, at most, boundary-cases of interpretive theory, and in this sense, the *Tractatus* not only prescribes for interpretation a logical form; it also proposes for it a declaration of independence, affirming interpretation as at once a science – rather than a conclusion of impression or intuition – and autonomous: not subject to other authority.

Spinoza thus clears a space for a conceptual and beyond that, for a social definition of interpretation. For the first time in the post-classical world, the question "*When* is interpretation?" becomes meaningful. This is, on one hand, a skeptical moment: even to raise that question – to recognize the act of interpretation – is already to presuppose the possibility of alternative interpretations; like the phenomenon of style, any one interpretation requires that there be more than one. But more importantly, on the other hand, it posits an *object* of interpretation – the meaning which a problematic surface at once conceals and provides evidence of, and which the "candid" reader (p. 118) whom Spinoza takes as an ideal, newly supplied now with the instrument of interpretation, can expect to reach and to know. The history of interpretation is thus also, we learn, the history of the concept of meaning.

These several elements of Spinoza's theory of interpretation coverge in effect on what I shall be referring to as the secularization or historicization of the text: the text, and then the process of interpretation based on it, and then the meaning derived which is based on *that*, are all viewed as historically contingent, as *possible* rather than necessary. This axiom in Spinoza's theory of intepretation – an axiom, in his view, for *all* theories of interpretation – is epitomized in the distinction Spinoza emphasizes between meaning and truth. The interpretation of a text, Spinoza insists – even of the Bible, and all the more so for other texts – depends not on the truth of the meaning disclosed by that process, but only on the recovery of meaning itself, irrespective of whether that meaning conforms to doctrine. Interpretation, in other words, need not – cannot – answer to authority.

Having established the methodological distinction between meaning and truth, Spinoza then moves to locate interpretation within the context of politics – a last step that brings the full sweep of his modernist turn into view. Having argued for the interpretive autonomy and contingency of the text, he now argues in the other direction, that this textual independence does not bring with it *social* autonomy. Quite the contrary, in fact, since the historicity of interpretation reveals interpretation as one contingent and social activity among others: like those others – like *every* public act – it thus requires a social or political warrant. The process of interpretation, in other words, presupposes a justification not only on logical grounds – that is, in terms of evidence and exposition – but also on social grounds – that is, in terms of its political possibility. Spinoza thus argues, on the one hand, for a textual purism in the process of interpretation; on the other hand, for a political definition of the context of interpretation. That these apparently conflicting impulses are consistent – more than this, that they are necessary to each other – is at the crux of Spinoza's account.

The Grounds of Interpretation

Spinoza's intention to search for meaning in the Bible "solely from [the Bible] itself" is emblematic of his effort to secularize Scripture[5] – to identify it as an historical object as it had previously been viewed, in accounts of its origins or meaning, as exempt from historical categories. This step of secularization is decisive for Spinoza's theory of interpretation; its consequences affect each step in the process of interpretation, from the first moment of inquiry to the last one of knowledge. Indeed, without this secularization, there would be no need or even possibility of interpretation, since textual meaning would then appear either as gratuitous or as imposed by an external authority – both of these quite independent of the text itself. With it, the very institution of religious authority which includes texts among its "subjects" is challenged; any authority now attributed to texts must be quite distinct from sources external to them. To be sure, even in this new setting, the Church may still go about the business of providing interpretations – but those must now be judged, like any others, without the "benefit of clergy". Once inside history, in fact, the process of interpreting Scripture is identical to that of interpreting other texts. We encounter in the former as in the latter the problem of the recovery of meaning – a problem which in Spinoza's account is itself defined as historical (and secular) since his theory of interpretation historicizes the method as well as the object of interpretation. Then, too, in this same sequence, the meaning which interpretation aims at is also shown to be historical – constituted, Spinoza proposes, by the combination of authorial intention and extra-authorial context at the moment when the text enters history, that is, when it is written.

This sequence of issues which lead up to a definition of textual meaning begins, however, with the need to establish the historicity of Scripture itself: meaning would not be contingent if the text were not – and conversely, if the text is contingent, meaning must be. The first step in this sequence is thus sufficiently important for his argument as a whole to lead Spinoza to make it the motif of the "Preface" and the opening chapters of the *Tractatus*; it recurs in later parts of the work as well. Given his emphasis on going "back to the text itself," it is evident that Spinoza would look mainly to the Bible for evidence of its own historicity; his strategy here depends on the construction of an enthymeme in which the (dangerous) conclusion of the historicity of Scripture is suppressed, to be drawn by the reader himself. The two premises of the argument are clear: the minor premise – the assertion that God is One – requires no discussion and would be accepted without question by Spinoza's readers. If it could then be demonstrated (for the major premise) that Scripture represented the work of more than one writer (whether in the role of author or editor), the conclusion to be drawn would be sufficiently obvious to go without saying: Scripture *could* not be exclusively the word or work of God. It would then follow that Scripture is scripture – located in history and open to the essentially historical process of interpretation.

The first requirement for this proof, then, is to show that more than one hand had been involved in the formation of the Bible – and it is worth noting (without putting too much weight on it) that at least some of the evidence used by Spinoza to prove plural authorship is, against his own prescriptions, not drawn from the Bible itself. In his discussion of miracles (chapter VI), for example, Spinoza mentions the inclination to superstition of many readers of Scripture (the "masses"); and he intends here not only to reiterate that much of the Biblical text was written *for* superstitious readers, but also to call attention to the plurality of interpretations given it by those readers. Even among interpreters who rely on external authority for interpretation, in fact, there is no concensus; authority also, it seems, moves in sometimes conflicting directions – and here again, Spinoza's conclusion is muted but clear. If even the religious conception of Scripture which assumes its single (and divine) authorship leads to diverse interpretations, then a theory of historical interpretation would be warranted on practical grounds alone – to adjudicate *those* differences. The discrepancies among these interpretations have to be confronted as if they were historical differences, since there is no other means of understanding – or interpreting – them. More to the point, the plurality of interpretations itself suggests the possibility of contradictory or at least of ambiguous meaning and then, beyond that, of an uncertain, if not necessarily plural authorship: could a text that was divinely inspired lead to conflicting interpretations? Such issues, although not in themselves conclusive, reinforce Spinoza's own suspicions; at the very least, they show that however authoritative the Biblical *text* is, there is no single authoritative *understanding* of it. There are only disagreements among professedly authoritative sources – that is, interpretations of textual meaning.

This symptomatic and to some extent external argument, however, is preliminary in Spinoza's account to the evidence of the plurality of voices disclosed in Scripture itself. On the one hand, Spinoza reminds his reader, "God has no particular style in speaking;" (p. 31) therefore, he concludes, since the Prophets *do* speak in different styles[6] – in language and tone, even (as between Samuel and Jeremiah, for example) in the doctrines they teach (p. 40) – we recognize the historicization of the words of the Prophets and thus the need for interpretation in order to discover the origins and purposes of those words; that is, to discover their meanings. The consistent patterns of these differences, moreover, indicate that prophecy is a function not of reason (which for Spinoza is one and universal), but of the imagination, which varies from person to person and is also inferior to reason.[7] The prophetic message, then, is not theoretical but moral or practical, and this explains the differences in "voice" among the Prophets: they address the particular contexts in which they find themselves. Insofar as God speaks through them, even He adapts Himself to the various conditions which surround them. Certain common themes do recur in their prophecies, but for the question of Biblical authorship, this is less important than the differences among them, and less important still than the *fact* of those differences. It is that fact, after all, which provides Spinoza with an unlikely starting point for a theory of interpretation.

The principal evidence for this starting point appears in the Biblical narrative itself. The traditional ascription of the single authorship of the "Five Books of Moses," Spinoza argues, is at odds with statements in the books themselves. (Spinoza's evidence here had, of course, been noted previously, in rabbinic as well as in secular commentary.) So, for example, we read there of Moses' death and his failure to reach the promised land; what stronger evidence than this could there be that the claim of *Moses'* authorship is doubtful? (p. 124) Such references, to be sure, might mean only that someone other than Moses had been the author (and indeed Spinoza inclines to the view of a single *editor*) – but Spinoza's purpose would be served here also by unsettling the tradition: Moses is not, after all, one among many "possibilities." Or again: Spinoza cites Abraham's reference (in Genesis XIV: 14) to the city of Dan – a name, according to the Bible itself, not given the city until after the much-later death of Joshua (p. 124). Spinoza adds a number of similar examples of anachronism and historical inconsistency; viewed cumulatively, these represent for him sufficient evidence for the conclusion that the Biblical text had been constituted by accretion and by the work of various hands, not by "monogenesis."

It might be objected here, to be sure, that where the role of God, even as indirect author, is at issue, arguments from diversity or even from inconsistency only beg the question. For if we ask if it is *possible* for a single divine author to have written a text which incorporates disparate points-of-view or which includes historical assertions which in conventional terms would be impossible, surely the answer here must be "yes." (A version of this apologia would appear in the later reaction of the Church to the alleged evidence of fossils for the question of creation: a God who created the world would surely be capable of creating fossils as part of it.) Spinoza does not, however, invoke the principle of God's omnipotence as an axiom of his theory of interpretation, not because he denies this (he does not), but because to invoke it in the context of reading is to deny not only the possibility but also the need for interpretation – and that, after all, is for Spinoza, a given.

For most texts, we do not have to consider, before undertaking to interpret them, whether they have the status of historical objects – but for the Bible, that probability had been consistently denied.[8] Spinoza's first argument in the *Tractatus*, then, is not part of his interpretation as such, but a condition for his theory of interpretation and indeed for all such theories – intended to establish their *possibility*. The evidence he adduces that the Bible is historical, that various hands had contributed to it and so *must* have acted historically, is thus presented as a methodological premise for his own Biblical interpretation and as a clue, more generally, for the theory of interpretation. And although it is true, as Strauss points out,[9] that Spinoza's argument here, strictly speaking, begs the question, the fact also remains that between his position and the alternative he is disputing, there is no arguing. All that Spinoza can do in criticizing the conception of Scripture as a single and ahistorical text is to show what additional consequences the reader who holds this view must accept – and this he surely does.

A second methodological premise that underlies Spinoza's theory of interpretation is the distinction between meaning and truth. This distinction is introduced in Spinoza's attack on Maimonides' theory of Biblical interpretation (Cf. especially chapter VII), but the failure to recognize the distinction is associated by Spinoza with virtually the entire tradition of religious commentary and interpretation, Christian as well as Jewish. The confusion against which the distinction is directed is, in Spinoza's view, quite fundamental: if the interpretation of Biblical meaning is required to conform to doctrines asserted independently of the Bible (that is, if we determine meaning only on the basis of what we already hold to be true), the interpretation arrived at in effect begs the question and is not, strictly speaking, an interpretation at all. Thus, "In order not to confound the meaning of a passage with its truth," Spinoza writes, "We must examine it solely by a reason that acknowledges no foundation but Scripture itself." (p. 101) Maimonides, in contrast, asserts that wherever a question arises about Biblical meaning, the interpretation to be assigned must at least avoid conflict with the truth as it has previously been defined; meaning thus depends not on the text but on truth ordained by an external authority and not itself part of the text. And this, Spinoza objects, is the way neither to meaning nor to truth. (We see in this objection here a version of a more general accusation of circularity against Biblical interpretation: "Everything in the Bible is true, because it is the word of God; we know that it is the word of God because the Bible says so . . .")

Among the examples which Spinoza cites as misbegotten by Maimonides' conflation of truth and meaning, one in particular stands out because of its more general implications for the theory of interpretation. This is Maimonides' defense, in chapter XXV of the *Guide*, of the doctrine of the creation (as opposed to the eternality) of the world. Maimonides' argument is that since the philosophical proofs (mainly Aristotle's) for or against the eternality of the world are inconclusive, *therefore* he will take the Biblical statements concerning the creation of the world as literally true – even though, if they were interpreted metaphorically (as he interprets many other Biblical statements), they are consistent with the doctrine of the world's eternality. Spinoza objects here that if Aristotle's proof of eternality had been compelling, Maimonides would then apparently have been willing to attribute *that* doctrine to the Bible by interpreting the Biblical statements about creation not literally but metaphorically (p. 115). Virtually *anything* could be demonstrated by this method of interpretation, as it is based on sources distinct from the Bible itself (and which are also, as it happens, themselves secular and historical). Maimonides in thus moving outside the text, makes a "candid" reading of the text impossible; so far as the process of interpretation is concerned, Maimonides' method is "harmful, useless, and absurd." (pp. 117–18) If meaning depends on truth, there seems little point in reading – or interpreting – at all: the conclusion is already known.

It should be noted that although the distinction between truth and meaning is thus methodologically fundamental for Spinoza's theory of interpretation, this does not prevent Spinoza from involving a conception of truth in his own interpretation. Indeed, he speaks of the method he employs as the "true method," requiring "only the aid of natural reason" (p. 113), and he is evidently appealing to the same standard of truth here that applies, in his view, to all reasoning. The criterion of truth adduced, moreover, applies not only to the conception of a method, but to the determination of particular meanings which follow from that method – but it is important to recognize that neither of these uses violates the distinction between meaning and truth. To argue in defense of a *method* is quite different from identifying the meaning of a text with "truths" external to it: the former enables interpretation to proceed; the latter is an a priori deduction that prevents interpretation.

Again, the two related methodological premises which Spinoza thus emphasizes – the historical status of Scripture and the distinction between meaning and truth – are preliminary to his own interpretation. But in arguing for them as conditions of Biblical interpretation, Spinoza also establishes them, I have suggested, as conditions for the theory of interpretation more generally. For one thing, it is at least arguable that even if *only* the Bible were held apart as outside history, the interpretation of other historical or secular texts (even those which ostensibly have nothing to do with religious doctrine) becomes problematic. Given the primacy of the ahistorical text, a condition of the interpretation of other texts would be their compatibility with – more precisely, their subordination to – Scripture. To this extent, the meaning and interpretation even of mundane texts would be dependent on Scripture; they would be freed from this only when Scripture itself was secularized. Furthermore, we know that it is not only *religious* authority that can impose itself on the process of interpretation – and a further implication of Spinoza's formulation of the meaning-truth distinction would be to reject the determination of textual meaning by the use of *any* external framework invoked as a key to interpretation. Insofar as a text is historical or contingent, so also will be its meaning; and this suggests that to impose on it categories of interpretation determined indpendently of the text may well be at odds with – or more simply, miss – the text itself. (This would, in more contemporary terms, argue against the imposition of ideological frameworks such as Marxism or psychoanalysis in the process of interpretation.)

Taken together, the two methodological conditions lead into the skeptical "moment" which for Spinoza evokes interpretation – Biblical or otherwise – in the first place. For as soon as the contingent status of the text is recognized, the possibility is also implied of alternate meanings – a possibility which in effect *asserts* the obscurity of the text even if there is no other evidence of it. And for the Biblical text, of course, there *is* ample other evidence. To be sure, not every text requires interpretation: a text *may* be clear and distinct. But the historicity of the text entails that the need for interpretation is always in principle possible – and thus that the fact of interpretation is always actual. For an ahistorical text, interpretation will always be gratuitous; for the historical or secular text, interpretation becomes inevitable. Thus, too, the question of what meaning is that interpretation aims at is always present.

The Recovery of Meaning

That Spinoza is less concerned with the "meaning of meaning" than with the logic of the theory of interpretation – in contrast to the opposite balance in twentieth-century writings about interpretation – is due largely to the problem that Spinoza initially faced of secularizing the text. One consequence of that starting point – and of his success in dealing with it – is that, for better as well as for worse, Spinoza is untroubled by the questions which later become central to the analysis of meaning. Thus, he moves quickly to locate the meaning that interpretation attempts to disclose in the "aim or intended aim of the author" (p. 111), and his reasoning here is forthright. Insofar as meaning is historical (and then, expressive), it is also the product of a human mind, most immediately the mind (and intention) of its author. This is not, it must be noted against potential objections (like that registered in "The Intentional Fallacy"[10]), a psychological thesis which presupposes impossible access to an author's mind. The aims or intentions that underlie meaning, including authorial meaning, are for Spinoza quite objective, to some extent external to the author himself. The determination of meaning involves a grasp of "what the time and occasion [of writing] demanded" – that is, the historical context of discourse. That context, moreover, includes reference to linguistic usage as well as to the more general social and historical conditions. Thus, Biblical interpretation presuppposes access to the language of the Bible and the "environment" (p. 103) in which the latter appeared, as well as to the lives of its authors and the "fate" of their writings – Spinoza's telling term for what is currently referred to as their "reception." Only when such information is assembled and complete is the text established as an object for interpretation. This stage is evidently still preliminary to the process of interpretation, although interpretation is also, in a sense, involved in *it*: the text to be interpreted must first be determined or established – the procedure designated in nineteenth-century Biblical criticism as the "lower criticism." For Spinoza's own examination of the Bible, this includes defining the meanings of terms taken from a sometimes archaic vocabulary, and also the specific determination in the Biblical text of its levels of discourse – for example, the differences between literal and metaphorical meaning (an issue whose significance had been recognized by even the earliest Biblical commentators, for example, Philo). Until these questions are resolved, the text is not ready *to be* interpreted (although it is evident that they are themselves tied into the process of interpretation).

The assembling of the historical data which constitutes the "aim or intended aim" of the author sets the stage, then, for the "act" of interpretation and the conception of meaning which is its goal. Meaning, placed in this framework, has two principal features which are apparently so self-evident in Spinoza's view that they require no argument. The first of these is that meaning is fixed temporally – more specifically, that it is fixed at one time, at the time of the writing (perhaps, more accurately, at the time of the "thinking" if that could be distinguished from the writing, but in any event no later than the writing.) The second feature is that meaning is objective: it is ingredient in the words of the text, as real as the words themselves, and thus also commonly and equally available to any interpreter. Spinoza does not ask whether interpretation would be impossible if meaning did not have these characteristics; he seems not to consider the possibility that meaning might *not* have them.

Where meaning occurs as so defined, then, it is in principle, if not always in practice, recoverable as objectively "there." The interpreter, in Spinoza's view, characteristically "looks for" (p. 100) or "seeks" (p. 128) or (as he succeeds) "perceives" (p. 101) the meaning of the text (*the* meaning) which is there to be discovered. For some texts, to be sure, or for some individual passages, there may be no meaning at all: contradictions or other types of obscurity are always possible, and the text in which they occur would to that extent be meaningless. There may, furthermore, be parts of a text which are unintelligible for historical reasons: words or phrases whose meanings have been lost, allusions that cannot be traced, and so on. In these cases, although meaning *exists*, it is not accessible – and for Spinoza this second source of unintelligibility joins the first one as applicable to certain parts of Scripture: "I do not hesitate to say that the true meaning of Scripture is in many places inexplicable, or at best mere guesswork." (p. 112) (For an interpretation to conclude that the meaning of the Bible was at certain points inaccessible would have been no less a threat for much of Spinoza's audience than the doctrine that he *does* find accessible there.)

A presumption of the objective and fixed meaning of a text (if there is meaning at all) is thus central to Spinoza's theory of interpretation; as objective and fixed, moreover, such meaning should be accessible by the same process employed by the understanding elsewhere. The comprehension of nature, in fact, affords a useful model of reason at work: " . . . The method of interpreting Scripture does not widely differ from the method of interpreting nature: – in fact, it is almost the same." (p. 99) The force of the analogy is soon made clear: like the interpreter of nature, the interpreter of Scripture is required to begin from and return to the object of interpretation for evidence and confirmation. Like the interpreter of nature, the interpreter of Scripture also proposes to infer from the object interpreted certain "fundamental principles." (p. 99) The aim of interpretation, then, like the aim of all science, is to move from the more immediate to the more intelligible, uncovering the general principles on which the particulars depend. For Spinoza, those principles – the common themes on which otherwise diverse statements converge – *constitute* textual meaning.

The view of the process of interpretation which is fostered by the analogy between the interpretation of nature and the interpretation of Scripture is useful not least because it explains why the conciseness of the "meaning" of Scripture (in Spinoza's version of that meaning) is assured by the method itself. Rigorous interpretation will lead the interpreter to the "fundamental principles" on which the other elements that appear in the text depend. It follows from this stipulation that the more fundamental the principles arrived at, the fewer and more comprehensive they will be. Ideally, then, from the point of view of the science of interpretation, there would be *one* such principle – and it is altogether consistent with this that Spinoza, notwithstanding the apparent multiplicity of "meanings" in Scripture, should conclude that "From the Bible itself we learn, without the slightest difficulty or ambiguity, that its cardinal precept is: To love God above all things, and one's neighbours as one's self." (p. 172)

The basis on which Spinoza justifies this conclusion makes still more explicit what he means by a "fundamental principle" of interpretation; for immediately after his statement of the principle, he adds: " . . . If the Bible had ever put forth a different doctine [than to 'love God,' etc.] it would have had to change the whole of its teaching. . . . The Bible would not be the work we have been examining, but something quite different." (p. 172) The principle, then – *any* such principle – must satisfy two requirements: first, that it be consistent with whatever else appears in the text (not that it should entail everything else, only that it should not be controverted by anything else); and second, that if it were altered, everything else in the Bible that follows from it doctrinally would also have to be changed. (Spinoza's emphasis here reappears in such formulations as Frye's: "The first postulate . . . [in the study of literature] is the same as that of any science: the assumption of total coherence."[11] In satisfying these conditions, meaning becomes an axis around which the text revolves; meaning comes to represent in effect the "intention" of the text, and Spinoza almost seems here to shift the "aim or intended aim" that he initially located in the author to the text as a whole. What is presupposed or entailed by the principle(s) that constitute meaning is itself also part of that meaning, although it is not likely to be as concise: "As this cornerstone ["To love God above all things . . . "] is intact, we must perforce admit the same of whatever other passages are indisputably dependent on it, as for instance, that a God exists, that he foresees all things, that He is almighty, that by His decrees the good prosper and the wicked come to naught, and finally, that our salvation depends solely on his Grace." (pp. 172–3)

To be sure, the adequacy of Spinoza's *specific* interpretation of Biblical meaning must be judged apart from the statements of his method or theory of interpretation – including in the latter even his first stipulation that "the meaning of Scripture is only made plain through Scripture itself." (p. 117) It might be further objected that the interpretation of the Bible which concludes with the brief "principles" cited above reflects more on that specific text than on Spinoza's conception of interpretation, and indeed Spinoza explicitly asserts that the knowledge (or meaning) conveyed by the Bible is minimal. It may seem ironic that Spinoza's theory of interpretation should be founded on a text whose main purpose is *not* to provide "meaning," a text in which "doctrines are very few and very simple . . . for we know that Scripture does not aim at importing scientific knowledge" (p. 176) But this only reinforces the sense that he is presenting here a general method of interpretation: it is no reflection on the method used to determine meaning if it shows, in a particular case, that meaning is minimal or even absent. In any event, this objection is a textual version of an *ad hominem* argument (*ad librum?*); the crucial question is whether Spinoza fairly applies his own method, not whether the method had been cut to fit (or distort) the text. One thing that is quite unmistakable about the Bible for Spinoza is its status as *requiring* interpretation; only where there is unclarity is interpretation necessary – and for Spinoza, as for the rationalist tradition more generally, unclarity is most likely to occur in writing that is highly figurative, emotive, or prescriptive, that is, in writing that is non-cognitive. It is just such writing that, in Spinoza's view, mainly constitutes the Biblical text.

With the exception of one last step – into the *politics* of interpretation – the sequence so far outlined completes the theory of interpretation which had begun with the methodological requirements of secularizing the text and establishing the distinction between meaning and truth. These conditions are then joined to a conception of meaning and finally to a method of interpretation by which meaning is arrived at. For reasons that have been pointed out, these elements not only comprise Spinoza's own theory of interpretation, but also disclose his view of what is involved in *any* theory of interpretation. They thus represent a theory of theories of interpretation – again, quite aside from the particular interpretation of the Bible that is taken as exemplary.

This further, still more abstract implication makes it all the more notable that Spinoza's theory of interpretation which depends entirely on the condition of secularizing the Biblical text, finally concludes by demonstrating that the Bible may *yet* be sacred. The sense in which the Bible may prove to be sacred although *also* secular is closely tied to the earlier distinction in the theory of interpretation between meaning and truth. Here, too, the criterion depends on consequences or use: "Words gain their meaning solely from their usage and if they are arranged according to their accepted signification so as to move those who read them to devotion, they will become sacred . . . . From this it follows that nothing is in itself absolutely sacred, or profane, or unclean, apart from the mind." (p. 167)[12] A claim for the Bible as sacred, then, can be warranted neither by reference to its origins (of which we may know little more than what, circularly, the Bible itself tells us) nor because Biblical "meaning" is intrinsically sacred (since there is, on Spinoza's account, nothing intrinsic – sacred or otherwise – about meaning), but by its consequences, as the text evokes a response of piety. The test that "By their fruits shall you know them," thus turns out, in Spinoza's view, to be applicable first to the Bible itself.

Spinoza's conception of a "sacred text" has significant consequences for the traditional status of such texts which had been accorded that status on the basis of their alleged origins outside of history. The shift to the consequences of such texts means, for one thing, that in principle any text, whatever its origins, may turn out to be sacred. Obviously, then, there may be more than one such text; furthermore, texts that are judged to be sacred have this status only contingently:

since history or use determines that status, the status itself may change as history or use do.

Spinoza's theory of interpretation may appear now, and to some extent, even in his own time, to be quite conventional. His "organic" conception of the text and of interpretive meaning, with its emphasis on the properties of unity and coherence, had been indicated first by Aristotle in the *Poetics* and the *Rhetoric* (and even earlier, although less systematically, by Plato); *after* he wrote, it was carried to extremes that Spinoza himself could hardly have imagined, as in the metaphors of nineteen-century Romanticism which found itself claiming the rationalist Spinoza as one of its forebears. More recently still, the conception of textual meaning as objective and temporally fixed (linked to authorial intention and historical circumstance) has, post-modernly, been challenged as ideologically naive. Indeed even the traditions most directly indebted to Spinoza's theory of interpretation, for example, the "higher criticism" of the nineteenth-century, begin to move towards a position opposed to Spinoza's, that is, towards a justification for subjective criticism. For Spinoza himself, it is clear, no "hermeneutic circle" would impede or diffuse the recovery of objective meaning; whatever the practical difficulties of establishing meaning, they do not, in Spinoza's view, lead (as Schliermacher, for example, was to conclude) to an "infinity" of the elements of meaning with the implication this carries that interpretation is never conclusive. (For Schleiermacher, the postulate of infinite evidence implies that interpretation, no matter how much it succeeds, must also fail: there will always be something more to be interpreted.)[13] By contrast, the possibility of knowledge for rationalist epistemologies is real and constant, and so, too, the prospect of historical and thus of interpretive knowledge is constant and actual for Spinoza. Interpretations can, of course, be mistaken – but this very possibility testifies to the objectivity of meaning: without such objectivity, mistakes could not occur.

In these respects, again, Spinoza's account of interpretation may now seem passé, too reasonable to be true. Yet there are other sides of Spinoza's theory of interpretation which cannot be patronized in this way. It is not only that what now appears as a largely conservative theory of interpretation and meaning was in its original appearance radical – but that certain aspects of what made it radical at the time, beyond its critique of the tradition of Biblical reading, continue to claim that role for it now as well. Spinoza located the occasion of Biblical interpretation in the same skeptical moment presupposed in the interpretation of obviously secular texts. With his denial of the privileged position of the Bible and Biblical commentary, Spinoza thus also posed a challenge to the role of all authority in interpretation; he thus – then and now – set the requirements for a general theory of interpretation, something that could not even begin to be done so long as the "proof-text" of the theory of interpretation had itself been exempted.

There remains one last feature of Spinoza's theory which is only intimated in what has been said so far; this is his view of the "politics of interpretation." Spinoza's theory of interpretation, I have suggested, began in reaction against a traditional view of the theory of interpretation in which the authority for interpretation came from a source outside the text. That view of interpretation, Spinoza demonstrates in the first part of the *Tractatus*, is inadequate even on non-political terms; the text itself defies any interpretation from authority. But the relation between politics and interpretation is not itself dissolved with this objection; the connection between the two is in fact intrinsic, and this is attested by a structure underlying the several other layers of his theory of interpretation. The denial of *one* version of the politics of interpretation – for example, that meaning depends on an external authority – is not a denial of the political commitments of interpretation; it means only that a more adequate politics must be identified – since finally, in Spinoza's view, interpretation as such entails a politics. It may seem odd that Spinoza should postpone this sweeping conclusion until he has outlined what might by itself seem a full theory of interpretation – but in terms of the theory itself, this becomes less odd or mysterious. Let us first, his strategy here goes, show that (and how) interpretation is possible logically and what it entails structurally; *then* we can see what the practice of interpretation, interpretation in motion, requires as it touches on other activities or practices, including, most basically, the politics in which it is set. The latter connection, again, is intrinsic, since *any* kind of practice in the world of the interpreter implies such a connection – for the interpreter himself and for the act of interpretation. For interpretation, then, politics is inevitable: the question confronting any theory of interpretation is not whether it *has* a politics, but what its politics are.

The Politics of Text and Understanding

The deferral so far in this account of the topic of the politics of interpretation mirrors a similar deferral in the *Tractatus* itself. Spinoza moves through 15 chapters (of the 20 in the book) before he raises the question of what relation there is between the politics and the theology which are so matter-of-factly joined in the work's title. When the question *is* introduced, moreover, it appears abruptly, following immediately the apparently unrelated discussion in chapter XV of the relation between theology and reason, and beginning, furthermore, with the most fundamental issue in political theory (that is, in chapter XVI, "Of the Foundations of a State ... ") In effect, then, we find here a second starting point of the *Tractatus*; if a bridge exists between the five chapters which comprise this last "part" of the *Tractatus* and the first and larger section, it will emerge from the juxtaposition of the two parts rather than from any explicit statement of method made in either of the parts.[14] And indeed this *is* what we now find, together with an even stronger assertion that what is at stake in the *Tractatus* is a general theory of interpretation. As the political theory that Spinoza outlines is a *general* theory of the relation of the state to the individual, it is not only Biblical interpretation that appears as requiring a definition of political authority, but the process of interpretation as such.

To be sure, Spinoza, in his discussion of politics, does refer to Biblical politics in particular – but the analogy between this and his earlier discussion of Biblical interpretation further underscores their common implication in a general theory. Just as Spinoza had argued that a precondition of Biblical interpretation was that the text had to be secularized or historicized, made independent of religious authority, so, too, it is necessary for him to show that the Biblical politics – and thus the social context in which the Bible had traditionally been interpreted – no longer holds, for if it continued to hold, this would itself be an argument against the autonomy of the text. It is important, then, that none of the different stages that Spinoza identifies in the history of Biblical political organization, ranging from what he takes to have been the democratic covenant between God and the Jewish people at Sinai to the theocracy of the Kings in the Divided Kingdom – should be found to be still binding even on the Jews, let alone on anyone else. Thus, anticipating Locke's refutation in the *Two Treatises on Government* of the hereditary rights of kings, Spinoza argues that whatever claims the Biblical forms of government may once have had no longer hold; the chain of inheritance has been broken, and the terms of the original agreements are thus dissolved. He thus purports to block appeals to the continuity of Jewish religious authority as a basis for Biblical interpretation involving sources other than the Biblical text itself. The eventual decline of the theocracy of the Kings of Judah and Israel did not occur accidentally, he suggests, but unavoidably – because of an internal conflict that would eventually doom *any* theocracy. When the commitments of political and religious authority are conflated, they act only to undermine each other – and the main purpose of Spinoza's politics of interpretation is to prevent or to deny this conflation.

A parallel – and in terms of his own position, more pertinent – objection is directed by Spinoza against any argument for continuity that might be based on the democratic agreement which he associates with the covenant established at Sinai. Since Spinoza himself will be proposing a democratic politics of interpretation, it is crucial that he should be able to demonstrate a discontinuity between that form of government in the Biblical past and any agreement or covenant it might lead to in the present. His argument here is quite explicit: in leaving Egypt, the Hebrews also left behind the laws that bound them to the state there; they thus entered (or re-entered) the "state of nature" (p. 219) and were then free to accept the covenant at Sinai. Acting "as in a democracy, all surrendered their rights equally . . . all were equally bound by the covenant . . . [and] all had an exactly equaly share in the government." (p. 222) But *this* democratic covenant turned into a theocracy after Moses' death (the covenant had been made with him as God's representative) – and with his death, its initial legitimacy could no longer provide a warrant for its continuing authority. The state that had been brought into existence by the original covenant was thus dissolved; in order for it to be revived, the parties to the covenant – including, of course, God – would once again have to give their consent.

The claim for continuity in Biblical political authority is thus rejected by Spinoza for much the same reason that he also denied the framework of religious authority for interpretation. Like the interpretation of texts, the analysis of political structures must start from the facts themselves – and thus from *their* beginning. Thus, chapter XV (on "The Foundations of a State . . . ") begins with a compressed account of the concepts of human nature and natural right which are presupposed in all political theory (Spinoza's account of the former closely resembles that of the *Ethics*). On this account, the individual is the unit on which social existence and the state depend, and for the individual – whether inside or outside the state – his *conatus* or will determines the direction he moves in: " . . . It is the sovereign law and right of nature that each individual should endeavour to preserve itself as it is, without regard to anything but itself. . . . The natural right of the individual man is thus determined, not by sound reason, but by desire and power." (pp. 200–01) Political forms of authority that encroach on this "right" of the individual can be empowered, then, only with the consent of the individual. This anticipation of the Social Contract theory is, for Spinoza, a requirement for legitimate political organization: "In this manner, a society can be formed without any violation of natural right, and the covenant can always be strictly kept – that is, if each individual hands over the whole of his power to the body politic.... A body politic of this kind is called a Democracy...."(p. 205)

To be sure, the suggestion here that the citizen hands over "the *whole* of his power" to the state argues for an apparently non-democratic imbalance of power between the state and the individual – an imbalance evidently at odds with the classical liberal conception of natural rights as inalienable. Spinoza seems in this sense, moreover, to promise little protection for a politics of interpretation or indeed for almost all other political freedom. The extent of the sovereign's authority is further extended insofar as the sovereign is entitled to assume as his right everything not explicitly denied him in the agreement by which he holds power. It is not, moreover, for the individual citizen to decide which of the laws promulgated by the sovereign are to be obeyed. (If citizens could decide this, "the rights of the state would be dependent on everyman's judgment and passions." (p. 212) – a conclusion which for Spinoza amounts to a *reductio ad absurdum*.) This conception of legal sovereignty and power is in ways more extreme even than that of Hobbes: within the state, no less than outside it, the individual has only as much "right" as he has power. Thus even if self-preservation should require disobeying the law, the individual has only as much right to this as he has the power to act on it, and he obtains this power either by the inability of the state to enforce *its* will, or by having earlier made provision for such exceptions (in which case, they would, strictly speaking, be legal). In this sense, then, *anything* that a sovereign does may be said to have been willed by the citizenry: "For if they [the citizens] had wished to retain any rights for themselves, they ought to have taken precautions for its defense and preservation; *as they have not done so...*" (p. 205; emphasis added) What the citizenry have not tried to do or what they have tried to do but failed to, implies consent to whatever is enacted at the moment.

This conception of political authority may seem to promise no more protection to interpretation than what the personal inclinations of the ruler amount to. But it is also at this point that Spinoza introduces a distinction that stands at the basis of his "politics of interpretation." For the sovereign has power (and right) over the domain of *actions* – and interpretation takes place not in the domain of action, but in the domain of thought. Interpretation stands with respect to texts as thinking stands with respect to all human actions or commitments – and external authority of *any* kind, according to Spinoza, can thus claim no more hold on interpretation than it can on thinking itself. Since, as Spinoza postulates, there can be only as much political right as there is power; and since no one can have the power to coerce thinking (or interpretation), the right to interpretation is and remains a right of the individual. Whatever the authority of the sovereign, it can "never prevent men from forming judgments according to their intellect." (p. 258) Moreover, since no one – including governments – should attempt to do what cannot be done, political authority must allow the individual citizen the freedom of thought and interpretation which he would assert for himself anyway. As rights do for Spinoza elsewhere in his ethics and metaphysics, political right also follows fact.

Spinoza did not need to be told, of course, that rulers, political systems and social structures (e.g., the Church) may attempt to control thought and interpretation. But such attempts have consistently failed and the reason for this is quite fundamental. Since "Every man's understanding is his own" (p. 251) – and Spinoza goes even further than this, risking his rationalist credentials: "Brains are as diverse as palettes" – any attempt to impose understanding is *bound* to fail. Obviously, Spinoza is not claiming here that the sovereign may not attempt to do this; the sovereign would, moreover, be quite within his rights in doing so, since he is entitled "to treat as enemies all men whose opinons do not, on all subjects, entirely coincide with his own . . . ." (p. 258) But the attempt to control opinion, Spinoza contends, is bound to fail – and if only because of this, it would also work against the government's own interests. Coercion of this sort is in fact less likely to assure consensus or to enhance the sovereign's power than it is to cause people to be "daily thinking one thing and saying another, to the corruption of good faith, that mainstay of government, and to the fostering of hateful flattery and perfidy, whence spring stratagems, and the corruption of every good art." (p. 261) The means of coercion in this context are self-defeating; they "only succeed in surrounding their victims with an appearance of martyrdom, and raise feelings of pity and revenge rather than of terror." (p. 265)

The claims that the state may be justified in suppressing or punishing opinion and yet would find it impractical – in some sense, then, wrong – to do so may seem at odds with Spinoza's commitment to the principle that "ought implies can." But this potential inconsistency is also resolved by his conception of interpretation as it is intertwined with his political theory. On the one hand, Spinoza argues, the sovereign gains authority from his contractual agreement (whether "willingly or under compulsion" (p. 204)) with the individual citizen. On the other hand, the sovereign has good reason (although, again, no obligation) for not exercising his authority in such a way as to diminish it – for example, by bringing it into conflict with the wills or ideas of the members of the society which he cannot control. The state and the sovereign, in fact, are not concerned with meaning or interpretation or truth – but with action; political structures thus assume a "non-cognitive" role analogous to that earlier ascribed by Spinoza to religious doctrine. As religious prescriptions are necessary for the conduct of a community, so other, more obviously "secular" instruments are required by the state in the conduct of *its* affairs; it thus becomes a secular analogue of religion. In neither of these is truth or understanding a central factor; *that* remains always and finally within the domain of the individual, determined by his capacity for the light of reason – which he possesses by virtue not of political or religious authority, but by nature. The just sovereign will thus also be the prudent sovereign, allowing freedom of thought – and interpretation – that he could at best only attempt to control, and always, on Spinoza's account, at his cost.

This restriction of the domain of interpretation to the individual mind obviously is not meant to be a defense of interpretive anarchy (any more than Spinoza would offer a defense of political anarchy). Spinoza's view, as has been mentioned above, is closer to the other end of the political spectrum. The sovereign, again, has the right to do as he wishes and is able to; but the legitimacy of this power extends only to the *actions* of his subjects, not to their thoughts which remain always, inalienably, with the individual. " . . . The individual justly cedes the right of free action, but not of free reason and judgment." (p. 259) The sovereign, then, who wishes at once to maintain sovereignty and to govern "without any violation of natural right," accords to his subjects the freedom of thought and opinion – the same freedom which Spinoza himself had exercised in the *Tractatus*. Any such act not only takes place within a political framework; it is itself political, in part because it presupposes a political warrant, but more importantly, because the political presuppositions are implied in the interpretive structure: to be *able* to interpret freely is a function on the one hand, of politics, on the other hand, of reason itself. The particular political structure involved or stipulated – like any particular theory of interpretation – may vary; but the fact of the relation between the two is constant. Where there is interpretation, there is politics – and one has only to reflect, from our own vantage point, on the contemporary array of theories of interpretation – leading in one direction to the anarchic skepticism of deconstruction; in the other, to the authoritarian determinism of formalism – to see how closely intertwined with them are conceptions of political structure. A theory of interpretation which locates its source of authority in intuition will be committed to a politics of intuition as well. So, too, a theory of interpretation – like Spinoza's – which implies autonomy for the text and for the reader will be necessarily tied to a politics in which "candid reading" is possible, that is, where the text can be read in its own terms.

It might be objected here that Spinoza's own position, far from politicizing interpretation, seems in fact to insulate it from politics because in the end, interpretation is intended for him to be immune to obtrusion from the outside. It is clear, moreover, that the sharp distinction that Spinoza draws between thought and action is open to dispute. Modern totalitarianism has provided harsh evidence that state-power may extend beyond the control of its citizens' actions to their thoughts as well; the Stoic version of rationalism on which Spinoza bases his model of the individual mind asserting itself against external force is, if not refuted, certainly held up to question by political and technological developments which Spinoza (and the Stoics) could have had no inkling of.

But the relation between politics and interpretation cuts below these objections, and we see this in the contrast between Spinoza's political commitments and the two principal alternatives to it – the same ones that Spinoza had reacted against initially, at the level of the text. The first of these would assign the power of thought and interpretation to a supra-individual or corporate body – a version of the hierarchy exemplified for him in the Church (and which appears now in the varieties of totalitarianism). The second alternative is that of a revelatory or self-disclosing text which requires no intermediary process or interpreter. In the first of these there is only politics and no interpretation: the text itself has disappeared. In the second, there is no politics and only interpretation. On Spinoza's account, the process of interpretation implies a political structure; it is itself iconic with that structure – and this is the case, in Spinoza's terms, not only because of his particular views of politics and interpretation, but as exemplary of the intrinsic relation between them. Even when interpretation (as it is for Spinoza) is a "public" act, it is a function only of the individual mind, for the conception assumed here of the individual is political. And if this is the case for the privacy of interpretation, it would hold *a fortiori* for conceptions of interpretation which involve other members of the social context.

Here too, then, Spinoza's view of Biblical interpretation is exemplary of a more general connection between interpretation and politics. The principal theories of interpretation which Spinoza rejected had denied their political identities; this denial enabled them to claim that in some privileged sense, they were not interpretations at all. Once the first of these denials is shown to be false, however, we know also that the second is also false.

Spinoza thus makes a case for the politics of interpretation not only as it happens, but as inevitable. This means that the question to be asked of any theory of interpretation is not whether it has political presuppositions and consequences, but what they are. Modernism insists on, even takes for granted, the centrality of interpretation, not only for texts, but for epistemology and ontology as well; it does this to an extent that Spinoza could hardly have anticipated and that, certainly in its postmodernist version, he undoubtedly would have disputed. To be sure, some of these most recent formulations – from the deep heremeneutics of Heidegger to the poststructuralist claims of liberation (from author and from text) – agree with Spinoza in viewing interpretation as autonomous and thus as independent of external framework of meaning. This new autonomy, however, is a shadow of its earlier Spinozistic self – since its protest against external sources leads it also to deny to interpretation even an *internal* structure. Interpretation here becomes anything you make it – a condition not very far removed from the immaculate conception of texts and from the corresponding assumption of political anarchy that are both (and for the same reason) rejected by Spinoza.[15] From a starting point in which interpretation is entirely subordinate to the social institutions of power, we now, postmodernly, face a prospect in which interpretation is not only detached from the historical and thus from the political context, but self-sufficient (even, as things turn out, when there is no self). And here Spinoza has, I believe, a continuing lesson to teach: that as politics without interpretation will be blind, interpretation without politics must be empty. The world which the postmodernists describe, where interpretation is itself both subject and agent, may be artful and enticing in every detail; it only does not happen to be the world we inhabit. Among the other necessities imposed on that world, we find the necessity of interpretation; we also find – not because of that necessity, but in addition to it – the *possibility* of interpretation. In this sense, modernism may also be sufficient to the postmodern day. And Spinoza was radical enough in his break with the past to know this, not only about his present but about the future and our present as well.

Notes to Chapter Eleven

1   Translated as *A Theologico-Political Treatise*, by R. H. M. Elwes. (New York: Dover Publications, 1951 (1883)).

2   Edwin Curley suggests that Spinoza might have authorized publication of the *Tractatus* prior to that of the nearly-completed *Ethics* in order to "prepare the way" for the latter. (See *Collected Works of Spinoza* (Vol. 1), edited and translated by Edwin Curely (Princeton: Princeton University Press, 1985), p. 350.) The fact that the *Ethics* was published posthumously (and so far as Spinoza could know, might not have been published at all) seems to count against this view; it is unlikely, in any event, given Spinoza's frequently expressed distrust of "mass" readers, that he would have been more concerned about the reception of the *Ethics* than about that of the *Tractatus*.

3   See, for example, Arthur Hertzberg, *The French Enlightenment and the Jews* (New York: Columbia University Press, 1965), pp. 29–46, and Julius Guttman, *Dat U-Madah* (Jerusalem: Magnes Press, 1953), p. 223 ff..

4   Cited in Hans Frei, *The Eclipse of Biblical Narrative* (New Haven: Yale University Press, 1974), p. 19. Consider also Luther's statement, "The Holy Spirit is the plainest writer and speaker in heaven and earth," which Frank Kermode reacts against in "The Plain Sense of Things," in Geoffrey H. Hartman and Sanford Budick, eds, *Midrash and Literature* (New Haven: Yale University Press, 1986).

5   In referring to the Bible or Scripture, Spinoza includes both the "Old" and "New" Testaments, but his principal emphasis, both for examples and for criticism, is on the former. This has led some commentators to view the *Tractatus* as using the issue of interpretation as the means for an attack on Judaism (see e.g., Emanuel Levinas, *Difficile Liberté* (Paris: Albin Michel, 1976), p. 144) – although Leo Strauss argues against that conclusion (*Spinoza's Critique of Religion* (New York: Schocken, 1965), pp. 19–20.)

6   Acknowledgement of this had long been part of the interpretive tradition, extending at least as far back as Maimonides. See Alexander Altmann, "Ars Rhetorica as Reflected in Some Jewish Figures in the Italian Renaissance," in *Essays in Jewish Intellectual History* (Hanover, New Hampshire: University Press of New England, 1981), p. 101.

7   Cf. in elaboration of this point Shlomo Pines, "Spinoza's Tractatus Theologico-Politicus and the Jewish Philosophical Tradition," in I. Twersky and B. Septimus, eds, *Jewish Thought in the Seventeenth Century* (Cambridge, Massachusetts: Harvard University Press, 1987), p. 501.

8   Michael Fishbane calls attention to the fact that numerous examples appear *within* the Bible of "free" (what I have been calling contingent or historical) interpretation. (See "Inner Biblical Exegesis," in Hartman and Budick, *op. cit.*) This, if anything, underscores the persistence of the dominant tradition of "non-free" interpretation of the Bible as a whole which Spinoza criticizes.

9   Leo Strauss, *op. cit.*, pp. 123, 143.

10 See William K. Winsatt, *The Verbal Icon* (Lexington: University of Kentucky Press, 1956).

11 Northrop Frye, *Anatomy of Criticism* (Princeton: Princeton University Press, 1957), p. 16.

12 The connection asserted by Spinoza between meaning and use will be familiar to twentieth-century readers of certain versions of pragmatism, operationalism, and positivism. (For a summary of these views, see William Alston, "Meaning and Use," *Philosophy Quarterly* XIII (1963), pp. 107–24.)

13 See Fr D. E. Schliermacher, "The Hermeneutics: Outline of the 1819 Lectures," translated by Jan Wojcik and Roland Haas, *New Literary History*, IX (1978), p. 14.

14 Spinoza does assert a connection more explicitly elsewhere (see *Ethics*, Part IV, Proposition XXXVII, Scholia 1 and 2), but those brief statements do not provide a full basis for – and in certain respects seem at odds with – the conjunction in the *Tractatus*.

15 Consider the distance between Spinoza's view of the role of interpretation and that, for example, of Harold Bloom, when he asserts that "... there are *no* texts, but only interpretations." and "words ... refer *only* to other words." ("The Breaking of Form," in Harold Bloom, *et al.*, *Deconstruction and Criticism* (New York: Seabury, 1979) pp. 7, 9 (emphasis original). So, for example, Spinoza, after conceding that "words are a part of the imagination": "... It is not to be doubted that words, as much as the imagination, can be the cause of many and great errors, unless we are very wary of them." (*The Emendation of the Intellect*, translated by Edwin Curley, *op. cit.*, p. 38). For Bloom, by contrast, there is no basis on which to *be* wary.

12

The Praxis of Criticism

"How do I get to Carnegie Hall?" the stranger asked.
"Praxis, baby, praxis," the native replied.

When Hegel announced its death, he predicted that art would be survived first by religion and then by philosophy. He did not even mention criticism, and although history may yet live out the terms of this prophecy, the odds are not promising. The artists, it seems – certainly the artists of writing: the poet, dramatist, novelist – may indeed soon live only underground, invisible except for traces that require great expertise to identify; perhaps, like the Lamed-Vavniks, responsible through their selfless labors for keeping the rest of us alive and sane, but never known to us, not even discovered to themselves. But the critic, he who used to live in the Cloak of Humility, in the modest role of Handmaiden – an appurtenance, a reflection, a critic always *of* somebody or something – bestirs himself now, and finds an audience reading every move.

The turn, it seems, came with a discovery arrived at through an invalid but quite practical syllogism:

Premise 1: Art criticism is about art. (By definition)
Premise 2: Art is about art. (Cf., e.g., the Russian Formalists, the Abstract Expressionists, the Structuralists, the Poststructuralists, the Deconstructionists, *The Anxiety of Influence*, etc..)

Conclusion: Therefore criticism is also art.
(Things about the same thing can't be far apart themselves.)

The logic is troublesome, of course, but we can hardly fault history for choosing cunning when the alternative is consistency. In any event, reasons may be good even when they are not sufficient, and those are what I am after here. How has criticism come so to celebrate itself? Are its new claims possible in addition to being actual? The story is worth the telling, because even if it turns out to change nothing in the life of criticism (we can probably count on this), it may still affect the understanding with which criticism sports, plays, but cannot do without. Ours.

A Tale of Two

Since criticism has put little of itself into a body, we should not be surprised that it wears so many faces. The term, originally meant for "judgment," invites equivocation: Do we expect from it a verdict? An interpretation? Simply a reaction, *any* reaction? Each of these definitions, and others, has been suggested; no single motif runs through them. For example: one response to what is placed before us, one manner of judgment, is to see, and then to say, how it is made – more specifically, how it is well made. The technological impulse here has a legislative, even a moral tone, adding the attraction of taboos to the promise of order. Mainly cookbooks now deploy this manner of judgment, which served Aristotle, however, in a recipe for tragedy. There is, in any event, no ready way to elide this one purpose with that other one of appreciation, where criticism proposes to reveal to feeling the circle formed by the parallel lines of a text; or with that other, still more speculative one, which sets out, on formal grounds, the possibilities and impossibilities of literary genre. And there is no need to, either; only the housekeeper who insists that the way to keep a room clean is not to use it would tidy criticism up by telling it what tasks it should not set itself.

Still, as reality has joints for the carving (so Plato arranged the menu), we ought to have our plates ready. All the more so, since in the criticism familiar to us, reality and appearance in its conclusions are so difficult to tell apart that the test we finally have to rely on, after logic and argument have had their way, is the unhappy one of indigestion: some judgments just will not go down. As well fail to locate formal differences in the immediate variety of criticism, however, we can attempt to see what more latent purposes that variety turns out to serve. And here, the matter is simpler, not historically (since in their own version of the state of nature, the functions of criticism compete with each other and encroach in disorderly fashion), but conceptually, where two alternatives are logical complements: we find the process of criticism either an end in itself or as a means to some other end.

We might, in other words, first assume that critical judgment, as intentional, has the purposes it says it has. But seen close up, those purposes turn out to be more than the saying admits, with boundaries so blurred that we can hardly tell how many, let alone where: explicative criticism, interpretive criticism, evaluative criticism, and so on. To find an order here requires that we move up a logical step, asking how to characterize the variety itself; and then a two-fold division appears, at a point on which logic and history (for once) agree. Given the existence of criticism, there could be no other forms – and there *have been* these: to one side, criticism as instrument, a means merely, serving a further and so, one supposes, a higher end; to the other side, criticism and an end in itself, staking out, asserting its own claims. I speak briefly of these two together before speaking of each singly; it is not only their differences but what they have in common that will later evoke an alternative theory of criticism as *praxis*.

Like the history of slavery of which it is part, the idea of criticism as a means, or subordination, has formal variations within what at first glance is only a single and brute theme. For one example: the tradition here defers to the text as master – in its religious appearances, as Master; and as commentary surely is a critical genre, Biblical commentary takes life from the ideal of an absolute text where meaning is a function of every gesture of the text. (That each Hebrew letter is also a number makes this ideal more plausible – but was it not the idea of the absolute text, making every gesture "count," that preceded this too?) The potency of both meaning and its commentator is viewed here as inexhaustible – for the one, because of the infinite reach of its source; for the other, in the commentator's dependence on that source. The authority of the text in this version of critical subordination originally attests only to the power of its Author; but by a nifty move of Shamanism the authority of the Text survives even when its author, unsettled by the skeptical looks around him, begins to fail. His power, it turns out, is transferable (more, perhaps, an argument for than against the Author's grandiose claims; was it only an accident that the commandment against idolatry did not proscribe that one most extraordinary graven image – the written word?). Thus, as desacralization eats away at the spirit and inner life of the Church, the authority of its relics – of the past and its texts (the past itself becoming a text) – increases. So the viewer is surprised, in Titian's painting, to learn that the figure with clothes is Profane Love and the figure without them is Sacred – and so the Renaissance assumes the humanistic mission of reconstructing texts, of paring away the interpolations, notes, doodlings, absentmindedness of the scribes and clerks who had been keepers of the authorized presence and who had taken so seriously the claims of incorporeality by that presence that they would not believe that its own words could be a violation.

The purpose of this modern scourging was purity, quite in the ritual sense. Plato's meaning (even Plato himself) is there in the text. But to reach it (and him) means to erase the marks of hands that have touched it, to authenticate the text – preferably, because less hermetically, by extra-textual means. So histories are traced, the search is on for the provenance of manuscripts, biography comes to life – all the proto-versions of fingerprinting and carbon – 14 dating that later appeared as instruments of the same process of identification. The critic whose work turns into this process is not even obliged to read, still less to understand, the text he submits to. He has only to prepare and serve it; the consuming comes later, at other hands. It is always a mystery, with such habits, why critics know as much as they do – as much a mystery, that is, as why cooks tend to be fat.

Criticism as subordinate has not yet discovered a nonlinguistic medium, a distinctive, impersonal guise which, like any other uniform, would mark it as servant, the member of an order; but it aspires to this goal. Like the first rule of the physician, "Do no harm," the first maxim for criticism in this role is "Don't block the view." The second maxim (and there are only the two) is the refrain of Goethe dying: "More light, more light." Only so, we understand, is the object to be perceived – and that, for criticism in this office of servant, is to be. The light itself is not supposed to be part of the view – an intense, even masochistic expression of humility on the part of the agent. It is the *object* of vision, the text, that wants attention; the critic has only to make it – more precisely, to leave it – visible.

We should be in no hurry to believe that the rush of political liberals or religious antinomians has made obsolete the role of the critic as dependent on the *nomos*, the law of the text. The Lower and Higher Criticisms of the nineteenth century left much textual reconstruction to be done and other to be redone (there is no limit to *that*, after all); the innovations of science have provided formulae, technological devices, and a spirit which substantially increase the means of criticism as an instrument. If we ask, in fact, why critical formalism should now be in vogue when form itself is so abused in the culture, part of the answer undoubtedly lies there: form is most readily available as a means. The American "New Criticism," now itself a relic, gave good value to this disposition. Intention was false to the text, affect was false, paraphrase was heretical: there was only the object to be served, the text itself. The formulas of irony, paradox, tension – a critical do-it-yourself kit – were intended as much to get the critic out of the reader's way as to provide literary toeholds. Such self-abnegation may not have been as noticeable in the New Critics as they supposed (their own names, after all – Tate, Ransom, Brooks – endure, and not only as titles). But their readings were devout even when they were not consistent: criticism must serve art; what the critic asserts is not meant to survive by itself; the original text is the thing – complex, meaningful, complete, real. Criticism, reflected from these features, is a medium, to be read *through* (in the way that glass is seen through).

The passion represented historically in this ideal of discourse as transparent may seem greater even than the allure of the original *object* of criticism. But noncritics as well are familiar with that preference for talking about somebody or -thing even when, by a slight shift in direction, the body or thing might have been addressed directly. It is the role of voyeur that the reader chooses here – perhaps, as Barthes supposes, part of the pleasure in reading *any* text, but doubled, if that is so, for the performances of criticism where we read someone else's reading of a text. The pleasures of suspicion, distance, even dominance (what pleasures, after all, would the voyeur have if he knew *he* was being watched?) begin to assert themselves here, to separate off; the reader, then the critic, begin to think of themselves. So the slave, even the slave who has been willing, finds the will taking on a life of its own, claiming the role of master. We may think of a medium as passive – but we may not, in that, be thinking the idea that the medium has of itself. And thus we find intimated the second view of criticism, in which the ideal of transparency and the role of servant give way to claims of authority, to self-assertion – a declaration of independence by words themselves.

Here, too, there is a history – in part, the history of commonsense, which is often only the recounting of brute necessity. For how, we ask (not yet referring to an actual history), *could* the critic be invisible even if he wanted to be? The critical display takes up space, its words take time. Where the words of an original source are supposed to matter, can talk about those words escape calling attention to the talk, to its own means? Can a text be read aside from *all* contexts?

The critic himself, after all, adds history to what he sees (his own history, for starters). And although his audience might well deserve some indemnity for collaborating with the critic, it would hardly be reasonable to expect or even to invite the critic to jump out of his skin.

Such questions have been repressed by the ideology they dispute, but they keep turning up nonetheless. They were most clearly on view in the historical parallel between the decline of authority and the greening of a self-conscious self propelled forward in the seventeenth century. Should we identify a point, for reference at least, in Descartes' dreams? That moment is already overdetermined, but no matter: not only the irony that the master of reasons, of clarity and distinctness, discovers his method by way of a dream touches us, but the fact that he becomes master *in* the dream. He thus challenges the longstanding subordination of the dreamer to external source: for Joseph and his brothers; for Socrates, appealing on his last morning to a dream, in order to call his disciples beyond the incapacity which a lifetime of teaching has failed to cure. The dream is traditionally a form of commentary, a subordination – but then, in Descartes, we find the dream asserting itself, asking rather than giving deference, a reality on which the waking experience turns out to be commentary, not the other way round, "I dream, therefore I am," Descartes could have argued – since his thinking, too, might have been dreamt, and would remain thinking nonetheless.

Descartes did not dream of Matthew Arnold; there is no reason why he should have. But for this second version of criticism, because language more than reason is his medium and because he rarely doubted either what he was talking about or what he said about it, Arnold appears historically as the preface to an ideal. Criticism in the Victorian age, where everything that language can name is also assumed to have a proper place – metaphysical etiquette – is the means by which we place ourselves in the world. Speaking about what things are is very important for their *being* what they are; and not only, then, does criticism move up to the very boundaries of art, art itself turns out to be a function of criticism. What matters in literature is thus also, whatever else it is, criticism; one could hardly require a stronger reason for deferring to criticism as an end rather than as a means, for attempting to look to it rather than through it. "Is it true," Arnold asks, "that all time given to writing critiques on the works of others would be much better employed if it were given to original composition? Is it true that Johnson had better have gone on producing more *Irenes* instead of writing his *Lives of the Poets*? . . . "

And although Arnold's denial of those possibilities is admittedly equivocal, the very question he asks clears a space that such writers as Ruskin and Pater then occupy with no equivocation at all. So Pater, for example, at once absorbing and parodying Arnold, brings the critic into full view: "The first step towards seeing one's object as it really is, is to know one's impression as it really is. . . ." The form of prose and not only that of poetry, Pater argues in his essay on style, compromises art – and how then could the prose of criticism be left out? The object itself when not viewed is unknowable; it is the view, *our* view, which always and unremittingly occupies us.

This impulse toward authority for criticism comes, moreover, from art as well as from the critic (who might be suspected in such claims of serving himself rather than art). The tradition here is if anything older than criticism itself, for in assuming criticism as a natural kind, we easily forget that if art had left it no space, criticism, historically, might never have begun. So, for example, commentaries on Homer seem obtrusions or at best redundant: Auerbach, writing about Odysseus' scar, intimates that had the Homeric style endured, interpretation need never have come into existence at all. But style did not stay constant (would there even *be* style if there were only One Style?). Turning inward, speaking more about itself and less about the world, art begins to pose and soon to leave over questions. Responding, commentary takes on body – and then, obeying the law of conservation (of energy? of inertia?), the body acts to preserve itself.

The differences between the two views of criticism,[1] then, are firm, not historically, perhaps, where the lines of distinction rarely are clear, but conceptually. What is at issue between these ideas? Do they contradict each other – or is their evident disagreement mainly verbal or stipulative? Is the dialectic they combine to make – mammoth, incessant as it has been – the history of discourse or reason itself? The language we summon with such questions is metaphysics, however disguised – for in it we speculate about how certain fundamental structures, the "beings" of art, have anything to do with criticism. And the place to confront that general question seems then to be first with one of the two views we have been discussing, and then with the other.

Aesthetic Distance: The Myth of Immaculate Conception

The eighteenth century is the age of the encyclopedia, and of the ideas which had to be born in order to make an encyclopedia possible, one of them was the possibility of putting the objects of knowledge at a distance, constructing frames which focus, and thus celebrate, confirm, the viewer's field of vision: an order is disclosed not only in or among the objects, but *of* them as well. Museums are also encyclopedias, moreover, laid out in space rather than time, more explicitly than books putting frames to work: insulating the divisions between objects, making arrangements of and between artists or periods or topics, putting up nameplates (names themselves being an early version of the frame). The first impulse for museums admittedly seems to have been rather different, but not inconsistently so. The ruler of empire must have a place to store his acquisitions and, still more important, to show that he has acquired them. So Napoleon becomes himself a treasure of the Louvre; Catherine the Great, of the Hermitage; the Mellons (kings of Oil and Aluminum), of the National Gallery in Washington. But what is first meant to impress by sheer mass and force also invites an order of some kind for the storing. And then distinctions appear which have to do with the character of the objects rather than with accumulation, as though the original un-sorted heap, imitating the life around it, had decided to differentiate itself, to stake out an identity.

The original impulse – indeed, all sense of origins – is soon blocked in the museum which, after we once cut through the pieties about honoring the past, turns out to recognize only the present (more like conquering the past). Just as the intentions of the frame quickly re-place an initial character of intensification – inclusion – with the quali-ties of detachment – exclusion – so seriality or history in the museum turns into a single and large present tense. Objects in the museum, originally intended for specific and varied settings, move into the setting which is a denial of settings. And what then do we know of the objects in the museum? Only that they are marked off, separated from others of their own kind and, all the more, from others of different kinds. Their value? For one, their uniqueness, their individuality. (Not only do we name *them*, we insist on the names of their makers. Forgeries are the one form of subversion feared by museums, since if they were easily and convincingly made, museums with their "origin-als" would be nothing but warehouses. Even a version of Angst is understandable as the condition of museums and their keepers – the consciousness that good forgeries are those that hang undetected.) We assume that there is no way of replicating them, not even of produc-ing others like them in spirit but different in detail. Nor, furthermore, because they are separated in this way, can we measure them by practical standards of use or profit: what they do, what they make, even what they make of the viewer. It is a world apart – and so the frame which starts off quite modestly circling around, embellishing an object, ends egocentrically, pointing to itself. (Narcissus might indeed have been beautiful – but that fact by itself would not have told his story.)

So goes the only slightly mythic account of the origins of the "Museum Theory of Art" – less mythic as an account, in any event, than what the theory asserts. Kant lived immaculately, but hardly, we suppose, in his origins – and why should we credit more to his theories that to what he was unwilling to keep out of them? Yet this is the ideal to which criticism-as-subordinate looks: seeing as fragmentary, incomplete, dependent – opposed in each of these respects to the *object* of criticism which is complete, autonomous, removed from need and consequence, untouched by history, by intention or by consequence. "Ohne Zweck," Kant says about aesthetic judgment "without purpose" – stepping off the distance between that experience and the critical revisions or practical extensions of it, which like almost everything else man does, everything now except the sheer, self-contained aesthetic pleasure, becomes *all* "Zweck." What are the metaphysical features of the objects of aesthetic judgment? For one thing, their remoteness, their difference from others, as though they could *only* be defined negatively, by what they are not, a negative ontology. For a second thing, their willingness (in anyone else, this would be called desire) to give themselves away – insulation, frames, and all. The viewer has only to strike a posture, present himself to art in a clear show of disinterest – and art must respond. Admittedly, in answering this fastidious invitation, it turns out to have not much to show, but it cannot be faulted for holding anything back. The distance, then, is everything, the means by which the object steps outside history, outside measurement: it alone tells us what it is. That is why criticism not only can afford to be transparent, mere light, but *must* be: it is the object that is supposed to sparkle, not the critic. When the critic aspires to a character that is more than transparent, he becomes an obstruction.

An extended family of ideas is related to this theme of subordination in criticism. So, for example, *Organic Form* – that biological metaphor which first assumes the literal perfection of nature: everything in its place, to change one feature is to change them all, all surrounded, made coherent, by an impermeable membrane (an aid, surely, in immaculate conception). This sense both of necessary connection and of completeness nourishes the status of criticism as subordinate, since the critic, reflecting on the unities of art, can hardly expect to maintain them, let alone to extend the circle of their unities to his own words. Art and criticism as subordination are thus brought together, joined by Organic Form, but ironically; they are made for each other in the way that unequals (social classes, numbers) often combine to constitute what looks like a whole, but is in fact only a set of differences.

Or again: *Faculty Psychology*, the distinctive aesthetic faculty, in particular, also known as Intuition, the Aesthetic Sense. Disengagement, after all, disinterest, is hardly the first or most evident among human impulses: we see this in the characteristics themselves, since "engagement," "interest" must, we suppose, logically precede them. So we then reify capacities to make room for another one, for a form of address which denies the first ones, moves beyond them, making a virtue out of the lack of necessity (of art). Thus a faculty of aesthetic judgment or sensibility is set up; and criticism in its role-as-instrument, even though it mediates for art, must find a different place for itself; the only real difference, when we are talking about faculties, is between one faculty and another – and this means that whatever criticism is, it is not art.

Fiction and nonfiction. The Greek myths were not, we may believe, myths for the Greeks. Only at first true and then, slowly, false. But that is a different difference from the one between fiction and nonfiction, where nonfiction may be either true or false and fiction would be – neither? Both? Something more? Something less? Is *poetry* fiction? But it is too personal, too committed in its claims. Is *drama* fiction? But it is too impersonal, makes too abstract a claim. The truth of the matter is that with the distinction between fiction and nonfiction we hope to aestheticize truth altogether; fiction has nothing to do with fact, and nonfiction thinks of truth as bits of information.[2] It is fair enough, then, that fiction should come to suggest decoration, baubles, the novel as it connotes novelty, diversion, romance – the tint of scandal, the hint of a second and mysterious presence. Life, "real" life offers no such possibilities: the distances are always too short.

The intention of each of these designs is to leave intentions behind, to assume the otherworldly character which frames exemplify in themselves. Practical purpose, desire, even theorizing, abstract thinking, are if not menial, certainly mundane. Only when we move beyond them, infusing each moment with the possibility of a Sabbath outside worldly time, does man come alive, free. Those moments, art provides. Criticism, then, another mundane task, can only serve; it paves the roads that mark the distance. The language is different (ordinary); the direction is different (away from itself); the purpose is different (mainly, that there *is* one). Art is real, and criticism is only approximate; art speaks for itself, and the voice of criticism speaks only for the other. Does art in this view have parents? A lineage? Does it impinge on the history of the reader or even invite his attendance? Does it bear any other imprint of human touch? So, in adding up the answers "No," we find ourselves reinventing the immaculate conception.

Derrida Overriden (Or: How Original Is Original Sin?)

It requires strong will and brute force to preserve the naiveté and sweet innocence in this idea of a text which both speaks and then interprets its own words – the same power which Fundamentalists ascribe to the Bible (even for them, after all, that is the one text for which this is true). What, after all, could words be which had no history? Even the *concept* of a text has a beginning (and probably, in the future, also an end). Sentences, we know, exist in a time that periods and commas mark, and words themselves are flesh, body; no medium that they comprise could ever be quite transparent, give itself away. And this holds as well for the other elements ingredient in words: alphabets, phonemes, the mechanical apparatus, even the shape of writing, con-texts. So long as criticism is discursive, there can be no escape from these conditions – and although it may not be clear to what extent such features obtrude on the idea of criticism as invisible, ancillary, there can be little question that barring a constant miracle, they do in fact obtrude.

For the last hundred, post-Hegelian years, a group of writers have, in a variety of languages and idioms, been making exactly this claim; they come together in as fine a point as we are likely ever to be impaled on in the words of Derrida – using his name now metonymically, even beyond what he himself recommends for authors' names, to cover a range of his own writings and those of a group with affinities to him.[3] The diet here is rich: if Berkeley's tarwater could nourish the astringencies of British empiricism, Derrida must concentrate on creams and sauces, where the taste is for blending, for nuance, for the sustaining power of the soupçon (so Heller speaks of the nineteenth- and twentieth-century "philosophers of suspicion").[4]

Exactly that traditional concept of the text which has been described, with its frames, class hierarchy, authoritarian claims, is the starting place of Derrida's thought, what he reacts against. The spaces that purportedly divide history or experience or writing as a series of texts, marked off from one another by enough distance to allow each of them to observe the others, to parse them, turn out for Derrida at each step to be only new occasions, breeding grounds, for myth, ideology. Criticism in the large becomes mythic insofar as it poses as representational, claiming a pristine object on which it – openly not pristine – reflects.

No, when Derrida thinks of texts, he thinks rather of The Text (as Heidegger insists on Being and World rather than on beings and a world: so the acquisitive impulse for "Das Kapital" overcomes older linguistic and social antagonisms). We think of *that*, textuality, in parts or pieces only if our thinking about it was fragmented to begin with; there is no way of establishing boundaries for discourse, because the space of reflection or consciousness required to mark them off is itself part of the artifact. We may not know exactly why a particular construction (like the myth of aesthetic distance itself) should have been made – but we know something better: why *all* constructions, including that one, are made. And the reason is precisely the opposite of detachment or disinterest, much more in the line of an unresting *conatus*, a common will: to power or at least to pleasure and feeling.

No text, or the reflection or consciousness in which it starts, is for Derrida more rarefied or transparent than its object: every occasion of discourse, every moment is assertive, opaque, "thick." And thus, although the sum of such moments, at some mythic latter day, may be imagined to constitute a whole (Derrida is uneasy with this prospect, perhaps because he will not be there to see what he so long, with such self-denial, postponed), there is in any event no completion or detachment before then. Expression and representation make an inevitable mark, a differ*a*nce in what they express or represent – so Derrida anticipates the alteration by spelling *difference* with a difference (we shall surely hear someday about the influence of the Beatles on French thought). Thus, texts which are purportedly about other texts turn out in the end (which comes immediately) to be mainly about themselves (if, this is, they are about anything at all).

Derrida stands at an extreme in asserting this position which also has been stated here in extreme form (he is, it must be said, more radical a proponent than a practitioner; he writes about many historical figures – Plato, Husserl, Condillac – deferentially [*e*, not *a*] and lucidly). But although Derrida's account is extreme, parts of the conception of criticism (finally, of reading) which he maintains are not isolated or unique in the history of criticism. I have mentioned the quite different figures of Arnold, Ruskin, and Pater, and their claims for the hegemony of criticism; variations on that theme occur, sometimes argued, sometimes tacitly, in critics as diverse as Johnson and Lukacs, Dryden and Trilling. These writers share a moral, finally a metaphysical, premise in their conceptions of criticism: namely, that since the critic, and what he relates literature to, share the life that literature has as its subject, criticism is itself literature, and the critic, an artist. The generic distinctions between the two expressive forms, even the fact that viewed as literature, criticism seems a peculiarly hybrid and ill-formed genre as compared, say, to the poem or the novel – these finally make little difference, since what sets any genre off is the fact of its alien character rather than *what* is alien about it.

I do not mean to suggest by these parallels that Derrida is the bearer of a tradition. In addition to his distrust of the very concept of tradition, he would have a specific objection to being identified even with this tradition which is in some obvious ways close to him – not because its indictment of the notion of the pristine text is misplaced but because the indictment is not radical enough. Arnold, for example, defending the critic's role, still promises for the critic (and *his* readers) a view of the object "as it really is"; Lukacs, acknowledging the literary significance of criticism, still views its characteristic appearance in the essay as a "preliminary" to (we assume) something else. But for Derrida, even these modest vestiges of the logocentrism of philosophical realism must be shed as well. It is too much to hold that a text, in addition to speaking with its own voice, may also defer to another; the self-assertiveness must be everything, the only thing. Derrida, with Heidegger, fondly recalls the death of metaphysics. Think, for example, of the traditional concept of substance, what underwrites the definition of things in the world – and realize that what this substance presupposes in the way of form or definition is itself the merest of fictions: there *are* no forms to be grasped. The hardworking mill of logocentrism – in Plato, in Aristotle – found its grist in mistaking grammar for metaphysics, in a power of the imagination which did not recognize itself as imaginative. The very idea of reason as dominant or even as isolable in human nature is also a fiction: consciousness or reason are effects, traces, the detritus of will. Thus, it is not only that man lacks the capacity to detach reason from the will, to see or to know without motive – but that there is nothing, no thing, to see or to reason about: no nature, no natures, not even real fragments, which, after all, are themselves entities. As Kant's version of the Copernican Revolution shifted the design of philosophy from ontology to epistemology, from the question of what there is to the question of how we can know what there is, Derrida gives the Revolution one more turn, from epistemology to aesthesiology: from how we can know, to the question of what is left to experience when knowledge is cut out of it. (The next step, of course – not very far off – must be anesthesiology.) The several faculties of mind devised to support the naiveté of aesthetic distance are replaced by one: the capacity for pleasure which is itself a function – more literally, a symptom, of the will.

The two great moral influences on Derrida, it comes as no surprise, are Nietzsche and Freud. Together with them, he looks for the "Happy Science" that, once and for all, will not only assert that metaphysics is dead but will by its own example make that claim good. But is this in fact what we find in Derrida? Only if we agree that continuity is metaphysically less charged than discreteness; only if we agree that the concept of the One is coherent and without presupposition while the concept of the Many is not; only if we agree that the cure for naiveté (like a belief in the immaculate conception) is the abyss of Original Sin.

Upending the Mean (i.e., Praxis Makes Perfect)

The temptation is strong to take an economic view of the two ideas of criticism that have appeared here – to split the difference. And this is in fact a way that has been taken. The ideal of subordination – Biblical and classical commentary, formal and formulaic criticism – has, despite itself, left traces of elaboration, new texts to be added to the old: Maimonides on the Torah, Aquinas on Aristotle; Leavis on Lawrence, Wimsatt on Johnson. The weights on the first side of these balances may not equal those on the second, but there is no question that they exist, and a similar balance appears in the other critical ideal which had hoped to elide the written past with the writing present. We recognize the past here not only as translated into the present but for itself as well. Arnold's critical ideal – to "see the object as it really is" – may be question-begging, but his nostalgia for the object is real enough; and to read Arnold on Byron, or later, Trilling on Arnold, *is* to look backward at their objects, as well as around, at the critic himself. So the liberal imagination does better, certainly *more*, than it had promised.

But this mood of compromise in practice has no counerpart in its principles, which, as between the two views of criticism, oppose each other by precept and not only by inclination. This theoretical antinomy is a division which must, I believe, be overcome if criticism is itself to be coherent. As in any antinomy, resolution will not come here by finding one or the other of the opposing principles false, or by finding the whole to be a contradiction, but by discovering a ground on which the two conflicting claims are together intelligible as well as separately true. For *of course* we read criticism becuase of the importance of the objects about which it speaks; and *of course* we turn to criticism for the sensibility and thought of its own authors. A conception of criticism on which one or the other of these findings is implausible is itself, prima facie, defective. The problem, then, is to devise a structure that can house them both.

Such a structure is available in a view of criticism as *praxis* or doing,[5] in contrast to the concept of *poiesis* or making, which is, I should claim, responsible for the appearance of contradiction in the Antinomy of Criticism. The *poiesis–praxis* distinction is recognizably Aristotelian, although the account given it here is in its central thesis at odds with Aristotle's; namely, that art – more specifically litera-ture, including criticism – is to be understood as *praxis* rather than as either the product or process of *poiesis*. Three parts of the concept of *poiesis* in particular drive the antinomy, and it is their contradictor-ies in the concept of *praxis* which, I propose, resolve it.

1   *The Ahistoricity of the object.* The object of *poiesis* – what is made – is set apart from both its maker and from the context of its making – and also, consequently, from its audience or critics. Histor-ical origins may be invoked as a means of explaining or understand-ing it, but those origins are always subordinate to the later appear-ances of the object which are significant instrumentally, either for producing certain practical effects or for realizing a special quality of experience. The maker himself is detached from what is made; the object has no continuing or internal consequence for him.

2   *The lack of deliberation.* Poiesis excludes deliberation, that is, the use of general principles in the choice of means – the principles themselves subject to revision in light of the choice itself. *Poiesis* appeals to two alternative procedures in avoiding the one of delibera-tion: the particular may be seen as an instance of general rules (so, the cookbook reading of Aristotle's *Poetics*); or, no general rules may be held to apply at all (*poiesis* here looks to genius or inspiration as a source). Deliberation contributes, in opposition to either of these, the continuing presence for the act of criticism of the "doer": as doer, the critic is as contingent as are his choices, and he is, in fact, contingent *on* them.

3   *The discreteness of meaning and evaluation.* The things made by *poiesis* are fixed at a moment. Since they are also solutions to a

problem, they are judged as realizing that goal or failing to do so, and the critic's judgment here, like the success or failure itself, is attached to the moment, the problem *to be* solved. It turns out, to be sure, that both the problem and the solution are, in this view, given to the critic by the literary work itself. And as those works are individuals, separate from others, so the judgments and interpretations of them will also be.

These three features of *poiesis* are especially noticeable in the appearance of criticism as subordination. In contrast to the viewer with his dependene, the object, on that account, is self-contained; everything it requires – whether as a poem or a table – it provides for itself. Designed to serve an end – pleasure, usefulness – there is no reason why if that end could be otherwise realized – by an illusion or deception, by substitution, even by removal of the purpose – the object made could not be forgone. (This argument applies also to criticism itself.) To make something, in this sense, is to dissociate both maker and user (or viewer) from the object. Maker and user are each essentially complete without the object; they may be touched, but they are not altered by changes in its status. The role of the critic is to enable, to provide for a consummation: he serves the object (like a waiter at table). The critical process, furthermore, although an activity, is in another sense passive: the object meets certain standards or not; the critic may make do *with* it, but he cannot make *it* do anything not first suggested by the object itself. And finally, the object does not endure for the viewer beyond the encounter itself except as memory (or perhaps desire, but in any case, not as present and contingent). All of these presuppositions we have seen exemplified in the conception – the immaculate conception – of criticism as subordinate.

On the other hand, the ideology of *poiesis* is broader even than the role of criticism as subordinate, and we see this quite clearly in Derrida precisely *because* of the sweep of his attack on criticism in that role. Like the account which he indicts, Derrida's account presupposes a disjunction: either knowledge – and thus criticism, as a form of knowing – must, like its objects, be clear and distinct, or it cedes any claim as knowledge (so, we might say, the dream of Descartes is still dreamt). The idea of criticism as subordinate commits itself to the first term of this disjunction: insofar as critical judgment is clear and transparent, it reveals the equally clear and distinct outlines of its objects. It is thus mimetic, representational. Derrida rejects this argument with the counterclaim that critical judgment, *all* judgment, is opaque. But in then concluding that criticism fails as knowledge, he accepts the original disjunction: a candidate for knowledge must be clear and distinct, or it has no claim to the title. Thus only the fact that there is *no* knowledge in this sense prevents criticism from qualifying; the objection has nothing to do with the criterion. What passes as knowledge in criticism turns out for Derrida to be, like other knowledge, a function of the will that prizes clarity and distinctness as it does anything else – from an interest, a *self*-interest, in the object rather than in truth.

This view is aestheticization in precisely the sense ascribed above to *poiesis*. In it, the consummation of action alone matters, directed to a "consumer" interested only in acting *on* the object involved. The relation involves no past or context other than that of immediacy – no integration of subject and object (because they belong to different orders), no mingling in a common project (not because they have nothing in common, but because there is no project). Where *poiesis* more traditionally presents itself as one activity of several open to man, one in which he is capable of making a mark that then, by dissociation, becomes a monument for him and of him. Derrida's reaction only extends this view to define man *himself* as *poiesis: he* is the object made, his *own* monument.

To this view, criticism which sees itself and its objects as aspects of *praxis* stands exactly opposed. The critic who addresses the literary text (more generally, the work of art) as a doing or action rather than a making, shapes his own work to fit: both the object and the critical judgment on it thus become "performances". *Praxis* implies a continuing relation between agent and action: the action is intelligible only insofar as intention and consequence appear as parts of it; the doer is himself judged in terms of what he "does". Thus, history is integral both to the work of art and to the critical process; nothing in either of them is intelligible apart from it. Because *praxis* involves deliberation, furthermore, its conclusions are both assertive and evaluative; and those qualities, too, rub off both on the work of art and on critical judgment. In the sense that action is always an embodiment of the agent, so the work of art too becomes a personification; it is thus distinguished not only from involuntary or chance acts but also from the larger class of actions regarded as independent of their origins. Intentions are significant in these actions, as the language if not the theory of criticism has always known; that the intentions appear mainly as intentions of the work of art rather than of the artist only defers the question of the relevance of origins. No *specific* history (for example, the artist's) may be presupposed for understanding a literary work, but that is far from denying the significance of all or any history. Thus, the presuppositions of *praxis* – the continuous articulation of a self, the internal relation between subject and object, the idea of creation as itself a process – openly dominate critical discourse in the same way that, before that, they dominate the process of art. The work of art, in other words, is itself subordinate, and so, by that fact, is the work of criticism.

The shift from *poiesis* to *praxis* also has implications in "applied" criticism where the general principles cited are visible and testable. I have, for example, spoken of *praxis* as involving assertion and evaluation – both of them denied by *poiesis* with its emphasis in critical judgment on a "science" of sensibility or will. It requires no very subtle notion of assertion, in fact, to see its presence in the work of art. "The very form of a literary work," Trilling suggests, "is in itself an idea" – and surely some, if not all of the burden of proof falls on the denial of this claim, to show what either ideas or literary works could be when this affinity is denied. Again, a constant issue for criticism as *poiesis* has been the admissibility of moral criteria to the judgment of art: the latter seems diminished without them, but incoherent with them. No such incongruity occurs, however, if the structures of art are intrinsically, and not only in the eye of the beholder, related to moral action. A fictional penumbra surrounds the concepts of character and of person in general; this is only slightly denser when the moral concepts by which we address them are applied to art and to the work of criticism.

Poiesis also has difficulties in explaining historical change in critical interpretation and evaluation. Insofar as the work of art is taken to be ahistorical, its significance should be accessible at a moment, even at the first moment; it follows from the same premises, moreover, that, like judgment, critical categories are closed. But it is clear that critical consciousness, even of the individual critic, *does* evolve; critical categories contrived long after the original "fact" of the work of art may yet be apposite. This would not be surprising (indeed it is entailed) in the conception of art or criticism as *praxis*, since the consequences of *praxis* are integral to the doing: those consequences can be estimated when they are still incomplete, even at an early point; but all such judgment is defeasible. (So the maxim cited by Aristotle in the *Ethics*, "Call no man happy before he is dead," applies to art as *praxis*: call no art happy – or beautiful – before history is over.) This same challenge to the ideal of organic forms also makes sense of the history of criticism as a history, where the alternative is an artificial consistency – high fiction – of inclusions and exclusions, produced from the standpoint of a mythical "ideal" observer. The latter alternative simply denies basic characteristics of the artistic medium. Like the political conceptions of Utopia, art on this account is assumed to involve completeness, irrefragability; as with the other ideal and its exemplifications, art never lives up to this one – and it is clear that art often has not even attempted to.

I do not, with these comments, mean to suggest that the ideal of criticism as *praxis* is new, but only that it has often been denied and still more frequently, obscured. Some of the adherents to that ideal have been named: Trilling, Arnold, Pater; and others might be added: F.R. Leavis, Burke, Howe. The strong differences among these critics would itself refute any claim for an orthodoxy, but the features of *praxis* that I have cited are important elements in the work of each of them. There is also one group of critics who *as a group* have significantly represented the concept of *praxis*. I refer here to the tradition of Marxist criticism which, as in Lukac's work on the historical novel, in Goldmann's work on Racine, in Benjamin's work on the "mechanical reproduction" of art, has established a major and recognizable point of critical view. With so many critics at work, with such various practical results, often at cross-purposes to the ideologies professed, nominalism is an understandable temptation: it may seem more than enough to undertand and judge them and their work individually. But there *are* generic distinctions within criticism itself – and why should we mince words here? Whatever novel or important words can be said about the history or logic of linguistic forms, the interrelation of genres, the migration of literary symbols, the psychological sources or corollaries of criticism, the science of literature – all of the central promises of recent critical theory – nothing in these statements makes sense without the understanding of art and then of criticism as social action and gesture, as an awareness of history and *its* facts. This holds true for the critic's conception of him no less than for his conception of what he is a critic of. Few of us escape dreams of life as Robinson Crusoe – of difference, of removal, or shrugging free from history. But no more, more certainly, can we escape.

Non-nonviolent Criticism: Breaking into the Text

The tradition of criticism as *poiesis* holds to an ideal of nonviolence: in it, the critic's main concern is to avoid violating what is there – for criticism as subordinate, out of deference to the object; for criticism as autonomous, for *amour-propre*. Measured by these principles, criticism as *praxis* is non-nonviolent criticism: its role is *precisely* to obtrude into the work. The critic, and indeed as the critic personifies the act of reading, all readers, "force" the work – not by imposing criteria or understanding, but by hitting upon the opening which the work leaves and leaves necessarily, notwithstanding the gestures it makes toward closure. It is as if *praxis* were founded on a principle of incompleteness, an artistic version of Godel's theorem: there is always a gap in the text, a requirement for an added presence in the person and grasp of the reader. The physical boundaries of the literary text are thus misleading. To view them as circumscribing the literary work is as false as it would be to say that the identity of a person is marked out by the reach of his arms and legs. In reading, we read ourselves, not in the sense that perception inevitably bears the mark of the perceiver (although this is undoubtedly, but more generally true); not even in the sense that words are always directed at someone, an implied audience (since also this, as true, is true of all words); but because the text in its composite expectation is always looking at the reader, always counting on him. He may, of course, refuse the overture – but he can hardly object that he had not been invited.

This denial of artistic closure may seem perverse – factually false for deliberately "seamless" works of art such as *Madame Bovary* – and a priori extravagant; all in all, perhaps no more than a stipulation. I concede something – but even then, not much – to the last of these claims: no theory, and not only this one, avoids a commendatory element. Insofar as this qualification is true, however, it is not *all* that is true about the theory – and that becomes evident in the examination of literary appearances, even of those works most consciously devoted to the ideals of *poiesis* and its distancing effects. Narration itself, we need to recognize, offers peace in its usual forms of repetition and continuity only after violence; events do not *occur* as narrated; they collect themselves under coercion, not spontaneously. Kierkegaard's parable about the tortured shrieks of the artist which, echoing from his prison, reach the ears of an audience as sweet music is surely true for the *material* of art even if we may often doubt it for the life of the artist himself. Undeniably, art often (and deliberately) conceals art – but we know this, too, only from art itself; and that *knowledge*, as well as the concealment, unavoidably figures in the attention we give art. Art, whether representational or not, has a look to it, much in the way that a face has. And what would a look – or face – be without the assumption which starts at the beginning of its history, that it would be seen? Still less, it seems, than invisible, since not evocation, not assertion, not even form would in solitude, out of all sight, be conceived as possible.

And so also for the process of criticism: the boundaries – of texts and contexts – utilized as levers by criticism are themselves projections of the critical judgment: another way of saying that what criticism criticizes cannot be dissociated or understood apart either from its history or from the person of the critic. The critic in addressing an object unavoidably speaks also of himself, thus challenging the line in critical perception between subject and object. The critic is responsible for what he says, not just because he has said it, but because what he says is unintelligible except as it acts on others. If it does not, he is not a bad critic – he is a noncritic: the distinction is worth preserving.

There is even a specific critical method dictated by these principles, although this is not the place to do more than mention it. The critic as he conceives and then tests critical possibilities is looking for a ground to the literary work – what makes its appearance, his experience, possible. The first step in this direction is in terms of coherence and consistency – reconciling the families of possible meaning both within and outside the work, excluding alternatives. What is left from this for the second step is the reconstructed look of the work in which, by that time, the critic himself appears. Having forced an entrance in the opening lines of interpretation, he easily – unavoidably – looks out of the work thereafter. Mirrors, self-portraits have had a peculiar fascination for painters, who would have their work not only reflect, but reflect the act of reflection. The writer has no such ready means of disclosure; he is often forced to tease or to taunt the reader, daring him to find the reflections as if to suggest that there are none. It is an artifice, this challenge: the critic, seeing it, is even *meant* to see through it; with true poetic justice, he makes his way through it, by its own means, until he has the work at ground level, at *his* ground level. The critic is obliged not only to see very well, but also to see through and around, a seeing that involves a motion of the body – his body – not only of the eye, for neither, now, can (or should) criticism conceal criticism. What this amounts to, and what, I should argue, criticism must always mean is that "art is short, life is long." Why, I wonder again and again, should the critics be so reluctant to admit this? Isn't it their life, too?

> The mind never makes a great and successful effort, without a corresponding energy of the body.
>
> *Thoreau*

Notes to Chapter Twelve

1 For statements of the work of criticism as subordination, cf. such works
   as Cleanth Brooks, *The Well-Wrought Urn* (New York: Reynal and
   Hitchcock, 1947); John Crowe Ransom, *The New Criticism* (New York:
   1942); Northrop Frye, *Fearful Symmetry* (Princeton: Princeton University Press, 1969); William K. Wimsatt, *The Prose Style of Samuel Johnson*
   (New Haven: Yale University Press, 1941). And for classical examples of
   the role of criticism as coordinate with art, cf., e.g., Matthew Arnold,
   Essays in Criticism, First Series (Boston: Ticknow and Fields, 1865);
   Walter Pater, *Appreciations* (New York: Macmillan, 1905); J. E. Sping-
   arn, *Creative Criticism* (New York: Harcourt, Brace, 1925). Cf. also
   George Watson, *The Literary Critics* (Totowa: Rowman and Littlefield,
   1973) for a history of the relation between these (among other) types of
   criticism.
2 See for the argument of a sociological origin for the literary distinction
   between fiction and nonfiction, Lennard J. Davis, "A Social History of
   Fact and Fiction," in Edward W. Said, ed., *Literature and Society*
   (Baltimore: Johns Hopkins University Press, 1980).
3 Cf., e.g., Jacques Derrida, *Of Grammatology,* translated by Gyatri
   Spivak (Baltimore: Johns Hopkins Unviersity Press, 1976); *Writing and
   Difference,* translated by Alan Bass (Chicago: Univesity of Chicago Press,
   1978), and *Glas* (Paris: 1974); Roland Barthes, *The Pleasures of the
   Text,* translated by R. Miller (New York: Hill and Wang, 1975) and
   Image-Music-Text, translated by Stephen Heath (London: 1977); and the
   related – although not always historically or consistently – work of the
   "Yale School": e.g., Harold Bloom, *A Map of Misreading* (New York:
   Oxford Unviersity Press, 1975); Harold Bloom et al., *Deconstruction and
   Criticism* (New York: Seabury, 1979); Geoffrey Hartman, *Criticism in
   the Wilderness* (New Haven: Yale University Press, 1980), Paul de Man,
   Allegories of Reading (New Haven: Yale University Press, 1979).
4 And so Derrida is also one of the least quotable of writers, posing a
   constant challenge to his reader: take all, or perhaps nothing – but at
   least not piecemeal. Even Hegel, more openly a disciple of the Whole, did
   not manage this side of his writing so efficiently.
5 Marxist writers in particular have paid attention to the fundamental role
   of *praxis,* but in general it has been understood, even when applied to art
   or criticism, to be (at most) an ethical concept. I am claiming here that the
   historical and systematic distinctiveness of art and art criticism itself
   discloses the applicability to them of the concept of *praxis* – and that the
   implications of this extend to other contexts as well. Cf., for general
   analysis of the concept, Kostas Axelos, *Alienation, Praxis, and Techne in
   the Thought of Karl Marx,* translated by Ronald Bruzina (Austin:
   University of Texas Press, 1976); Nichoals Lobkowicz, *Theory and
   Practice* (Notre Dame: University of Notre Dame Press, 1967); P. Mar-

kovic and Gojo Petrovic, *Praxis* (Boston: Beacon Press, 1979); Adolfo Sanchez Vasquez, *The Philosophy of Praxis* (New York: Humanities Press, 1977).

Index

*Index compiled by
Meg Davies*